ALSO BY GEOFFREY ROBERTSON

*Reluctant Judas: The Life and Death of the
Special Branch Informer Kenneth Lennon*

*Obscenity: An Account of Censorship Laws and
Their Enforcement in England and Wales*

Freedom, the Individual and the Law

Geoffrey Robertson's Hypotheticals (Volumes 1 & 2)

Does Dracula Have AIDS?

Robertson & Nicol on Media Law

The Justice Game

Crimes Against Humanity: The Struggle for Global Justice

*The Tyrannicide Brief: The Story of the Man
Who Sent Charles I to the Scaffold*

The Levellers: The Putney Debates

The Statute of Liberty: How Australians Can Take Back Their Rights

The Case of the Pope: Vatican Accountability for Human Rights Abuse

Mullahs Without Mercy: Human Rights and Nuclear Weapons

Dreaming Too Loud: Reflections on a Race Apart

*Stephen Ward Was Innocent, OK:
The Case for Overturning His Conviction*

An Inconvenient Genocide: Who Now Remembers the Armenians?

*Rather His Own Man: In Court with Tyrants,
Tarts and Troublemakers*

*Who Owns History? Elgin's Loot and the
Case for Returning Plundered Treasure*

Bad People – and How to Be Rid of Them: A Plan B for Human Rights

*Lawfare: How Russians, the Rich and the Government
Try to Prevent Free Speech and How to Stop Them*

THE
TRIAL
OF
VLADIMIR
PUTIN

GEOFFREY
ROBERTSON

Biteback Publishing

First published in Great Britain in 2024 by
Biteback Publishing Ltd, London
Copyright © Geoffrey Robertson 2024

ISBN 978-1-78590-867-5

10 9 8 7 6 5 4 3 2 1

A CIP catalogue record for this book is available from the British Library.

Set in Minion Pro and Interstate

Printed and bound in Great Britain by
CPI Group (UK) Ltd, Croydon CR0 4YY

FSC
www.fsc.org
MIX
Paper | Supporting
responsible forestry
FSC® C171272

To the memory of Alexei Navalny

'The sovereign who ... takes up arms without a lawful cause ... is chargeable with all the evils, all the horrors of war: all the effusion of blood, the desolation of families, the rapine, the acts of violence, the ravages, the conflagrations, are his works and his crimes. He is guilty of a crime against the enemy ... He is guilty of a crime against his people ... Finally, he is guilty of a crime against mankind in general, whose peace he disturbs, and to whom he sets a pernicious example.'

EMMERICH DE VATTEL, *THE LAW OF NATIONS*, 1758

CONTENTS

INTRODUCTION

Any potential reader who presumes to judge this book by its cover – i.e. its title, *The Trial of Vladimir Putin* – might find it a hypothetical too far, an exercise in wishful thinking. How could this political giant, with personalised power over Russia and almost 6,000 nuclear weapons at his beck and call, be made accountable to any court set up by other countries?

That was my view, on 24 June 2023, as I boarded a 24-hour flight from London to Sydney. The plane was equipped to receive Al Jazeera and CNN, which shortly after take-off were reporting that Yevgeny Prigozhin, 'Putin's chef', head of the Wagner Group of mercenaries who had been doing the deadliest work in Ukraine, had begun a 'march for justice' on Moscow. He had declared that Putin's justification for war – genocide against Russians by Ukrainian Nazis – was nonsense and that Russia was in no danger from NATO but more from its own venal and incompetent generals. By the time my flight reached Dubai, his army had reached the command centre of Rostov-on-Don, having shot down a number of army helicopters, and he was pictured being welcomed by its citizens. Putin appeared briefly on the screen, with the colour drained from his face and looking suddenly vulnerable, talking of treason.

I watched – no sleep was possible – as Prigozhin drove off towards Moscow. I was excited at the prospect of Putin's overthrow but terrified of the consequence of Russia's nukes coming under the control of this deranged figure. By the time we were over Perth, Prigozhin had stopped his march, just 200 miles short of the capital. A few weeks later, his plane crashed and burned, killing a few of his cronies along with the pilot, co-pilot and a 39-year-old flight attendant. (The CIA now believes the plane was sabotaged by the FSB, successor to the KGB, with a bomb fitted to its wing while refuelling.) In any event, the moment passed by the time we reached Sydney and I confess to an overwhelming feeling of relief, that Russia's nukes were still under the control of a bad man rather than a mad man.

But the episode demonstrated that Vladimir Putin may not be invulnerable. That was thought of Slobodan Milošević, when he was indicted by a UN tribunal, but the West failed to realise that he was silently despised by many decent Serbs who voted him out and dispatched him for trial at The Hague in return for the lifting of sanctions. Putin is seventy-one and can stay in power, constitutionally, for another twelve years, but age may take a toll and the Russian economy may tank as a result of sanctions brought about by his decision to go to a war which he may yet lose. International justice has no time limits: Radovan Karadžić and Ratko Mladić hid from it for seventeen years but ended up in its prisons convicted after fair trials. So did Hissène Habré, the torturer of Chad, who managed to stave off a trial for almost as many years. The gold medal for avoiding legal nemesis is held by a French Cambodian businessman indicted for funding the radio station in Rwanda which summoned the Hutu people to commit genocide ('the grave is only half full – who will help us fill it?'). For twenty years after his indictment, he hid in Nairobi and Paris, until dragged to court in Arusha, by which time dementia had set in and he could not be fairly tried.

If this is Putin's fate, it will still afford some consolation to his victims – the people of Ukraine. Crimes against humanity are unforgivable and unforgettable but justiciable because the records, many visual, still survive, collected by prosecutors and (in Putin's case) by a number of institutions in Ukraine and Europe, which have been busy amassing evidence of the war crimes committed by Russian forces in Ukraine as a result of Putin's invasion. Although he appears safe at present, with his generals and ministers paying him obeisance and having no political rival (Alexei Navalny having now been murdered or died from 'sudden death syndrome' at his prison in the Arctic Circle), change may come as it did with Milošević, and Putin may end up, years from now, shuffling into the dock like some old Nazi. But the dock of which court, and charged with what offence? The world must now prepare for this possibility and be ready to put him on trial for committing the greatest crime, causing the most casualties, since the Nazi blitzkriegs of the Second World War.

There is another reason for preparing a trial, namely the prospect of conducting it *in absentia* – without Putin being physically present. Such trials are frowned upon by many Anglo-American lawyers, who say they are not trials at all because a defendant by definition cannot contest the evidence or instruct counsel. But for all that, they are permitted in France and many other European countries – and most importantly in Ukraine. The UN's Human Rights Committee, arbiter of international fair trial standards, has accepted that *in absentia* trials can conform to such standards if 'accused persons, although informed of the proceedings sufficiently in advance, decline to exercise their right to be present'. This is subject to a condition that there must be a retrial should the absent defendant later appear to contest their conviction. A conviction of an absent defendant will give some solace to victims of the crime, although by no means as much as if they see the malefactor sent to prison, and will at least provide an authoritative judicial account of what happened.

Colonel Gaddafi's malevolence was exposed when his intelligence chief was convicted *in absentia* in France for blowing up a passenger plane over Niger. The same impact was not achieved by the Amsterdam court which convicted two Russian soldiers and a Ukrainian separatist *in absentia* for murder by shooting down Malaysia Airlines Flight 17, for one very good reason: they were not represented, and the more appropriate verdict, of manslaughter by gross negligence, was never argued.

If international law is to have any meaning, *in absentia* trials must be acceptable, so long as those indicted are properly defended by amici curiae – 'friends of the court', i.e. experienced advocates assigned to argue on behalf of a defendant who refuses to be present. This method enables questions of law to be properly adjudicated and available defences to be fully developed, albeit without the instructions of a defendant who insists on staying in their cell – or in Moscow. It allows the decision, where the court is composed of distinguished international judges, to have a certain force, both in stigmatising defendants and in giving some satisfaction to their victims. In Putin's case, any tribunal called upon to try him for the 'crime of aggression' will have all the facts and all his relevant speeches and writings. There would be nothing that he could add to his defence by his physical presence, because 'self-defence' requires an objective appraisal of the well-known facts, while his intentions were clearly stated at the time. So far as war crimes, however, these must be charged before the International Criminal Court (ICC) – one crime, the unlawful transportation of children, has already been charged in this way – but that court has no power to hear such cases in his absence, unless its member states amend its statute. This may well be the only way to bring Putin to trial, and so the case for doing so will be considered in this book as well as the more familiar, but obviously less likely, possibility of having him physically present in the dock.

●　　●　　●

Putin's war commenced with the invasion of Ukraine on 24 February 2022, and it has taken innocent lives, both Ukrainian and Russian, every single day it has continued. At time of writing, in early 2024, tens of thousands of Ukrainian civilians have been killed, about 1,000 of them children, and many more have been seriously injured, attacked by Russian forces with drones, bombers and tanks, taking the lives as well of many thousands of Ukrainian soldiers and defenders. Russian troop losses are estimated to be four times heavier – well over 100,000 – with legions more injured. Not a day goes by without some atrocity: the bombing of civilian homes and apartments (as seen regularly on television), a drone hit on a church or on children playing outside a pizza restaurant or a direct hit on a blood transfusion centre or a public hospital clearly marked on aerial maps as non-military targets but blasted nonetheless, by Russian commanders well aware they are committing war crimes with the approval of a supreme commander-in-chief who is more likely to award them medals than to prosecute them. In some war crimes, he is directly involved – for example, he has boasted about approving the transportation to Russia of Ukrainian children, for which his arrest is sought by the ICC.

In short, Vladimir Putin is a man who kills children and kidnaps them and bombs their houses, their parents and their families. He is the man responsible for starting this war, and he can be tried for two different classes of crime. The most heinous is the crime of aggression, which means that he ordered the invasion of a United Nations member state with force of the 'character, gravity and scale' amounting to a 'manifest' breach of Article 2(4) of the UN charter, which prohibits states from invading one another. The only defence – and Putin has notified the UN that this will be his and Russia's defence – is that of 'self-defence' under Article 51 of the charter, where the aggressor state (i.e. Russia) is itself reacting to a threat (from Ukraine or its NATO allies) and is in imminent danger of attack. This must be Putin's defence, if he is ever put on trial, and he will have to convince the court that the same defence advanced by US President George W. Bush for the invasion of Iraq, namely 'pre-emptive self-defence', is valid in law – i.e. that Putin's fear that Ukraine would join NATO and invade Russia was sufficient to entitle him to strike first. Aggression is a very serious crime – a person who starts a war is responsible for all the death, destruction and suffering that it brings in its wake. It carries the most severe sentence – death, for the Nazi leaders convicted of it at Nuremberg (where aggression was prosecuted as a crime against the peace), and life imprisonment for the likes of Putin today (international courts do not have the death penalty, although the US insisted that Saddam Hussein should be hanged and might apply the same reasoning to a tribunal charged with punishing Putin).

The problem of trying Putin for the crime of aggression, of which he is obviously guilty unless he can prove that he acted in self-defence, is that there is no court which has the power to try him. Only leaders of forty-five countries have specifically agreed to be bound by the ICC's limited jurisdiction over this offence, and Russia is not one of them. So there will have to be a new court created to do so and an 'aggression tribunal' is slowly being constructed in The Hague. The work is not easy: it must have the power (which can come only from international law) to invalidate any amnesty Putin has been given (and an amnesty will certainly be a condition of any peace treaty with Ukraine). The court would also need to have the power to sweep away head-of-state immunity (or the immunity of an ex-head, as Putin might be by then), an immunity which protects him from trial under local law in

Ukraine or in the courts of any other state. For that reason, the aggression court would need to be set up as a fully fledged international court acceptable to the International Court of Justice (ICJ), where Putin could challenge it. A 'core group' of thirty-nine Western states are at work on constructing such a court, and the European Union has donated €9 million to open an investigative office in The Hague. But the tribunal itself will take some time before it is open for business, and it is unlikely that Putin will agree, or could be forced, to attend. So it must be given the power to try him *in absentia*, if international law on the use of force is to be vindicated.

At the ICC, a second type of offence – specific war crimes committed in Ukraine – can be investigated, prosecuted and punished. War crimes have been settled for centuries and are enumerated in the Geneva Conventions and in Article 8 of the Rome Statute of 1998 which established the ICC. They include: the deliberate killing of civilians, by execution, bombing or other military means; the transportation of children; rape and pillage; the targeting of hospitals, churches and museums; bombarding towns, villages and buildings which are not military objectives; and launching unnecessary attacks knowing they will cause 'widespread, long-term and severe damage to the natural environment'. Russian forces have been accused of committing all these crimes and more, and they are all a result of Putin's war. He is the commander-in-chief, responsible for them all as the person who started the war by the crime of aggression but who must be connected to individual atrocities before he can be punished as a war criminal.

The court has issued an arrest warrant for one war crime which there is no doubt that he ordered because he has publicly boasted of it, namely the transportation of Ukrainian children to Russia. Other crimes were ordered by generals who are directly responsible for them, but Putin awarded them medals instead of investigating and ordering them to be tried and punished. He can be charged with 'command responsibility' for the crime itself, under a doctrine that punishes a leader for turning a blind eye to crimes they could stop or deter. The punishment is less than that for a direct perpetrator, but conviction would put Putin in prison for quite a few years. The ICC has no power at present to try him *in absentia*, so the prospect of him answering the arrest warrant in person will depend on whether, like Milošević, he is overthrown and sent to The Hague.

That much is clear from Putin's reaction to the court when it issued the warrant for his arrest for the illegal transportation to Russia of Ukrainian children. His spokesman declared: 'We consider all documents coming from this body as legally null and void ... The ICC is indeed on the road to self-destruction.' He followed with supporting quotes from Trump-era Americans like John Bolton, who hate the ICC and wish to destroy it lest it ever be minded to indict an

American. But the pretence that the ICC warrant would have no effect at all was belied, a few days later, at Putin's meeting with Chinese President Xi Jinping, when a supply of Chinese weaponry was expected to be offered for sale to Russia. But despite the routine declaration of friendship, China was not prepared to be branded as the supplier of munitions to a suspected war criminal. And then Putin's invitation to an important conference (of BRICS nations, the R standing for Russia) in South Africa was withdrawn. South Africa is a member state of the ICC, and its law in consequence required the execution of ICC warrants on any who came within its borders. Putin had the taint of an international fugitive, compelled instead to meet Kim Jong Un, the North Korean leader, to buy more weapons to kill Ukrainians.

Nonetheless, Putin's truculence and his nuclear power make his actual trial unlikely in the foreseeable future. In that case, the question is whether an *in absentia* trial is worth pursuing. It cannot be pursued at the ICC unless member states of the Rome Treaty amend its constitution (the Rome Statute) to allow such trials for indictments accusing Putin of war crimes. The ICC cannot, for reasons that will be explained, put him on trial for the most serious crime of aggression, which will require a separate court – an aggression tribunal – established so it can validly exercise international criminal law. Such a body was first urged within a few days of the invasion by former British Prime Minister Gordon

Brown and championed by President Volodymyr Zelensky, who has devoted a good deal of his legal resources to support the emergence of such a court at The Hague, with financial input from the US and the European Union for the International Centre for the Prosecution of the Crime of Aggression Against Ukraine, an investigative mechanism that will collect evidence for a prosecution. Assuming that it does then develop into a court with distinguished international judges and a hotshot team of defence attorneys appointed as amici to take every point in Putin's favour, would an *in absentia* trial and consequent authoritative judgment on whether he was guilty of the crime of aggression be worth more than the paper on which it is printed?

There is little doubt that a written and reasoned verdict, by unbiased and expert judges after a proper adversarial trial where evidence can be challenged before it is finally assessed, can carry weight in the world. The great result of the judgment at Nuremberg was to confound Holocaust deniers ever afterwards. An authoritative judgment on Putin, translated into Russian and Ukrainian, may serve to refute the suggestion by his propagandists that Ukraine was run by Nazis engaging in genocide, or that he had any lawful right to invade. Moreover, it would serve to vindicate international law by demonstrating that its breach had consequences, and by branding the instigator as a criminal, it would invite his diplomatic isolation and possibly even his overthrow by his own, shamed people. It might serve as a deterrent to other aggressors, like Ilham Aliyev of Azerbaijan, who was encouraged in 2023 by Putin's seeming impunity to annihilate the little democratic enclave of Nagorno-Karabakh, confident that a Security Council poleaxed over Russian aggression would take no action about his own. The trial proceedings would be covered in the world media and would increase knowledge about international criminal law and its constraints on cruel behaviour by combatants. International law imposes a duty on states to prosecute certain crimes against humanity, but that duty does not necessarily extend to putting perpetrators in prison – trying them *in absentia*, if there is no other way, would be a worthwhile and appropriate response to a manifest breach of international criminal law by a criminal like Putin with too much power to be arrested.

Vladimir Putin holds an extraordinary grip over political power in Russia – he bestrides his country like a colossus, unaccountable to its courts, its party of government, its bureaucracy, its compliant parliament or its lickspittle media. His advisers are self-selected, his opponents are in prison and his church worships his actions. There are many books and television programmes in the West that purport to analyse his mind and his motives and continue to treat him as a dictator – cold-blooded, capable and efficient. But this presents him as a politician conducting business as usual – the captain with a coterie of advisers steering the ship that is the Russian state.

There is little public sense that he is a criminal, the boss of a gang that has killed many thousands of innocent people for no reason other than to enslave their descendants and dependants and to seize their land, homes and even their ethnic identity. This is behaviour that decent people would describe as 'wicked' were it the objective of a run-of-the-mill mafia capo, yet this mud does not stick to the suit and tie of the little President of Russia as his genuflecting guests sit at the end of his long table in the Kremlin as he goes about the business of the state. The importance of a trial, to transform Vladimir Putin in the public eye from a statesman to a crime boss, may be symbolic, but it is a symbol that reflects the truth.

A trial, by procedures accounted as fair, is the means by which a finding of guilt normally results in punishment. Fair trials are not perfect for this purpose, but they are the best we can do. So long as they are held in the open, with capable teams of lawyers on each side, evidence probed and tested by cross-examination, both sides able to call witnesses of fact and of expert opinion before judges who are utterly independent of any state or any other power (military, commercial or religious), then the result will be reliable and will determine whether Putin has broken the law and, to the extent that the law lays down a rule based on a moral principle, whether he is a bad – or, if preferred, a 'wicked' or even 'evil' – man. Ordering an invasion that will inevitably kill tens of thousands of innocent civilians and hundreds of their children is, prima facie, a deeply wicked action, undertaken not by a statesman but by a mass murderer. It takes a trial to show the difference.

• • •

Chapter 1 of this book sets the stage, by explaining how international criminal law has developed since its initiation at Nuremberg and then through its legacy of 'ad hoc' UN courts in former Yugoslavia, Rwanda and Sierra Leone and eventually to the ICC. It will be necessary to give some background to the crime of aggression and its recent formulation and insertion into the statute of the ICC, which can only prosecute states that would never commit it, namely those which agree to be prosecuted if they do. The chapter will also explain the flaw in the UN charter, namely its reliance on the Security Council to save the world from 'the scourge of war' but the impossibility of that task when entrusted to 'permanent members' like Russia, China or indeed America, which can veto any action against themselves or their allies.

Chapter 2 further explains the crime of aggression and what has to be done to set up an aggression tribunal with the power to bring perpetrators which are not ICC members, like Russia, to account. Such a tribunal will need to circumvent some of the traditional problems in prosecuting presidents and foreign ministers that arose, for example, in the proceedings against

General Pinochet – namely, the diplomatic immunity that the law generally accords to such personages and the amnesties they usually grant to themselves or receive as a result of peace treaties. There are questions of law here of some complexity, which have been responsible for delays in the construction of the aggression tribunal proposed by Ukraine and many like-minded states. As this is a book for a general readership, I have tried to keep treatment of these legal issues simple without becoming simplistic, and have avoided the footnotes and case references that choke up law books on the subject.

Chapter 3 cuts to the chase with a description of how the prosecution case will play out, whether or not Putin turns up to hear it. It should not take long, at least if the prosecution sticks to the facts which show that this was not some 'special military exercise' but a full-blooded invasion from the start. The intention to occupy Ukraine can be proved by Putin's own speeches, before and after the invasion, and by photographic evidence of his tanks rolling towards Kyiv. His mindset will be evidenced by an essay he wrote in 2021 to the effect that Ukraine should be considered as part of Russia, and by his attempts, on the eve of the invasion, to grant independence to separatists in the Donbas area in the coal-rich east of the country. The prosecutor could charge Putin separately with aggression for his forcible annexation of Crimea in 2014, although this would extend the hearing and enable him to invoke a wider range of defences. His answer to the charge is anticipated in Chapter

4, as a 'dream team' of defenders would argue that his actions were justified by 'pre-emptive self-defence', a doctrine invoked (in fact, invented) by George W. Bush's lawyers to excuse the invasion of Iraq in 2003. The irony of Putin relying on a legal argument that Russia (along with the UK and Australia) then rejected as a perversion of international law is stark, but it is the only way that Putin could be acquitted.

War crimes, as set out in the Rome Statute of the ICC, are the focus of Chapter 5. They would be tried separately to the aggression charge and, in all probability, only if state parties to the Rome Treaty allowed the ICC to conduct trials *in absentia*. However, now that a number of countries permit war crimes prosecutions under universal jurisdiction laws, it is possible that peripatetic Russian officers and officials may be arrested on their travels and forced to have their day in a foreign court. Trials in Ukraine would be appropriate because that is where the crimes have been committed, but that nation has indicated its preference that any high-ranking suspects they capture should face an international process which cannot be accused of bias, and trials at the ICC come with a reasonable guarantee of fairness.

Chapter 6 looks at what Putin's punishment should be if he is convicted. Should he hang, like Saddam Hussein and others who have started wars? Thus far he has 'got away with it' and faced no serious consequence for a crime that has caused hundreds of thousands of deaths of Russian and Ukrainian civilians and soldiers. This book points to the fatal flaw in the structure of the United Nations, which leaves the General Assembly as a talking shop and gives all power to a Security Council that can be – and now is – hamstrung by a veto reserved to its five permanent members who use it to protect themselves and their allies from accountability for crimes against humanity. The very fact that the UN could not expel Russia, even were it to drop a nuclear bomb on Ukraine, because Russia would veto its own expulsion, demonstrates why it is not fit for its purpose of keeping peace in the world. In Chapter 7, I discuss other examples of how, influenced by Russian impunity in Ukraine, aggression by Azerbaijan has snuffed out the little democracy of Nagorno-Karabakh, and there has been no retribution for the military coup in Myanmar or the violent end of a transition to democracy in Sudan. The so-called rule of international law is no rule at all, unless some attempt is made to reassert it, and that alone makes the case for putting Vladimir Putin, in person or in his absence, on trial.

If the war against Ukraine in time winds down to become a 'frozen conflict', it is still important to have an authoritative verdict on who started it and who has to pay for it. If the aggression tribunal is clothed with the full power of international law, it could order compensation against Putin, whose personal wealth is reportedly huge, with assets spanning several jurisdictions. They could be stripped from him and paid to his victims in Ukraine, even were he convicted *in absentia*. If he is overthrown from within, by the army or the security services, his property will be at the disposal of a new regime and could appropriately be distributed to the families of soldiers killed in the war of his making. If he ends up being tried and convicted by the ICC, it has a trust fund and the power to gather up the ill-gotten gains of its convicts and redistribute the money to victims. No amount can compensate for the premature death of loved ones, but in the absence of imprisonment, orders for fines and sequestration provide some consolation.

I hope this book will encourage discussion of the merits of putting Putin on trial. This has so far been confined to international lawyers whose arguments, both pro and con, can be incomprehensible to the general public – and even to other lawyers. I have tried in this book to cut them down to size, avoiding the affectation of Latin citations and lengthy case precedents. The trial of Putin is not, in itself, a difficult exercise: it can be attempted in mock proceedings at schools and universities and by documentary dramas. A definitive judgment on the man can be made only in a real courtroom, but in the absence of such a tribunal, there is no reason why his guilt should not be debated by adjudicating on the legal arguments he would have to present if he was arraigned. It may also help to understand why, 2,500 years after the Greeks hit upon democracy, the world has proved incapable of stopping wars by punishing those who start them.

CHAPTER 1

THE NUREMBERG LEGACY

SOME HISTORY

International law is reckoned to have begun with the Treaty of Westphalia in 1648, which ended the Thirty Years' War in Europe. It was not much of a start, because it sanctified the autocracy of kings and princes, establishing, to the horror of the pope, that they could make treaties without his approval and go to war whenever they wanted in order to settle disputes. It embodied the absolutist philosophy of Jean Bodin, that tyranny was more congenial than rebellion and the greatest danger to the nation state came from tolerating talk about 'the people's liberty'. The best thing about the Treaty of Westphalia was that England was not part of it: the following year, it put its king on trial for tyranny – for making war on his Parliament and people, pillaging their towns and torturing his prisoners. Charles I refused to plead to the charge and participated in the trial only to argue that the court was illegitimate. On the scaffold, he claimed divine immunity – he had been appointed by God and since 'a sovereign and a subject are clean different things', his sovereignty was inviolable. It was regarded as a mistake to execute him; it lent a martyr status which helped his son to power eleven years later, when the nation had tired of rule by quarrelling politicians. But Charles I's trial, which ended a brutal civil war, is the first precedent for the trial of a head of state.

Why a trial, when Oliver Cromwell could so easily have put the king before a firing squad or have had him 'shot while trying to escape'? The army wanted vengeance on this 'man of blood', but their puritan leaders believed that evidence of guilt should be presented publicly, in the sight of God, and they even prosecuted a soldier who had tried to assassinate the king before his trial. Parliament, in fact, gave him a fairer trial than any yet held, with the right to have the best lawyers in the land, which he declined, preferring (like Milošević, who hid his lawyers in the court gallery) to take all the limelight. His lawyers advised that he could not be tried, as under Magna Carta he had to be tried by his peers 'and the king has no peers'. Cromwell replied by rounding up seventy generals, barristers, mayors and other civil worthies to form a jury. This mode of trial is not permitted in international courts, where experienced judges must deliver reasoned judgments and eschew the death penalty.

2

That was not the case in France with the trial by Parliament of Louis XVI the following century. His lawyers had studied the trial of Charles I and advised their king to adopt the same tactic of denying the jurisdiction of the court because the French constitution gave him immunity, but Louis doggedly insisted on trying to establish his innocence. This was a bad idea: he was convicted, and his speech from the guillotine was drowned out by army drummers. His trial was grossly unfair: the National Assembly had already declared him guilty, and then went on to rubberstamp its earlier verdict. When Britain defeated Napoleon, it saw no need to put him on trial – he was instead exiled to St Helena.

The first time that nations contemplated an international criminal court to try a head of state was in the aftermath of the First World War, when Prime Minister David Lloyd George came to the Versailles Peace Conference promising to 'hang the kaiser' for ordering the brutal invasion of Belgium which began the First World War. Up to that point, aggression had simply been a policy prerogative of sovereigns, notwithstanding Emmerich de Vattel and other jurists who had argued that starting a war was the worst of crimes (at least if it were lost). Article 227 of the Treaty of Versailles stated that Wilhelm II of Hohenzollern would be tried by a 'special tribunal', with five judges drawn from the victor countries (Britain, France, Japan, Italy and the US) on the charge of committing a 'supreme crime against international morality

3

and the sanctity of treaties'. Several months of legal and diplomatic arguments followed as to how this might be implemented. There had never been any precedent for a crime of
aggression, so the kaiser's lawyers might have successfully
objected that this was retrospective liability, unforeseeable at
the time of the invasion of Belgium in 1914.

More relevant to Putin today was the problem of head-of-
state immunity, entrenched in all national laws and which came
to bedevil the proceedings against Augusto Pinochet at the
end of the century. It would stop Ukraine from putting Putin
on trial in its courts, were he captured while still President of
Russia or if he surrendered after a coup. But an international
court, recognised as such, may pierce this immunity and proceed to put a head of state or former head of state on trial –
there have been many examples (see Milošević, Charles Taylor,
Radovan Karadžić, Jean Kambanda, Laurent Gbagbo etc.). The
$64 question, however, is what makes a court international? If
the 'core group' of states which are setting up an aggression tribunal gets this wrong, Putin will slip through their fingers.

Back to Versailles in 1919, where there were questions
about whether aggression was a crime at all. Most states were
happy to see the law develop in the direction of making it
an offence, but the US in particular, which had recently
fought an aggressive war with Spain over Cuba, was reluctant, despite the millions dead in trenches on the Somme,
to set a legal limit on its own future foreign policy. Britain

and France were insistent, and this first international criminal court began to take shape: the proceedings would be in public, with oral hearings and defendants having the right to counsel, and counsel who were entitled to examine and cross-examine witnesses. There was further agreement that the trial should be held in England, where the kaiser would be imprisoned in the Tower of London. America, however, was reluctant to go forward: its legal advisers insisted that the principle of head-of-state immunity should prevail, and President Woodrow Wilson was extremely concerned that his grand plans for a League of Nations would be stymied if Germany refused to join – as it might in fury if the kaiser were sentenced to hang. There was a reported altercation with Lloyd George, who asserted, 'I would like to see punished the man responsible for the greatest crime in history', to which Wilson replied, 'He is universally reviled – isn't that the worst punishment for such a man?' It is doubtful whether bombed Ukrainians would think it enough for Putin.

In any event, the stand-off was resolved by the kaiser, who sought and was granted asylum in a lakeside castle in the Netherlands, where he lived unhanged until 1941. It remains one of history's most intriguing hypotheticals, whether his trial for aggression would have given pause to Adolf Hitler.

Wilson's League of Nations was doomed from the start when his own country refused to join. In 1928, many nations signed up to the Kellogg–Briand Pact, by which they promised to renounce war as an instrument of national policy, but this was not legally binding and made no provision for trials of warmongers. The league would do nothing to stop Benito Mussolini invading Abyssinia and Libya, or Japan from invading Manchuria to establish the puppet state of Manchukuo. When a league commission awarded a sacked Jewish worker damages for discrimination, Hitler simply took Germany out of the organisation.

When it came to dealing with this perpetrator of the Holocaust, who had invaded most of the countries of Europe, something had to be done. But under the Westphalian principle of state sovereignty, nothing could be done except by Germany itself: crimes against Jews and other German nationals, committed pursuant to Nazi laws, could not be tried by other nations, and in 1945 lawyers in the US State Department and the British Foreign Office insisted that Westphalian state sovereignty principles should be upheld. But public outrage took hold after pictures from Bergen-Belsen and Auschwitz were released, and President Truman insisted that a way be found around the problem that had saved the kaiser at Versailles. The only way to do this was to create international criminal law: a trial of the Nazi leadership at Nuremberg, by a court with a constitution that abolished the immunity of leaders, diplomats and anyone else who had committed war crimes or what were called 'crimes against humanity'. Aggression, a crime which was arguably both, was prosecuted as a 'crime against peace'.

NUREMBERG

The charter for the Nuremberg trial was settled in London in 1945. It had been strongly opposed by Winston Churchill, who thought that Cromwell had made a mistake by putting Charles I on trial because it had made him a martyr and given him a platform which Hitler could exploit – using the witness box as a soapbox – to expound Nazi ideology. Churchill's favoured alternative was to draw up a list of fifty Nazi leaders, to be executed as soon as they were captured, having given them six hours to say their prayers. 'All sorts of complications ensue as soon as you admit a fair trial,' he warned. 'Hitler should die like a gangster,' he told the British war Cabinet, 'in the electric chair, no doubt available on lend lease' (the deal under which the US had financed the British war effort, at great profit to itself). The Churchill solution repelled Henry Stimson, the US secretary for war, and Franklin Roosevelt's successor Harry Truman, who had an idealistic belief in the 'beneficent power of law and the wisdom of judges'. He appointed Supreme Court Justice Robert Jackson to report on the correctness and the feasibility of a trial, and endorsed his memorable conclusion that to free them without a trial would mock the dead and make cynics of the living. On the other hand … executions or punishments without definite findings of guilt, fairly arrived at, would … not sit easily on the American conscience or be remembered by our children with pride. The only other course is to determine the innocence or guilt of the accused after a hearing as dispassionate as the times and the horrors we deal with will permit, and upon a record that will leave our reasons and motives clear.

The great powers were deadlocked on whether to try Hitler and the Nazi leaders – the US in favour, the UK wanting their summary execution. So the casting vote went to Joseph Stalin, who loved show trials as long as everyone was shot at the end. Charles de Gaulle voted in favour, and Robert Jackson, a US Supreme Court judge, was appointed as chief prosecutor of a special military tribunal to sit at Nuremberg with four judges (and four alternates) drawn from the main victor nations. 'Victors' justice' in one sense, although it might be said that victory had provided the opportunity to do justice on the authors of the Holocaust. There were some complaints about bias – but compared with the disgusting conduct of lickspittle Nazi judges, they were models of impartiality. When Andrey Vyshinsky, now Stalin's foreign minister, attended an official dinner in Nuremberg mid-trial and proposed a toast to 'the speedy trial and execution of all defendants', the British and American judges said that they choked on their wine. In the end, of the twenty-three Nazi leaders on trial, three were acquitted and twelve were given death sentences.

Churchill's concern about Hitler using the witness box as a soapbox was less compelling after his suicide and that of Joseph Goebbels and Heinrich Himmler, but it nonetheless has a relevance to the question of a trial for Vladimir Putin. He might not be permitted to make propaganda speeches but must be allowed to develop his defence that Russia was threatened by Ukraine and NATO, both in opening and closing speeches and in testimony. Although a question of law, the charge does involve politics and must allow him to explain his intentions at the time. At Nuremberg, Hermann Göring was permitted to advance the argument that the collapse in Germany of both capitalism and communism meant that a national resurgence was possible only by total support of Nazi ideology. His first cross-examiner, Robert Jackson, was driven to petulant rage by an inability to confound him: it took the French prosecutor, unemotional and clinical, to confront Göring with his signature on 'night and fog' decrees and other evidence of his guilt for participating in a crime against humanity.

Much will depend on the authority of the presiding judge: Milošević was given too much leeway at his trial to make speeches, but at Nuremberg, the no-nonsense English High

Court judge, Sir Geoffrey Lawrence, kept tight control. There is a remarkable moment, caught on film, at the beginning of the trial, when pleas to the indictments are being taken. Göring portentously rises from the dock with a stack of notes for a speech, but Lawrence cuts him short and the stout party collapses, cringingly mutters his innocence and returns deflated to his place in the dock.

Göring was the lead defendant, who influenced the others. Initially, he decided, like many later defendants in war crimes trials, that he should refuse to recognise the court – say no more to the judges than the defiant catchcry of one of Johann Wolfgang von Goethe's warrior heroes, loosely translated as 'kiss my arse'. But the fairness – or at least, fairishness – of the Anglo-American adversary proceedings gradually brought him round to participating and to taking the opportunity of providing his account to posterity. Putin, unless captured or surrendered, is unlikely to take this course: at most a diplomatic note will be sent to the court by Russia announcing his refusal to answer the indictment. If for some reason he ends up in the dock, he will have to choose – he could take the Charles I gambit and challenge only the power of the court to try him, or he could enter a full-blooded defence like Louis XVI. If he remains in Russia, the court will offer a Zoom appearance, which he is unlikely to accept.

Robert Jackson sagely observed that the Nuremberg trial succeeded mainly because of 'the Teutonic habit of writing

everything down'. The prosecution had access to all the documents generated by the Nazi government – internal memoranda, death camp records, night and fog decrees – by which
individual guilt could be determined. Putin's prosecutor will
not have this kind of evidence and will have to rely upon
inference from what can be proved and statements from
defectors at high levels in the military or from Putin's presidential guards. There is ample evidential basis for the charge
of aggression, and the ICC has already ruled that there is
sufficient evidence to arrest him for trial on the charge of
unlawfully transporting children, but forthcoming charges
of command responsibility for indiscriminately bombing
civilian residences and targeting hospitals and churches will
require some proof connecting Putin with the particular
atrocity, or at least of refusing to investigate and prosecute
those responsible. Does 'command responsibility' entail the
responsibility of a supreme commander for failing to punish
perpetrators of an atrocity he had nothing to do with? If
Putin is prosecuted for this lesser war crimes offence, the
ICC will have to decide.

The Nuremberg tribunal, however progressive its judgment, was nonetheless a creature of its time and some of its
procedures could not be replicated by an aggression tribunal
today. Most notably, its death sentences: although Göring
took poison on the night before his scheduled execution,
there is much to regret that a process which commenced

with Henry Stimson's call to punish the Nazi leaders 'in a dignified manner consistent with the advance of civilisation' should end at Hamelin Prison with English hangman Albert Pierrepoint slavering over Irma Grese ('as bonny a blonde as one ever could hope to meet') as he measured her for the drop. There would be nothing to stop states from giving the aggression tribunal the power to sentence Putin to death – the fate of Saddam Hussein (at US insistence) and of Nicolae Ceauşescu – so the question of capital punishment for aggression is considered in Chapter 6.

Nuremberg lacked an appeal court, a necessary feature of subsequent war crimes courts. It is notable how some major and lengthy war crimes trials can miscarry because some trial judges, although notable international law academics, have lacked the forensic experience to appreciate basic features of a fair trial. There will need to be an appeal court of five experienced and distinguished judges, on-call in the event of a conviction which the defendant will wish to appeal. International courts, following the European fashion, accord a right of appeal to the prosecutor, although this can be a device for keeping an innocent defendant in jail: surely if the three-judge appeal court has already acquitted, there must be a real doubt about a defendant's guilt? There was no 'defence office' at the Nuremberg court to ensure that all were competently defended. Most were not, by German lawyers outclassed by the Allied prosecutors. There were no English defence lawyers – the Bar Council, disgracefully and contrary to its much-touted 'cab-rank rule', refused to allow British lawyers to defend beastly Germans (members of the Krupp steel family had tried to retain a British KC). Putin should have enough to pay for his own defence, but if not, any amici appointed by the court must be appropriately remunerated by the court itself.

THE TOKYO TRIAL

There was a second war crimes trial – of leaders of the Japanese war in the Pacific which had ended only by the dropping of atomic bombs on Hiroshima and Nagasaki. It took place in Tokyo, before a dozen international judges presided over by Sir William Webb of the Australian High Court but with a prosecutor closely controlled by the US administrator of Japan, General MacArthur. MacArthur was determined to save the worst war criminal, Emperor Hirohito, who had approved all decisions of his Prime Minister, Hideki Tojo, including the attack on Pearl Harbor and the enslavement of 1 million 'comfort women' to serve the lusts of the Japanese military. MacArthur was obsessed with saving post-war Japan from 'communism and chaos', which he feared would ensue if Hirohito were arrested. To this extent, Tokyo was a mock trial: the twenty-five defendants loyally joined with the prosecution in this conspiracy to protect the emperor by never mentioning his name in court. When Tojo, in the witness box, blurted out that it was inconceivable for any of the defendants to take any action against the wishes of the emperor, this was edited from the transcript after he was called back the next day for a stage-managed retraction. The French judge said that the failure to prosecute Hirohito should have invalidated the whole proceedings, and Webb was of the view that because the leader of the crime, though available for trial, seemed to have been granted immunity, his accomplices should be spared the death sentence. Hirohito, however, lived on, and on the throne, sumptuously and safely for the next forty-three years. He masqueraded as a humble marine biologist, touring in 1971 to meet Queen Elizabeth and to the US in 1975, where he met Henry Kissinger and Mickey Mouse. As far as leading war criminals are concerned, he is 'the one who got away', and it is necessary to ensure that Putin is not the next one. The Tokyo trial does serve as a warning of how political considerations can defeat international justice. The US, at core group meetings to plan an aggression tribunal, has already served notice that it will not tolerate a court that could indict an American President.

The Tokyo trial had some achievements, serving the historical purpose of collecting evidence of systematic atrocities which, in their elemental bestiality, went beyond even Nazi contemplation. The Imperial Japanese Army soldiers had been allowed to impale women on stakes, after raping them and cutting their children in half. They dropped bubonic plague germs on the Chinese and boasted of their contempt for the laws of war by executing fallen Allied airmen alongside their parachutes and by sending Allied prisoners who survived captivity (27 per cent died, compared with just 4 per cent in German prisons) on death marches. There were some juristic achievements: unlike at Nuremberg, the defendants were provided with good American lawyers and permitted to challenge the legal basis of the tribunal on the grounds that it was imposing 'victors' justice' and *ex post facto* punishment for the crime of aggression. Most importantly, it gave rise to the 'command responsibility' principle when General Yamashita, convicted by a US military court for failing to stop or punish his troops when they run amok and killed civilians in the Philippines, had his appeal heard and decided by the US Supreme Court. It upheld his conviction and enunciated the principle that has been the basis for the indictments of a number of leaders. But just as historians, seventy-five years on from the war, have found ample evidence of Hirohito's guilt, so they have found evidence of Yamashita's innocence – he was 150 miles away and without communications when the massacre took place. This provides a warning to Putin's prosecutor: reliance on the command responsibility doctrine can fail, as it has in several ICC prosecutions, or worse, can convict an innocent commander.

AFTER NUREMBERG: THE 'AD HOC' COURTS

The Nuremberg trial had a major impact on the development of international law – transcripts of the evidence were delivered to members of Eleanor Roosevelt's committee who were drafting the Universal Declaration of Human Rights, which together with the Genocide and the Geneva Conventions formed the great post-war triptych of legal bastions against the recrudescence of the scourge of war. They were followed over the next half century by the 'good conventions' against torture, apartheid and the mistreatment of children and refugees, although none of those had any enforcement mechanisms – as someone said, looking at the killing fields of Rwanda, 'The road to hell is paved with good conventions.' This was the period when great powers and their diplomats regarded a pardon, not a trial, as the only way to remove a tyrant – dictators like the Duvaliers in Haiti (Papa Doc and Baby Doc) were allowed to leave their bloody stage with an amnesty in their back pockets and their Swiss bank accounts intact. Terrible crimes were committed, even genocide, without retribution: in 1971, the Pakistan Army executed the political leaders and intellectuals seeking independence for Bangladesh, killed several million of its people and organised mass rape for the purpose of ethnic cleansing, yet the US and other Western countries maintained a shameful silence, broken only by George Harrison's 'Concert for Bangladesh'. Idi Amin was another British-trained barbarian from this period who enabled the hostage-taking at Entebbe and killed judges who displeased him. His overthrow led not to a trial but to a welcome reception in Saudi Arabia, which hosted him and his wives in retirement in the name of 'Muslim hospitality'. Pinochet's torture chambers flourished quite openly, and as late as 1988 the UN said nothing about Iran's killing in prisons of many thousands of political dissidents.

It was the resurgence of a savage war in Europe in 1991 that brought the first post-Nuremberg tribunal into being. Ethnic cleansing of Muslims (and of each other) by Serb and Croatian armies and paramilitaries involved war crimes of torture and mass murder of civilians, this time seen on television throughout the world through pictures of 'an elegant cosmopolitan city, Sarajevo, systematically pulverised from a safe distance by cigarette-smoking, Sljivovica-drinking gun and mortar crews while they and the snipers leisurely targeted schoolchildren, bread queues, housewives doing their shopping, funeral ceremonies and the like'. There were diplomatic missions, which produced plans that failed to assuage the greed of the warring parties. The Security Council sent in its 'blue berets', its peacekeepers, but there was no peace to keep – they were captured and held hostage by General Mladić before he ordered the genocidal execution of 8,000 Muslim men and boys at Srebrenica. At the end of its tether, in 1993 the Security Council established the International Criminal Tribunal for the former Yugoslavia (ICTY).

This was achieved by using the Security Council's powers under Chapter VII of the UN charter, firstly to determine that the situation in the Balkans constituted a 'threat to the peace' and then to decide on a measure to give effect to this resolution, namely the establishment of an international criminal court to put an end to war crimes and punish the perpetrators. The International Court of Justice subsequently held that the Security Council could in this way create a valid court empowered to apply international law, albeit by a means that would not be possible were any of the 'big five' permanent members to dissent and veto the court – as Russia would in respect of any proposal for a court to try Vladimir Putin.

The ICTY, set up in The Hague, took some time to establish itself. There were disputes over its first prosecutor, until Nelson Mandela settled them by releasing Richard Goldstone from South Africa's top court to take the job. NATO did not support it, releasing a churlish statement that 'arresting Karadžić and Mladić is not worth the blood of one NATO soldier', and it took years before they were brought, bloodlessly, to trial. They are now serving lengthy prison sentences.

The ICTY was followed, in 1994, by the International

Criminal Tribunal for Rwanda (ICTR), the 'ad hoc' court set up in the same way by the Security Council to deal with the main perpetrators of the atrocities in Rwanda, where Hutu mobs had rounded up Tutsis and hacked 800,000 of them to death. US and UK diplomats disingenuously refused to call this 'genocide' because use of the 'G-word' would entail an obligation under the Genocide Convention to intervene to stop it, but once the war had ended, genocide could be admitted and the court was set up in Arusha (Tanzania) to punish politicians, civil servants and church ministers who had led it. Former Prime Minister Jean Kambanda pleaded guilty, and the main architect of the genocide, Théoneste Bagosora, was brought to justice. Most indictees were convicted, including the 'dear pastor' who Tutsis approached for protection in his church, pleading with him that 'tomorrow we will be killed with our families'. He wrote back: 'A solution has been found for your problems. You must die. God doesn't want you anymore.'

The ICTY and ICTR were described by the Security Council as 'ad hoc' courts, confined to the particular conflict, with a common appeal court in The Hague. Over the years they built up an impressive number of decisions on questions of evidence and procedure for international courts, which has been supplemented by rulings from ICC courts and the special courts in Sierra Leone and Cambodia and the Lebanon tribunal. There have by now been hundreds of trials conducted before international tribunals, providing a corpus of jurisprudence to resolve, as fairly as possible, issues which are prone to arise in adjudging allegations of war crimes and crimes against humanity. It has been one achievement of these courts to fuse different approaches of Anglo-American and European law – especially in regard to the admissibility of hearsay evidence, excluded in England but which can be of value to both sides at an international trial. The rules are now explicated in the textbook *The Right to a Fair Trial in International Law* by Amal Clooney and Philippa Webb and if followed by an aggression tribunal would provide a guarantee of even-handed justice.

THE SPECIAL COURT FOR SIERRA LEONE

The ICTY and ICTR were empowered by the Security Council, but in 2002 a different method of establishment was chosen to bring to justice those mainly responsible for atrocities in the civil war in Sierra Leone. This war was notable for the extensive recruitment of child soldiers, which was then not a crime in international law. Children as young as ten were brainwashed, drugged, armed with AK-47s and directed to kill prisoners – sometimes their own relatives. The most bestial of these factions, the Revolutionary United Front (RUF), introduced a new exhibit in the war crimes chamber of horrors – 'chopping' the hands of innocent civilians who had voted with that hand in a UN-sponsored election. The Special Court for Sierra Leone (SCSL) was the first to criminalise the recruitment of child soldiers, and even charged a government minister with the offence – the first instance of prosecution for war crimes committed by a victor rather than the vanquished. Notably, this court invalidated an amnesty for war crimes given to Charles Taylor, the President of neighbouring Liberia, on the basis that such crimes were unforgivable and hence a pardon was null and void in international law. Taylor was sentenced to prison for fifty years, a sentence he is serving in the UK, and his trial in The Hague came to international attention when supermodel Naomi Campbell and actress Mia Farrow attended to testify how Taylor had dispensed 'blood diamonds' from Sierra Leone after a dinner with Nelson Mandela. It provided an example of how international courts could be a power in the world, and led to hopes that the ICC, which opened in 2002, would exercise it.

The importance of the SCSL for any aggression tribunal to prosecute Putin derives from the way it was established. Although the Security Council resolved that the situation in the country was a threat to international peace, it did not use its power under Chapter VII of the UN charter to set up a court but instead left it to the UN secretary-general to do so by agreement with the President of Sierra Leone. This was a new approach – Nuremberg had been a military tribunal set up by victor powers, the ICTY and ICTR were creatures of the Security Council alone and the ICC was a result of a treaty between states. The SCSL, however, was established by a bilateral agreement between the UN and the Sierra Leone government. It was funded by voluntary contributions from about twenty member states, accountable to a management committee comprising representatives of the states and the UN legal department.

It was noticeably supported by the US – a major donor along with the UK and the Netherlands. It was thus independent of the Security Council and the Sierra Leone government, and entirely dissociated from the Sierra Leone legal system. This independence was important – unlike the Iraqi special tribunal which tried Saddam Hussein and the Cambodian Extraordinary Chambers for Khmer Rouge leaders, which were both embedded in their dysfunctional domestic systems. It was thus insulated from the Sierra Leone constitution (which would otherwise have required a referendum to establish it) and from local political pressures. It would provide a workable model for an aggression tribunal, if it were instigated or approved by the General Assembly rather than by the Security Council (which would never approve it, because of the Russian veto).

The SCSL was described as a 'hybrid' court because its prosecutor, registrar and the majority of its judges on trial and appeal courts were appointed by the UN, and the remainder by Sierra Leone, which appointed the deputy prosecutor. Cambodia was urged to adopt this structure but its President, Hun Sen, adamantly refused, insisting on having a majority of judges whom he could control, and did when it came to further investigations and prosecutions which 'his' judges blocked. It is even open to question whether the Cambodia court was 'international' in the sense required by the ICJ as a warrant for exercising international law, although this was never tested: the court, in relation to its Khmer Rouge defendants, simply proceeded to apply it. The Sierra Leone model remains preferable, although the question of whether any Ukrainian judges at all should sit on a trial of Putin is open to question.

THE ICC

Meanwhile, the ICC had been established by a treaty negotiated during a fractious five-week conference in Rome in 1998. In total, 120 states voted in favour, and only seven were opposed but these included the US, China, Israel and India (Russia abstained). Negotiations over the model for the court had see-sawed as diplomats from 'like-minded' nations seeking to create a court independent of the Security Council and endowed with jurisdiction over war crimes suspects anywhere in the world struggled against the US (joined by China and France), which wanted a court that would not indict their own nationals. President Bill Clinton had personally favoured a powerful body, but the Pentagon and Congress did not: it was noted that when his political power faltered over his affair with Monica Lewinsky, the Pentagon had its way, and by the end of the conference the US voted against having any court at all. Nonetheless, a sufficient number of states ratified the treaty (currently, the number is 123) for the ICC to come into operation in 2002.

Its power to prosecute was limited to those who committed international crimes on the territory of a member state or who were a national of a member state or else involved in a 'situation' referred to the court by the Security Council, which retained the power to block a particular prosecution for one year – a block that could be renewed year after year. This meant that the 'big five' permanent members could use their veto power to stop any ICC prosecutor from moving against their allies or themselves: Russia vetoed a British resolution to refer Syria to the court prosecutor (it needed its naval base on Syria's shoreline and did not want President Bashar al-Assad to be indicted) and America has twice vetoed resolutions calling for an Israeli ceasefire in Gaza. The US did, however, invite the Security Council in 2005 to refer to the court the situation in Darfur, where President Omar al-Bashir's troops were alleged to be committing genocide against the local population, and in 2011 came a rare moment of unanimity when Russia, China and the US supported a resolution to refer the situation in Libya (created by Colonel Gaddafi's threats to kill the residents of Benghazi) to the ICC prosecutor. Never since have the great powers given their unanimous approval to refer a case to the court prosecutor.

The ICC spent its first decade mainly prosecuting Congolese warlords, but it later conducted several trials of heads of state. The President and the opposition leader of Kenya were indicted for inciting pre-election violence which led to over 1,000 deaths, and they meekly turned up to the court – for a day – to accept its jurisdiction. But many prosecution witnesses were suborned and withdrew their accusations, to such an extent that the prosecutor could not proceed. Then came Jean-Pierre Bemba, head of a murderous faction in the Central African Republic, and Laurent Gbagbo, deposed President of Ivory Coast. Their trials foundered as well, and although Bemba was convicted on the 'command responsibility' principle, he was narrowly acquitted by the appeal chamber which found that he lacked the power and the opportunity to stop or punish crimes by his soldiers. The decision serves as a 'mind how you go' for those who wish to prosecute Putin for turning a blind eye to war crimes such as the bombing of civilians – they must prove that he actually knew of the crime to which he seemed indifferent and could have done something to punish it. It would be enough, however, if he saw it on television (e.g. the attack on Mariupol) or, like Charles Taylor, read about it in the memos he must have received from his commanders. The proceedings against Putin, launched by his arrest warrant in 2023, will be the ICC's greatest test.

From its inception by the Rome Statute in 1998, the ICC was clothed with jurisdiction to prosecute the crime of aggression – but only once the crime was satisfactorily defined. It was finally defined at the review conference in Kampala in 2010, and it came into operation in 2018, although only for the forty-five states, so far, which have agreed to be prosecuted if they commit it. These states do not include Russia, which is not an ICC member, and there is no prospect that the Security Council will refer the situation in Ukraine to the ICC prosecutor because Russia would veto the step. Hence the move for an 'aggression tribunal' as the only way by which Putin can be brought to justice for this, his gravest crime of all.

OTHER DEVELOPMENTS

There have been some international law developments of relevance to Vladimir Putin's prosecution, outside the ICC but nonetheless deploying its jurisprudence. The Lebanon tribunal was created to investigate and prosecute the car bombers who assassinated Prime Minister Rafic Hariri (and twenty-one bystanders) in 2005. It was set up by the Security Council under its Chapter VII power at the instigation of President George W. Bush, hitherto an implacable opponent of international justice. Its significance was that it conducted a trial *in absentia*, fair enough to acquit all but one suspect, who remains in Lebanon protected by Hezbollah. Its procedural precedents will be useful for any such trial of Putin.

Should Putin fall from power or be defeated by Ukraine and be forced to take refuge in another country, he might share the fate of Hissène Habré, who killed thousands of opponents while dictator of Chad in 1982–90. He was deposed and fled to Senegal where there was no extradition treaty to return him, but Belgium demanded to try him under its universal jurisdiction law. The ICJ, however, ordered Senegal to try him, which the country refused because of the cost. Human Rights Watch joined the pursuit and the ICJ held that there was an international obligation to put him on trial, irrespective of cost. Eventually, in 2016, the Extraordinary African Chambers did so – a court paid for by the African Union, Chad and international funding. It comprised mainly Senegalese jurists, with presidents of both trial and appeal courts drawn from other African countries. When his lawyers at one point walked out, the court replaced them quickly with amici who were given time and funding to master the defence brief. Habré was convicted of killing 40,000 civilians and sentenced to life in prison, where he died of Covid in 2021.

Any account of how international justice has girded its loins for the possible prosecution of a head of a state which is a permanent member of the Security Council must mention the opposition encountered from the start from the US Republican Party, very angry by the distant possibility that it might ever indict an American. When the ICC was under consideration, Jesse Helms (then head of the Senate's Foreign Relations Committee) threatened that any bill would be 'dead on arrival' in Washington unless it gave 100 per cent protection to American servicemen. He then promoted, and had passed, perhaps the most puerile US legislation ever: his 'bomb The Hague' bill, the American Service-Members' Protection Act, which gave the President power to use military force against any country detaining a US soldier on an ICC arrest warrant. It was supported by Dr Kissinger (the only US 'service-member' who might need protection) and claimed in its preamble that the ICC would inhibit the US military – from committing war crimes, presumably. Fortunately, George W. Bush in his second term resiled from this opposition to international justice: his administration largely funded the Lebanon tribunal and was a major supporter of the SCSL. His successor Barack Obama was on board with the ICC: although domestic politics prevented him from joining, America's votes in the Security Council have often been in favour of referencing conflict situations to the ICC.

But with the advent of the Trump administration, the irrational hostility of Jesse Helms returned full blast, especially from John Bolton, his old assistant and later Trump's national security adviser. He bullied American allies to withdraw their membership of the ICC when the prosecutor began to investigate allegations of rape and torture by US troops in Afghanistan, and it was his condemnations of the court that Putin's spokesman invoked to declare his arrest warrant 'null and void', while Dmitry Medvedev, channelling Jesse Helms, suggested that Russia should bomb The Hague if Putin were arrested. Trump's abrasive secretary of state, Mike Pompeo, dishonestly attacked the court as corrupt and revoked the visa of its prosecutor, Fatou Bensouda, so she could not enter New York to report to the UN. Trump went further, issuing an executive order banning ICC judges from entering the US and even banned the prosecutor's staff members, including a number of American lawyers. This disgraceful abuse of power was suspended by a federal judge and revoked once Joe Biden (who welcomed Putin's ICC indictment) attained office, but the court remains under threat from any future Republican President, who may have to decide between their own wish to indict Putin and their fear of a court that could ever indict an American.

CHAPTER 2

CONSTRUCTING A COURT

The US had been warning the world of the imminence of the Russian invasion of Ukraine for some weeks before it happened on 24 February 2022, and the Security Council, charged under the UN charter with securing world peace, was meeting regularly. On 31 January, there was a notable verbal clash between the two nations, with the US insisting that 100,000 Russian troops were ready on the border while the Kremlin's lying ambassador insisted that 'Russia had no plans to invade Ukraine'. Over the next three weeks, the US made some mention of sanctions but never once threatened Putin with prosecution for the crime of aggression, even after releasing details of his plans for Ukrainian leaders to be killed or sent to concentration camps. On 21 February, Putin held his televised State Security Council meeting, to formally recognise the independence of Donetsk and Luhansk and declare that Ukraine was committing 'genocide' against Russian-language speakers and to deny that Ukraine had any independent statehood. The UN Security Council met on 23 February: on their way to it, delegates heard that Putin had announced a 'special military operation' in Ukraine to 'strive for the demilitarisation and denazification of Ukraine'. The following day, as the tanks began to roll towards Kyiv, Russia vetoed a Security Council resolution critical of its action. Its opponents managed to have the resolution referred to the General Assembly, which voted 141 against five to condemn the Russian invasion.

By this time, just one week later, all states would have been informed by their international lawyers that

1. Russia's invasion of Ukraine gave rise to the crime of aggression initiated by its leader Vladimir Putin.
2. The only court with jurisdiction over this crime was the ICC, but it has no jurisdiction to prosecute non-member states (such as the US and Russia) without a referral from the Security Council.
3. No further action by the Security Council against Russia was possible, because any such action would be vetoed by Russia itself, a permanent member with absolute veto rights and nuclear weapons just in case.

THE FATAL FLAW IN THE UN CHARTER

The UN is unfit for its primary purpose of safeguarding

international peace. It transmogrified from the League of Nations, the international body set up on the initiative of Woodrow Wilson for this purpose at Versailles, which had been unable to prevent aggression – for example, Mussolini's attacks on Abyssinia and Libya, Japan's occupation of Manchuria and Russia's attack on Finland (although the league at least expelled the Soviets for this act of aggression). By 1939, war was on its way and the league collapsed. There was some debate over how to replace it, and H. G. Wells – the English writer and visionary – suggested an organisation of 'parliamentary peoples', democracies which would unite to protect 'the rights of man' and defend them against authoritarian assault. This might have been possible in 1939 but not by the war's end, after Russia had become the most valuable ally. At Yalta, Stalin insisted that Communist Soviet republics like Ukraine and Belarus should be admitted to a 'new world order' which would not defend democracy. What it would do, and this was its primary purpose, was to stop aggression. That was made clear by the opening words of the UN charter: 'We the peoples of the United Nations, determined to save succeeding generations from the scourge of war, which twice in our lifetime has brought untold sorrow to mankind, and to reaffirm faith in fundamental human rights.'

This purpose, set out in the preamble, is emphasised again in Article 1, where its purpose is declared to be 'to maintain international peace and security, and to that end: to take effective collective measures for the prevention and removal of threats to the peace, and for the *suppression of acts of aggression* or other breaches of the peace'. Its members go on to promise to 'live together in peace with one another as good neighbours' and to ensure that 'armed force shall not be used, save in the common interest'.

So the UN was pledged to act against the invasion of Ukraine. It could not do so because, as constructed, its General Assembly (then of forty-four members, now of 193) was not much more than a talking shop. The organisation's power to keep the peace is strictly confined to the Security Council, which is made up of fifteen states, ten of which rotate every two years, and five permanent members – the five allies that had suffered and sacrificed the most in the battle against fascism during the Second World War. Each was granted veto power over Security Council action, and as time went by, America, Russia and China sometimes used their veto to protect themselves or their allies. China, of course, was in 1945 run by the Nationalist government of pro-Western General Chiang Kai-shek. He was defeated by Mao Zedong in 1949 and fled the mainland with the remnants of his army, which he rebased on the island of Taiwan. It held China's seat at the UN until 1971, when it was replaced by the People's Republic of China.

However unrepresentative the Security Council permanent members are today (excluding India and Brazil, for example), the organisation is frozen – regular attempts to reform it are blocked by one or other of the great powers of 1945, threatening to cast a veto. The most obvious, and obviously right, reform would be a requirement that a veto could not be imposed by a permanent member state if it had a conflict of interest. Oddly, this is a requirement for voting on procedural issues but not on substantive resolutions. It would disqualify Russia from voting on a resolution about a war which it had started, or a resolution demanding a cease-fire or peace negotiations to end that war. However, there is no prospect of this reform ever being implemented, over the veto of Russia and probably of China and the US.

It will be appreciated from the above analysis that the UN is not a protector of Ukraine's democracy or anyone else's. It was set up to prevent war, and it matters not whether victim states are free or authoritarian. Ukraine deserves protection under the UN charter not because it was democratic or, as Putin alleged, run by fascists, but because it was a member state in good standing. The issue will be considered in Chapter 7: as the world becomes increasingly influenced by authoritarian regimes, is democracy worth a new organisation devoted to its values – a replacement, perhaps, for the UN itself, which is not capable of fulfilling that purpose?

The unfitness of the UN for its primary purpose of keeping the world at peace may be further gathered from the inability of the Security Council to deal with acts of aggression, and notably to enforce the fundamental rule in Article 2(4) of the UN charter: 'All members shall refrain in their international relations from the threat or use of force against the territorial integrity or political independence of any state.'

Force used against the territorial integrity of a state means an invasion, which is a precise description of the action of Russian forces on 24 February 2022, however much Putin may prefer the dishonest euphemism 'special military operation'. It was also designed to extinguish Ukraine's political independence, to extirpate or otherwise exterminate the democratically elected Zelensky and to replace him with a Russian puppet. There could hardly be any doubt of a prima facie case for the crime of aggression, against both Putin – who gave the order to start the war – and the state of Russia. It was the most blatant act of aggression since the invasion of Iraq by the US (Bush) and the UK (Blair), back in 2003. Zelensky keeps asking what can be done about this outrageous breach of the most fundamental principle of an organisation established to keep the peace, and the answer ('nothing much') is as follows.

The UN charter invites all members of the United Nations to meet as a General Assembly in session from time to time, but without the power to do anything other than debate and pass resolutions. The body charged under Chapter VII of the charter with taking 'action with respect to threats to the peace, breaches of the peace, and acts of aggression' is the Security Council. Its task is to determine the existence of such threats and it will 'decide what measures shall be taken … to maintain or restore international peace and security'. It may call upon the parties to cease firing or to withdraw, or may order its members to apply sanctions. If these measures are considered inadequate, it may invoke its Article 42 power to use such force as may be necessary to restore international peace and security, drawing upon armed forces that UN members undertake to make available, or choosing to set up a court to exercise international criminal law so as to punish aggressor states.

The Security Council would never consider action against Russia using the force permitted by Article 42, because Russia is a nuclear power, with more nukes even than the United States. Besides, Russia itself would veto such an action – the first catch in the UN charter is the rule that a permanent member may vote and veto in its own self-interest, as Russia would obviously do to stop any Security Council action against its interests or the interests of its allies like Syria or Belarus, or any attempts to set up a criminal court to try Putin. This fundamental flaw in the charter has been exposed by Russia's invasion of Ukraine: after an initial resolution, the Security Council went quiet. It should have been in constant session, doing its duty by at least discussing how to restore peace and putting pressure on Russia to negotiate with and/ or withdraw from Ukraine. Yet nothing happened. When

Russia took its turn to chair the Security Council in 2023, as the war was at its most intense, debate over it was sidelined – what should have been the first item on the agenda was quickly moved off it by Sergey Lavrov. The Security Council for two years has ignored the war that its primary duty was to stop.

The council's failure over Ukraine proves the UN is worthless as a guarantor of peace, because it cannot stop its permanent members from going to war and cannot require them to enter into peace talks once they do. The diplomats who designed the UN in 1945 did not appreciate this fatal flaw, namely the protection against aggression being entrusted to permanent members of the Security Council, several of which went on to acquire a long record for aggression – the US most notably in Vietnam, the Dominican Republic, Nicaragua, Grenada, Panama and Iraq, with Russia, not to be outdone, invading Hungary, Czechoslovakia, Afghanistan, Georgia and now Ukraine.

Any organisation that wants to be taken seriously must be entitled to expel members which break its fundamental rules. (Even the League of Nations expelled the USSR for attacking Finland.) The most fundamental rule of the United Nations is the rule against aggression, and the Russian war against Ukraine is a fundamental breach of it. The most obvious consequence, therefore, must be a sanction on Russia, by expelling it from the organisation. But where is the power to expel Russia from the UN? Article 4 of the charter makes membership open to all 'peace-loving states' which accept the charter's obligations and are able and willing to carry them out. Russia is not a 'peace-loving' state; it is a state which has declared war on a peace-loving state, and it is not willing to accept the charter obligations to bring aggression to an end. This means that it must be expelled – or does it?

Article 5 permits a member state to be suspended by the General Assembly, but only if the Security Council has recommended suspension. In relation to the war against Ukraine, the Security Council, to its shame, has taken no action at all and in any event would not recommend Russia's suspension because that would be a step that Russia would veto. This leaves only Article 6, which provides that a state that has 'persistently violated the principles contained in the present charter may be expelled from the organisation by the General Assembly' – and Russia has violated these principles every day since 24 February 2022 – but (wait for it) expulsion may only be 'upon the recommendation of the Security Council', which Russia would of course veto. It follows that Russia cannot be expelled from the UN, whatever it does. Even were it to engage in nuclear warfare with Ukraine, it would suffer no expulsion from the world community, however well deserved this expulsion would be.

A NEW AGGRESSION COURT?

So it follows that the Security Council will never establish an 'ad hoc' court like the ICTY and ICTR to punish Russian aggressors because Russia will veto any such action. The worst crime in the world committed by Putin, resulting in hundreds of thousands of deaths, cannot be dealt with by the Security Council or by any court that it establishes because it will not establish a court displeasing to Russia.

That became apparent within a few days of the Russian invasion. The first to call for action under international law was Gordon Brown, the former British Prime Minister, who urged the world, or a 'coalition of the willing', to set up a special 'aggression court' outside the ICC and the malign influence of the Security Council, in order to prosecute Putin and any other of his ilk (such as Alexander Lukashenko, his ally). This was widely acclaimed as a very good idea, and international lawyers around the world were retained or freely offered opinions on how such an aggression court might work. It was a difficult and controversial task, and it took over fifteen months before an 'International Centre for the Prosecution of the Crime of Aggression Against Ukraine' opened its doors in The Hague to collect evidence for a prosecution, but states have not yet agreed on the model for a court that could undertake the prosecution. Thirty-nine of them, including the US and many from Europe, have formed a 'core group' to design such a tribunal.

Any such court obviously must have jurisdiction (i.e. the power) to do so under international law. Ukrainian courts have such power but only under their domestic law. There is a provision against aggression in their criminal code – and if ever Putin were to be captured or surrendered, there would be no country more willing to see him punished. But – the first problem – he could never be punished, or even tried, because he is (or was) a head of state and, by immemorial convention of international law, heads of state have immunity; they do not allow each other to be put on trial. This is a principle that applies to trials in state courts, such as Ukrainian courts, which are bound to afford such immunity to foreign ministers as well, so Sergey Lavrov cannot end up in the Kyiv dock. The reasons for such immunity go back to the diplomatic niceties of bygone ages, to heraldic traditions and the divine right of kings, but they protected the kaiser and are hardwired into law and, as the British proceedings against General Pinochet showed, can take years to unravel. But as things stand, there is general agreement that international courts, but not the domestic courts of individual countries, can override any head-of-state immunity that Putin might assert.

That position has been reached as a result of the principles laid down by the judgment at Nuremberg, approved by the

UN General Assembly shortly after the trial. Hitherto, 'sovereign immunity' had attached to every leader, out of respect for the 'dignity' of their government: courts in Britain and America ruled emphatically that their domestic courts must decline jurisdiction over sovereigns and their ambassadors, out of respect and comity, no matter how undignified and lawless their behaviour. This approach shielded the kaiser, but failed for the Nazi leaders who claimed protection because they acted as representatives of their state. The Nuremberg court famously rejected that argument:

> Crimes against international law are committed by men, not by abstract entities, and only by punishing individuals who commit such crimes can the provisions of international law be enforced ...
>
> The authors of these acts cannot shelter themselves behind their official position in order to be freed from punishment in appropriate proceedings.

And that, in a nutshell, is what did for Augusto Pinochet, the well-known torturer and former President of Chile, who came to England to take tea (it was actually whisky) with his friend Mrs Thatcher. He was arrested by Scotland Yard on a warrant issued by a Spanish magistrate to extradite him on charges of authorising torture, and the courts decided that his immunity as a former foreign head of state could not prevail to protect him from prosecution for committing crimes against humanity. Sovereign immunity, based on respect for the dignity of foreign governments, must give way to a legal obligation to either put on trial or to extradite for trial any person reasonably accused of violating the fundamental provisions of international law – torture, in his case (backed by obligations in the Torture Convention), genocide, mass murder and, *a fortiori*, the crime of aggression.

And only international courts can override amnesties, the like of which Putin would doubtless be festooned before surrendering or resigning. So quite apart from all the other objections (it would not look good for Putin to be tried by Ukrainian judges, for example, who would inevitably have family or friends affected by the war), the problem of getting him to trial before a local Ukrainian court (or any other local courts – Poland has offered) is overwhelming.

Putin's thoughts have already turned to immunising himself against legal action – in December 2020, he had his servile Parliament, the Duma, pass a law which prohibited legal action against any Russian President, even in retirement. This permanent pardon would be valid only in Russia – courts in other countries would find it an illegitimate way of suspending the criminal law in relation to future crimes (a President would not be prosecuted, for example, for murdering his mistress). Perhaps Putin already had in mind a plan to commit aggression against Ukraine, and his lawyers will certainly be considering how a more cast-iron amnesty could be inserted in any peace agreement eventually made to end the war. Amnesties have long been a welcome way to end hostilities but have more recently been condemned by human rights groups as allowing perpetrators to walk free (usually, with their Swiss bank account free from seizure). The turning point came with an amnesty agreed at Lomé to pardon leaders of a faction in Sierra Leone that committed the worst of war crimes: the UN secretary-general had his representative insist that it could not pardon crimes against humanity, and the UN court – the SCSL – subsequently agreed.

This underlines the importance of ensuring that the aggression tribunal operates under international law rather than Ukrainian law. If there is an amnesty for Putin in a peace agreement with Ukraine, it would be binding only on Ukraine, but that might exclude that country from participating in the tribunal, no matter how vociferously Zelensky has advocated its establishment.

This consideration counsels against the suggestion that a Ukrainian court could be 'bigged up' to look international – perhaps transferred to The Hague and with a few foreign judges? This has been suggested by some states – like the US – which for political reasons have to 'show willing' for a Putin trial but do not want to create a precedent for an 'aggression tribunal' which might catch some future American

President who decides to invade a state like Saddam's Iraq or the Taliban's Afghanistan. This is an irrational fear – the tribunal's jurisdiction would be limited to crimes committed on Ukrainian territory. Nonetheless, the US is a member of the 'core group' of states meeting to plan an aggression court, and it has been arguing for an 'internationalised' Ukrainian court, set up in The Hague and awaiting Putin's arrival, as if by parachute. Such a court would not be possible, in any event, because it would require a change in the Ukrainian constitution, which has been frozen during hostilities and by martial law. And it would carry the danger of not being recognised as capable of dispensing international law because of its anchor in the Ukrainian legal system.

So the sensible model for an international court is one where the 'international' element is provided by an agreement with the UN. The General Assembly could endorse an agreement establishing the court concluded between Ukraine and the UN secretary-general, which would be modelled on the agreement between Sierra Leone and the secretary-general which set up the Special Court for Sierra Leone. The court would have a mandate to prosecute those 'most responsible' for aggression – it could feel the collar of Lavrov, Medvedev and Lukashenko, for example. It would exclude head-of-state immunities and the like, by a formula similar to Article 27 of the ICC Rome Statute:

This statute shall apply equally to all persons, without distinction based on official capacity. In particular, official capacity as a head of state or government, a member of a government or Parliament, an elected representative or a government official shall in no case exempt a person from criminal responsibility under this statute, nor shall it, in and of itself, constitute a ground for reduction of sentence.

It should, in fact, constitute a ground for a heavier sentence, for any perpetrator of an aggression that results in many deaths and injuries of soldiers and civilians. The definition of the crime, now encased in Article 8 *bis* of the Rome Statute, would likely be reflected in the proposed tribunal's statute. Provided that its proceedings conformed with international fair trial standards, the aggression tribunal should pass muster as an international court if its status were ever called into question before the ICJ or in enforcement proceedings before any other court or by a defendant's appeal to the appeal panel of the tribunal itself.

The ICJ – the supreme judge of international law – has not set out the qualifications it expects for an international court. The best precedent is the Special Court for Sierra Leone, which decided that factors such as its independence from the local court system, its UN-agreed statute, its UN-member-states' funding, international judges and legal provisions all pointed towards its status as an 'international' court. It had no connection whatsoever with local courts, as a matter of power or personnel. An aggression court, set up by an agreement with the Ukrainian government, would sit like other international courts in The Hague and would be financed by voluntary donations from UN member states – the EU has already donated $9 million to fund an investigative mechanism which opened in July 2023. The US, in November 2023, donated a paltry $1 million. It made a great fuss about the importance of the exercise but was not prepared to give enough money to ensure it would flourish.

There would not need to be any conflict between the ICC and the aggression court – a relationship agreement could provide for cooperation on, for example, sharing of evidence. The ICC would have jurisdiction over Putin in regard to war crimes, if he could be proved to have committed them (as alleged with the kidnapping of Ukrainian children) or to have turned a blind eye towards the perpetrators (as alleged in the second charge of having 'superior responsibility' for the exercise). An arrest warrant has already been issued by the ICC over these two charges relating to Ukrainian children, and more will likely follow alleging his complicity, or at least insouciance, towards bombings of civilians and executions of prisoners of war. If he is captured, he may well be tried alongside those in lower orders of the command structure in relation to a particular atrocity. If he is not captured or surrendered, he will not be tried at all for war crimes by the ICC unless its members amend the Rome Statute to make provision for trials *in absentia*.

But provision for trials *in absentia* should be made for the aggression court, which must be constructed on the assumption that a prosecutor will usually be unable to force heads of state, generals and foreign ministers to attend for trial. Russia has not only a multitude of nuclear weapons but the world's third largest military, so it is idle to think Putin will be dispatched to The Hague unless overthrown by a coup or some other upheaval of the kind presaged at one point by Yevgeny Prigozhin. Putin is now constitutionally able to stay in power until 2036, by which time he will be two years older than Biden's present age but but not likely to retire to any place where he could be snatched by the West. If Russia's economy and financial institutions suddenly collapse and his surrender becomes a condition for the lifting of Western sanctions, as was the case with Milošević, a new government might give him up, but even this is a most unlikely prospect – it would involve too much national humiliation. So the aggression tribunal, if it wants to do business, will have to prepare for a trial *in absentia*.

As already noted, many Anglo-American lawyers think that a trial *in absentia* is not trial at all. Defendants – however guilty the prosecution evidence may show them – cannot be there to refute it or offer explanations. Every inducement would be offered to Putin to attend, or at least to appear on a Zoom link to answer questions, but he is unlikely to fall for this: his tactic will be to avoid any action that might be construed as cooperation with the court. For all that he will complain (and Russia will complain on his behalf) about the unfairness of an *in absentia* trial, this complaint, as we shall see, can have little or no force in a trial for aggression, where the facts about the invasion are clear as are the aggressor's intentions – in Putin's case, stated in his speeches and writings and even in his sycophantic interview with American TV show host Tucker Carlson. Putin's 'self-defence' defence must be decided objectively – there is nothing that he could add to it from the witness box.

His case will come to the courtroom at the initiative of the prosecution, who will acquaint the judges with Putin's relevant public statements and anything their witnesses might say about his responsibility for the chain of command, but the defendant himself will not condescend to communicate. He will have, it is to be supposed, 'the right to silence', an English curiosity (now abandoned in England but treated with veneration in Commonwealth countries and international courts) which entitles a man who has given orders to kill thousands to stand back and laugh in the face of his prosecutors – they cannot ask the judges to infer his guilt from his reluctance to answer questions about it. They can, however, ask them to infer it from the proven facts, which in Putin's case should be quite enough to establish a prima facie case for the crime of aggression.

PROCEDURAL ISSUES

The aggression court will need a management committee – probably made up of delegates from donating countries and a few experts in running international courts. Then a court registrar or CEO must be appointed – the most important appointment. The court in Sierra Leone worked because of the masterful administration by Robin Vincent from the Lord Chancellor's department, who was then appointed to run the Lebanon tribunal but died before he could lick it into shape. In an international war crimes court, the judges are usually part-time and the registrar is central to the organisation of the court, ensuring that it has adequate defence counsel and that its funding arrangements are satisfactory. In the case of the Special Court for Sierra Leone, defendants challenged the voluntary funding system on the grounds that the money might run out. The court rejected the challenge but commented that if the court was left without money to afford a fair trial, 'it should not attempt to do so'. The trial of Putin would come at a price: the government of Ukraine obtained quotations suggesting that could be as low as £15 million, but it would probably be three times as much. If he turned up, of course, the cost would triple again.

The big question for this court, more than for any other international criminal court, is whether the identity and nationality of the judges causes any realistic apprehension that they will be biased. At Nuremberg, they were all nationals of the Allied powers, in that sense delivering 'victor's justice', although it was more a case of victory enabling justice to be done for the Holocaust. What will be required to judge Putin will be diligence, experience and learning, and dozens who have served as international judges have those qualities. But a trial of Putin, even in his absence, might be seen as biased if the judges, however independent in their work or their character, came from Ukraine or even from NATO nations. That would mean a bench of trial judges called, for example, from South Africa, Trinidad and Brazil. In a hybrid court, like that in Sierra Leone, the judges were two-thirds international and one-third from Sierra Leone, but there was nothing to stop Sierra Leone appointing international judges to its reserved seats and this would be the case if Ukraine had the right to make some judicial appointments. Nonetheless, the issue remains live and if judges from Ukraine or NATO nations are chosen, their independence and impartiality must be conspicuous.

Much will depend upon the personality and competence of

the prosecutor, who will inevitably become the public face of the court and bear responsibility for crucial decisions over the preparation and presentation of evidence. They will be subject to obloquy stirred up by Russian trolls, whether Putin is physically in the dock or not, and will need fortitude to withstand this barrage and a track record of conducting trials with exemplary fairness. Nationality should not matter, although it has been a debilitating factor in other international courts – the first, the ICTY, saw a number of good candidates objected to on this ground until Mandela saved the day by releasing a judge from South Africa's Constitutional Court to whom no country could object. Richard Goldstone worked with a deputy, Graham Blewitt, who had much experience in preparing belated war crimes prosecutions in Australia, and thanks to their leadership, the court overcame its obstacles (including sometimes its judges) to move on to meet its targets.

The target of the aggression tribunal will be Vladimir Putin, who plainly meets the leadership qualification for prosecution for aggression, namely that he was in a position to exercise control over, and to direct, the political and military actions of Russia. There would be reason to indict his accomplices who also meet this test – for example, the twenty or so ministers and generals present at the televised State Security Council meeting of 21 February 2022 who supported his plan to annex Donbas as a prelude to the attack on Ukraine three days later. They could argue, in their defence, that Putin was all-powerful and they had no freedom to countermand his orders or even to disagree. Intelligence material from the CIA and M16 might cast light on these accomplices who certainly gave no public indication that they were acting under any duress and have continued loyally to play leadership roles in the attacks on Ukraine, to oversee targeting decisions and to overlook war crimes by those under their command.

In reality, Putin's chief aiders and abetters in his crime of aggression have been his propagandists – those who spread on state television the Kremlin's lies about Nazis and genocide. Even more influential for most ordinary people was the Russian Orthodox Church, headed by Putin's close friend and alleged former KGB colleague Patriarch Kirill, who served as principal cheerleader for the war. These people had equivalents among the Nuremberg defendants such as Hitler's propaganda chief Joseph Goebbels and the editor of antisemitic newspapers, Julius Streicher. Journalists do not have leadership positions over the military or political establishment of the state and may not therefore be subject to prosecution for aggression because they would not have the leadership requirement for the crime. This is a serious defect in the ICC definition, which requires urgent attention, although the Rwanda tribunal decisions establish that those responsible for media that urges genocide are guilty of aiding and abetting the crime. Although Kirill and other state media propagandists lack the leadership status necessary for committing the crime of aggression itself, it is arguable that they can be tried alongside the leaders for incitement and conspiracy.

VICTIMS' RIGHTS

It will be a matter for those who establish the aggression tribunal to decide whether victims should have representation and hearing rights before it. This is deprecated in British courts because it looks like a second prosecution, loading the case against a defendant, and so 'victim impact statements' can be introduced only after a conviction. But in France and in other countries, including Ukraine, victims have certain rights to participate in court proceedings. This became a problem in the trial of Klaus Barbie, the 'butcher of Lyon' extradited to France to stand trial for the brutality of the Gestapo: relatives and representatives of his victims disrupted proceedings both in and outside the court, looking at times like a lynch mob. Some international courts do allow victims' representatives to make legal submissions, but there is a danger that an adversary trial will seem, in public perception, unbalanced if victims' understandable desire for retribution on the author of their suffering starts to infuse the proceedings. The aggression tribunal must give a fair trial, which means that the case for many millions of Ukrainian victims of Putin must be left in court, to the prosecutor.

But should a selection of such victims be called to testify to their sufferings from Putin's aggression? The prosecution will have to weigh the undoubtedly dramatic forensic force of their testimony against its marginal relevance (the court can take judicial notice of the suffering without hearing evidence of it), and to call victims and witnesses to the devastation caused by years of war would extend the time of the trial considerably. This kind of evidence can have its downsides, and the prosecutor will doubtless be aware of what happened in the Milošević case, where victims of Serb paramilitaries were put on the stand first, in the expectation that they would make a poignant impact, but they were confused and outclassed by the crafty self-defendant, himself (like Putin) a trained lawyer. The victims' voice should be heard at the sentencing stage of the proceedings for the crime of aggression, but not at the trial itself.

Aggression trials must be distinguished from those for war crimes under Article 8 of the Rome Statute, where victim testimony is highly relevant. If a commander (or a supreme commander) is charged with ordering (or failing to investigate) the bombing of a cathedral or a school, victims (both relatives of the dead, injured persons and witnesses) must be invited to tell their story of the atrocity. If Putin ever faces trial for the offence with which he has been charged, the forcible transportation of children, he will certainly face the evidence from the children he has been accused of transporting. They will be some years older, but the experience is likely to be seared into their memories and live again in their testimony.

Finally, there is the question of punishment in the event of conviction. Notwithstanding the death sentences passed at the Nuremberg and Tokyo trials, international courts ever since have eschewed this form of punishment (but see p. 144). Given the gravity of the crime of aggression, Putin should be imprisoned for the rest of his life. He could serve the sentence, by agreement with the ICC, in the jail of a willing state party to the treaty establishing a tribunal – like Charles Taylor, who is languishing in the cells of a British prison. The sentence can be imposed after a trial *in absentia*, subject, of course, to Putin's rights to a retrial if subsequently apprehended. An interesting power, which should be vested in the court, is to order compensation to the victims of his war – to Ukrainians certainly, but Russians as well if they are relatives of those conscripted to fight. Russia is unlikely to comply, but according to Alexei Navalny, Putin's assets are huge and span a number of jurisdictions where they are held in the name of cronies – an aggression tribunal order could allow local courts to trace and seize them.

At the time of writing, European countries have managed to seize and freeze upwards of $300 billion in Russian assets, which remain nominally in the ownership of the Russian state or its oligarchs rather than the banks which hold them. There could be no successful objection to the use of interest money or the frozen funds for the benefit of reconstruction in Ukraine, and some politicians (including the UK foreign secretary) have urged that they should be used for that purpose.

The ICC has a trust fund with state donations supplemented by the seizure of the ill-gotten gains of its convicts, and a similar body should be set up for the tribunal. It could be merged with the body established in 2023 by the EU's Council of Ministers which is based in The Hague with funds from the US, Canada and Japan as well as the forty council members. Its registrar will record claims and submit them to an adjudicative body – sensibly, this could be the judges of the aggression court, which would have the power to make seizure and compensation orders. Money can never compensate for the human suffering caused by a war of aggression, but Holocaust victims and others have found awards of compensation a belated solatium, and if Putin is forced to pay personally, seizure of his money will provide a form of punishment, albeit much less than he deserves.

CHAPTER 3

THE CASE FOR THE PROSECUTION

The case against Vladimir Putin for committing the crime of aggression may be shortly stated, although long-winded lawyers have a habit of taking excessive time and it will be up to the presiding judge to confine them to proof of the relevant facts. They will open the case with an explanation of the law and go on to argue that its application means the defendant should be found guilty.

THE CRIME OF AGGRESSION

Aggression, as an international law crime, needs a little historical explanation. It was not regarded as an offence when kings invaded neighbouring kingdoms or when nations built-up overseas empires by merciless attacks on territories which were subjugated and colonised. The first to be considered for prosecution, for starting the First World War, was Kaiser Wilhelm, and British lawyers (notably the Attorney General, F. E. Smith) worked out a legal basis on which they thought he could be convicted. The crime for which he was to be hanged was for invading Belgium in 1914. But the Americans, who had joined the war towards its end, were not so bent on revenge and insisted that as head of the German state, he had immunity from prosecution. Woodrow Wilson was concerned that a public execution of their king would be so shocking to Germans that they would refuse to have anything to do with his grand plan for a League of Nations, so the kaiser was allowed to claim asylum in the Netherlands.

Despite Wilson's support for the league, America refused to join it, but in 1928 it joined with other nations in the Kellogg–Briand Pact, a diplomatic exercise by which they renounced war as an instrument of national policy and undertook to rely instead on 'pacific means' to settle their disputes. This was one reason why Hitler's aggression, by invading other states before and during the war, was prosecuted at Nuremberg as 'a crime against the peace', for which his main Nazi commanders were convicted and executed.

The United Nations, in due course, approved the Nuremberg charges and a new definition of the crime, anchored to a breach of Article 2(4) of the charter, which lays down that 'all members shall refrain in their international relations from the threat or use of force against the territorial integrity or political independence of any state, or in any other manner inconsistent with the Purposes of the United Nations'.

This will be the first rule declaimed by the prosecutor. The judges will, of course, be well aware of it, but the UN charter is not widely read and for the television audience, hearing it read slowly and emphatically, and probably twice, it will sound like a precise description of what Putin has done to Ukraine. But there will be more, because the prosecutor will have to explain how this rule, purportedly binding on nations by virtue of the UN charter, became a criminal law, for the breach of which political leaders of these nations could be sent to prison.

The story really starts at Nuremberg, when the Nazi leaders were prosecuted and convicted for 'crimes against the peace': the Movietone newsreels of their tanks invading one country after another were admitted as evidence, together with wartime declarations by Hitler and the defendants and documents establishing the annexations. The crime was not carefully defined and was not charged subsequently in respect of aggression by the United States and the Soviet Union during the Cold War. When it came to setting up the International Criminal Court by the Rome Treaty in 1998, the crime of aggression was explicitly included as within its jurisdiction (by Article 5), but an empty space was left for a definition which ICC members would settle later. It took them until their conference in Kampala in 2010 to do so, and even then the power to prosecute was delayed until 2018.

Most of the delay was caused by the UK and France (ICC member states) and lobbying behind the scenes from the three most powerful non-members – America, Russia and China – all concerned to ensure that their leaders could never be prosecuted. As permanent members of the UN but non-members of the court, they could veto any referral to the ICC by the Security Council, and they made sure that the ICC's jurisdiction over aggression excluded aggression by non-members. Critically, the ICC is prevented from exercising jurisdiction over the nationals of non-state parties even when they commit a crime on the territory of a state party – distinguishing aggression from all other crimes under the ICC's jurisdiction.

However, any court established to try Putin would sensibly adopt the ICC definition, which the prosecutor would proceed to read at the outset of their opening speech. The prosecutor would tell the court that the crime of aggression was committed by a person who was in a position 'to exercise control over or to direct the political or military action of a state' (and Putin was certainly that) and who had been involved with 'planning, preparation, initiation or execution' of an act of aggression 'which, by its character, gravity and scale, constitutes a manifest violation of the Charter of the United Nations', i.e. of the prohibition in Article 2(4) on invading other states. The invasion of Ukraine was of a gravity and scale that constitutes a 'manifest violation' both because it was full-scale and because it was, on the face of it, unlawful.

The very reading of the definition, applied to what is publicly known about the invasion, does, so the prosecution would contend, fit Putin like a glove. He was in prime position to direct the military and political action of the Russian state, and the requirement that his act of directing the invasion must have a 'character, gravity and scale' that made it a manifest charter violation was amply fulfilled. It led to tens of thousands of deaths, the seizure of up to one-third of Ukrainian lands and had grave implications for food supplies and for the environment. It may be contrasted, on this score, with President Trump's act of aggression against Syria in 2020, when he attempted to deter its use of chemical weapons by attacking an air base, killing six workers but failing to immobilise the base, which was operational the next day. Although an act of aggression, it lacked the gravity and scale – it was not an invasion – necessary to be branded an international crime.

The Rome Treaty, as amended (Article 8 *bis*), lists a number of acts that qualify as aggression, including:

a. Invasion or attack of another state by armed forces
b. Bombardment
c. Blockade
d. Attack by armed forces on another state's army or air force

All of these acts of aggression against Ukraine have been

perpetrated by Russia and ordered by Putin and his generals. Aggression also includes use of mercenaries if they are fighting alongside the regular army, and there is ample evidence – on television, as well – of 'Putin's chef' Yevgeny Prigozhin recruiting from prisons those prepared to risk their lives as frontline fighters in return for release from their sentence. Putin actually admitted, after Prigozhin's attempted coup, that the state paid the salaries of his Wagner Group employees and paid them additionally with a pardon in return for surviving six months as cannon fodder.

There can be no doubt that Russia began a war of aggression on 24 February 2022, but at a trial this must still be proved. Putin's own declarations put beyond doubt that this 'special military exercise' was in fact a war of aggression. What was proved at Nuremberg by Movietone News extracts will be illustrated by clips from the BBC, CNN and Al Jazeera, recording Russian missile attacks from the early morning onwards on Kyiv, Kharkiv, Odesa, Kherson and other cities, their airports and military installations. The invading columns of Russian tanks can be seen leaving Belarus and heading towards Kyiv, and departing from Russia towards Kharkiv and from Crimea towards Kherson. Then came the paratroopers, the tanks and the ground troops in their tens of thousands striving, in the first few days of Putin's war, to capture the capital, Kyiv, and overthrow the Zelensky regime. The battle for Kyiv centred on its international airport and lasted for several weeks, as did the battles for other cities and towns. There is no shortage of direct evidence, from visual media on the ground reproduced on television in the West and in Russia itself (accompanied by false Kremlin boasts of success), that demonstrates the gravity and scale of the Russian aggression. Because aggression is a continuing crime, all its consequences up to the time of trial will be admissible in evidence, not to prove that Putin is guilty of specific war crimes (this comes in separate ICC proceedings) but to show the true 'character, gravity and scale' of the crime of aggression which makes it a 'manifest' violation of the UN charter. This includes not only the obvious consequences – all the death and destruction of the war – but the damage to the international rules-based order caused by the arbitrary invasion of a UN member state by a permanent member of the Security Council.

EVIDENCE FOR THE PROSECUTION

The trial will be televised and watched throughout the world: whether or not Putin is in the dock, visual reminders of the methods used as part of the aggression will serve to remind viewers of its brutality. Yet the prosecution would be wise not to dwell on this aspect for too long – some prosecutions of political leaders and generals have gone on for an unconscionable time (in the Milošević case, for example, an over-egged prosecution lasted for three years). It has been one of the most powerful criticisms of international courts – that their trials go on for years and the costs are exorbitant – and this is largely the result of prosecutors who strive to please the defendant's victims by including every possible charge and piling on witnesses to testify to facts that can be readily established, as in this case, by visual and documentary evidence.

The first tactical trial decision for the prosecutor will be how to open the 'live' evidence. The invasion of Ukraine will be proved by photographic evidence and declarations by the defendant, but someone from the Ukrainian government will have to testify to the timeline, i.e. the dates and broad details of further attacks stretching on for years, by the Russian forces with tanks, drones and aerial bombardments of cities and civilian homes, all to prove the 'manifest' gravity, scale and character of the aggression. The temptation will be to call President (perhaps by this time, ex-President) Zelensky, to relive that day of infamy, 24 February 2022. Any prosecutor would welcome the drama of his appearance to recount how on that day he refused a US offer to drive him out of Kyiv to safety: 'The fight is here; I need ammunition, not a ride.' Then to show his video address to the Ukrainian people: 'I am here. We are not putting down our arms. We will be defending our country, because our weapon is truth, and our truth is that this is our land, our country, our children and we will defend all this.'

This was a famous and courageous response to an act of aggression, admissible in evidence and sure to make a public impact were Zelensky himself to repeat it from the witness box. But prosecutors must be careful about 'politicising' the trial, seemingly to stack it emotionally in favour of Ukraine. Zelensky's appearance might also invite malevolent cross-examination. Putin's defence would seek to show that he was at the time trying to arrange for Ukraine to join NATO. The objective of a trial is to vindicate international criminal law by applying it as unemotionally as possible. It might be better to call a statistician, or a historian, to record the history of incursions and major atrocities on and after 24 February.

There will also be questions about calling evidence to prove that Putin's intention was regime change. This may be obvious, by way of inference from his attack on the capital Kyiv, but there is also likely to be live evidence from witnesses who could testify to Russia's (and hence Putin's) plans for the occupation. In burned-out Russian tanks were later found parade uniforms to be worn in a victory march down Kyiv's main avenue, and rations for Russian troops lasting only for the three days thought necessary to overcome Kyiv's resistance. Less certain have been allegations that the Ukrainian traitor Viktor Yanukovych, who had fled to Moscow in 2014, had been brought to Belarus in January, to be taken from there to Kyiv after a Chechen hit squad had assassinated Zelensky. Such allegations would be relevant (although not necessary) to prove aggression and may well be true, but unless there is hard proof, the prosecutor should resist the temptation to make them, remembering that truth is the first casualty of war and that a false witness will damage the respect that a trial conviction should carry.

Putin's intention, or as lawyers call it, his *mens rea*, can readily be inferred from his act of invading a sovereign state. His intention to breach the UN charter is obvious from the facts of the invasion – it was a war, and not some casual military exercise. The prosecution needs not prove that Putin had made any legal evaluation that the invasion was a breach, or a 'manifest' breach of the charter, but merely that he intended to initiate an act of aggression and knew that he was in a position to direct the political and military action of the state of Russia.

Of course, Putin may have imagined – and it has been widely reported that he was advised – that grateful Ukrainians, thrilled at being liberated from the neo-Nazi oppression of Zelensky's regime, would greet the invaders with flowers and kisses. This delusion may mitigate Putin's sentence, but it could not affect his liability for aggression, which came about through his deliberate act. An act which he admitted to on television and at public meetings. He claimed consistently that the invasion had been to eradicate the Nazis who were running the country and that it was necessary to stop genocide in Donbas and to prevent Ukraine from joining NATO. At the United Nations, his ambassador notified the secretary-general that Russia would rely on the defence provided by Article 51 of the charter, namely that of self-defence, which would therefore have to be his main defence at trial.

The prosecution could provide an account of Putin's intentions, from his own mouth. His claim that Ukraine was governed by Nazis was calculated to draw on popular legends about Russia's victory over Germany in the Second World War, but it was demonstrably a lie. Zelensky himself is Jewish, and in the last war several million Ukrainians had died fighting for Russia against Nazi invaders. It is difficult to understand how people, unless they had been brainwashed, could have swallowed Putin's lie – initiated from the Kremlin and promoted by pro-government media, which never mentioned the evidence that proved the contrary, namely the results of the 2019 Ukrainian election. The parties that could be claimed as 'neo-Nazi' were comprehensively defeated – they obtained only one seat between them in an election totally dominated by parties led by pro-European liberals – Volodymyr Zelensky, Petro Poroshenko and Yulia Tymoshenko. In

2022, the truth is that there was no Nazi or neo-Nazi faction in power or likely to achieve power in Ukraine.

THE 'IMMINENCE' QUESTION

This claim about Nazis running Ukraine is not even a defence to a charge of aggression – you cannot invade a right-wing regime any more than a leftist dictatorship – and in any event is so obviously false that no good lawyer would attempt to raise it. But what will be argued is the defence Russia gave notice of to the UN secretary-general at the time it invaded: it said that it would rely on Article 51 of the UN charter which preserves 'the inherent right of individual or collective self-defence if an armed attack occurs against a Member of the United Nations'.

But what conceivable 'armed attack' had occurred against Russia at the time of, or before, its invasion of Ukraine? Russia referred in general terms to a threat posed by Ukraine but gave no details to suggest that such a threat was imminent – a minimum requirement imposed by international law before force can be used in self-defence.

However, to justify the invasion of Iraq in 2003, the US had argued that 'imminent' meant a threat that might come to pass at some future time – if, for example, it turned out that Saddam Hussein had weapons of mass destruction and was minded to use them. Putin's lawyers, ironically, would have to argue that this extended notion of 'imminence', called 'pre-emptive self-defence', devised by Bush lawyers in 2002–03, represented international law. And to avail himself of this interpretation, Putin would have to go further and show that the threat to Russia in February 2022 was of Ukraine joining NATO and NATO then preparing to invade Russia. The prosecution would argue that this interpretation of international law has only ever been advanced by the US (which appears to have since abandoned the interpretation) and Israel. It would also argue, moreover, that this threat was non-existent. Ukraine had never previously shown any actual belligerence, other than during the Russian invasion of Crimea in 2014, and in respect of the pro-Russian insurgents in Donbas – examples of the state defending its own territory. Although Putin said that he regarded Ukraine's willingness to join NATO as a threat, this was a mere possibility at the time. Indeed, when Zelensky raised it in 2019 for the first time – as an aspiration – he was slapped down by US President Biden, who said there could be no possibility of NATO admitting Ukraine until it had instituted anti-corruption reforms. And just before the invasion, in February 2022, German Chancellor Olaf Scholz had insisted that 'all parties know that Ukraine's NATO membership is not on the agenda'.

The prosecution could call evidence from political scientists and indeed from NATO members to show that in

February 2022, Ukraine's membership was out of the question precisely because it would come with a binding obligation to defend Ukraine were it to be attacked by Russia. This was not an engagement, with nuclear weapons up the Russian sleeve, that Britain or any European country had the stomach to risk. To succeed with a Article 51 defence, if the Bush interpretation were accepted by the court, Putin would have to show the likelihood not only of Ukraine joining NATO but of NATO then attacking Russia. The prosecution would argue that this ultimate prospect was improbable. It would be well advised to leave Putin to make his case and then to shoot it down in rebuttal both as a matter of law – 'imminence' means imminence – and of fact, being no more than baseless speculation.

GENOCIDE AND NEO-NAZIS

Another reason that Putin gave at the time for the invasion was that Ukraine had started to commit genocide, by threatening to wipe out the 4 million inhabitants of Donetsk and Luhansk. The prosecution would reply that Ukrainian action came nowhere near genocide as defined in the convention. Its army engaged in armed conflict with insurrectionists in the east in 2014, during the Russian takeover of Crimea, and there were several thousand casualties. But this soon became a 'frozen conflict', with very few deaths in the subsequent years leading up to 2022. The action of Ukrainian forces, in protecting Ukrainian territory, could not amount to genocide, which requires a determination to wipe out a national, ethnical, racial or religious group. The only person to satisfy that definition in 2022 was Vladimir Putin, who invaded with the intention of destroying a nationality, namely that of being Ukrainian.

Putin's false allegations of genocide have already proved counterproductive: they gave Zelensky's lawyers the opportunity to bring the war before the International Court of Justice, on a fast-track procedure to claim that genocide has not been committed by Ukraine and that the convention does not provide a basis for the use of force. Russia refused to attend the first hearing but asked the Netherlands to pass on its claim that the ICJ had no jurisdiction to hear the application. The court decided that it did and, being apprised of the suffering and deaths caused in the early weeks of the invasion, it ordered Russia to suspend immediately all use of force on Ukrainian territory. This was in mid-March 2022, just three weeks after the invasion had started, but Putin refused. His disobedience – to the order of the World Court – would be admissible at his trial to further prove that Putin's intention to invade was and remains deliberate; he had the *mens rea* to continue committing the crime of aggression, irrespective of the order of the court. By the time of Putin's trial, the ICJ will have decided the case, and is likely to rule against Russia, i.e. that genocide was not threatened in Donbas in 2022, thus pulling the carpet from under Putin's use of this pretext for his invasion.

The best evidence of Putin's state of mind on the eve of the invasion comes in the form of his 6,000-word essay, 'On the Historical Unity of Russians and Ukrainians', which he published in July 2021, written while sheltering in the countryside – during the Covid pandemic. It was the expression of a desire to 'make Russia great again' by absorbing Ukraine. It was not a real country, Putin contended, because Russians and Ukrainians were historically 'one people' who should be reunited to achieve their spiritual destiny. This essay would be put before the judges as evidence of Putin's motive to extinguish the state of Ukraine and the national identity of its people by an invasion which would kill many civilians and return the rest back to their pre-1991 allegiance to the Soviet Union, now an alliance to Russia. He located the spiritual beginnings of this engorged state (Russia, Belarus and Ukraine) in the adoption of Christianity by Prince Vladimir in the eleventh century and he castigated Vladimir Lenin for 'inventing' Ukraine by giving it relative autonomy in 1920. Putin's objective in this essay was to eliminate Ukraine and to 'make Russia great again' in consequence. It was a theme repeated in his speeches in the aftermath of the invasion: he could have no sincere belief in the need to denazify and to stop genocide, but he probably did believe in the historical unity of Ukraine and Belarus with Russia and that its people, sharing this spirit, would welcome his invading troops. But as a matter of international law, optimism that all will turn out right in the end does not provide a defence.

To further show Putin's determination and deliberation in committing aggression, the prosecution should cite his breach of the Treaty of Budapest, the 1994 deal by which Ukraine allowed its nuclear weapons – one-third of those in the world – to be destroyed, after the break-up of the USSR. With encouragement from both the Yeltsin regime and the Bush administration, Ukraine signed an agreement to do so and Britain, Russia and the US reciprocally pledged 'to respect the independence and sovereignty of the existing borders of Ukraine'. The US paid for the destruction, and Russia paid compensation for the loss of the uranium in the bombs: this agreement for the next twenty years was hailed as the highlight of post-Cold War cooperation. Zelensky, in the run-up to the invasion, quoted it continually but Putin took no notice, claiming it applied only to nuclear attacks. Plainly it does not: it requires the parties to refrain from the threat or use of force or economic compulsion against Ukraine and additionally never to resort to nuclear arms. Putin's interpretation was wrong but served as his pretext for ignoring the Budapest agreement. This is evidence of Putin's malign intent: the Budapest agreement was a contract for which Ukraine gave valuable consideration in 1994 but in 2022 wished that it had not.

FURTHER EVIDENCE

The only other evidence the prosecutor might call upon is to identify Putin as the lead, if not the only, maker of the decision to go to war. He has accepted responsibility in speeches and could hardly contest the point: the televised State Security Council meeting three days before the invasion shows him in total command of his generals and his ministers who (with one terrified and brief exception) readily acquiesced in his proposal to annex Donbas. If the prosecution wished to ram home the point, it could call testimony about the decision-making process in the Kremlin, perhaps insider evidence from defectors or whistleblowers demonstrating Putin's personalised power over every sinew of the state. But he is unlikely to dispute his command responsibility for the decision to go to war. Were he to be prosecuted together with others of his 21-member State Security Council, the video recording of the meeting on 21 February, three days before the invasion, would identify the individuals who could also be charged, on proof of their 'leadership' capacity – i.e. their effective control of the political or military power of the state. Alexander Lukashenko, President and effective dictator of Belarus, may qualify as Putin's co-defendant, because of his close cooperation with the invasion which was launched from his territory.

The prosecutor will certainly show to the court the interview that Putin obligingly gave in 2024 to Tucker Carlson, a former Fox News host and right-wing propagandist opposed to US support for Ukraine. This will be used, if Putin is prosecuted in person, as the basis for cross-examining him about lying about the causes of the war. If the trial is *in absentia*, the interview will make up for his absence by presenting his defence as best it can be presented. He was never confronted with facts that refuted his falsehoods and the occasion smacked of a carefully crafted 'examination-in-chief', where the jury is supplied with the best spin that can be put upon facts that the defendant cannot deny. For the first half hour, Carlson was regaled with medieval history beginning with Prince Vladimir in 988 and the subsequent progress of Ukraine and Russia together with one faith, one language and one prince. Ukraine was an artificial Bolshevik state 'shaped at Stalin's will' and after the break-up of the USSR, it made the mistake of going its own way. Putin admitted that the 'coup' in Ukraine in 2014 was the trigger for the invasion – 'We would have never considered to even lift a finger if it hadn't been for the bloody developments on Maidan' – which he insisted had been orchestrated by the CIA. The move towards NATO by the 'nazified' government of Zelensky had forced Russia to invade, but Putin would have been prepared to withdraw a few weeks later had Boris Johnson (as Biden's emissary) not intervened to stop Ukraine from agreeing to this peace plan. Putin's account was not challenged, even when irreconcilable with demonstrable facts, and his lengthy excursus into history was highly questionable and provided no justification for the war. His idea that Boris Johnson parachuted in to veto a ceasefire agreement was risible and his Nazification notion was fantasy. But the recording of his TV appearance would be of great value to the prosecution in any trial *in absentia*, because it would make up for his absence and remove the central objection to such trials, namely that the defendant's voice is not heard. The one problem with the over-friendly Carlson interview was recognised by Putin's advisers: several days after it was widely derided in the West, Putin said that he was surprised that it had been so 'soft', and he had wished for sharper questions.

CRIMEA?

The evidence for the prosecution will amount, prima facie, to Putin being guilty of a single charge of aggression: it shows that all the elements of the crime are satisfied in relation to the 24 February 2022 invasion of Ukraine.

The other big decision for the prosecution is whether to call any 'similar fact' evidence about Russia's conduct in 2014, when it invaded Ukraine to annex Crimea, or whether to charge this separately, as another crime of aggression that had the character, gravity and scale to qualify as an international crime. This could prove a two-edged sword because very little was done about it by the international community, giving Putin some reason to believe that a full-scale invasion might not be seriously opposed. In logic, this would not justify the later aggression and could be separately charged or introduced into evidence as part of his plan to conquer the whole country. But the prosecution should tread very carefully. The court will need to be told the historical background of how Ukraine was made a semi-autonomous part of the Soviet Union by Lenin, and in 1945 was made, at Stalin's insistence, a member state of the UN, with sovereignty and independence unchallenged despite the fact it was still a component part of the USSR. The freedoms later allowed by Mikhail Gorbachev encouraged nationalist and separatist feelings, and in 1990 Ukraine's parliament – its Supreme Soviet – adopted a 'declaration of state sovereignty', approved by 92 per cent of its people at a referendum held the next year. From that point, the sovereign state of Ukraine (including Crimea) was, as a matter of international law, independent. These facts can be proved without controversy. The Russian annexation of Crimea in 2014 is more complex.

This had come about after the unpopular pro-Russian President Viktor Yanukovych fled to Moscow after ordering police to fire on protesters, and eighty of them were killed. There had been demonstrations against him in Kyiv's central square, the Maidan, where crowds displayed popular support for politicians who wanted the country to join the EU. Putin was furious and directed that the Crimean Peninsula should be infiltrated by his soldiers, in green uniforms but without insignia – the 'little green men' who prepared the grounds for takeover by Russian forces from its naval base at Sevastopol. After they did so, the Kremlin held a referendum, with a predictably unbelievable vote of 96.7 per cent in favour of Russian occupation and annexation. (Whenever will those who rig referenda realise they should make the rigged results reasonably close?) In total, 100 member states of the UN voted to recognise that the peninsula still belonged to Ukraine, but Russia took no notice. The US imposed some sanctions, but in general Russia suffered few reprisals – the general feeling at the time was that 'Putin got away with it'. He also got away with 'little green men' in Donbas, the east of Ukraine where support for Russia was strongest, namely in Donetsk and Luhansk.

Russia's intervention in that conflict extended to supplying the Buk missile which shot down MH17 – the Malaysian airliner carrying many Europeans to a medical conference in Melbourne. Two Russians and a Ukrainian separatist from the gun team were later convicted *in absentia* for complicity in murder, but the verdict is open to question: they were unrepresented and so could not advance the legal argument that they should have faced lesser charges. There was initial bloodshed – up to 14,000 deaths – from fighting between pro-Russian locals and their 'little green men' helpers on one side and the Ukrainian Army on the other, but the eastern zone soon settled into the familiar 'frozen conflict', in which Russia had significant – but not majority – support by the time of its February 2022 invasion.

The question for the Putin prosecutor will be whether to widen the indictment, either to include a second charge of aggression to cover 2014 or to allege that the crime began in 2014 and continued thereafter. There is no doubt that aggression may be committed by infiltration of armed forces, whether or not they are in uniform, and that the annexation of Crimea was unlawful and constituted a form of aggression – the use of force to violate the boundaries of a UN member state. But the definition in the Rome Statute did not become operative until 2018, so the defence could argue that Putin was being subjected to retrospective punishment. Moreover, the time needed to prove his guilt would be lengthy and the facts more complex – although hostile annexation had always been a crime in customary law, the different areas of Donbas could claim rights of self-determination. The proceedings would take much longer – many months longer – than a trial confined to details of the 2022 invasion, and the outcome could not be foretold: the pathetic response by the

West would be used to claim that it was not a 'manifest' violation of the charter and the fact that a significant minority of residents of Donbas did wish to be ruled by Russia gave the conflict, however frozen, the character of a civil war.

The Russian action in 2014 was denounced by Ukraine as 'armed intervention' in breach of the charter, but Russia claimed it was an exercise in support of Crimea's right to self-determination. In fact, a minority of Russians in Donbas were seeking to form a violent separatist movement and if Russia had an international law duty, it was to discourage them. The only state support it had for the annexation came from Belarus, when Lukashenko argued that Ukraine had acquiesced: 'Why did they not stand up and fight if the land was theirs?' Because, Ukraine could easily answer, they had no wish to start a war with Russia. In cases heard about the annexation over the next decade, Russia has claimed to have been invited to enter by its acolyte Yanukovych. Aggression by invitation is an old trick used by the US in Vietnam and by Russia in Czechoslovakia. However, Yanukovych, although previously elected, was now on the run and had no control of the state. He requested Russia to save his skin but not his country, and after fleeing he had no authority to issue an invitation on behalf of Ukraine.

Sometimes, defences advanced by Russia for the annexation of Crimea sound like the defences they advance for the invasion of Ukraine, namely to protect against genocide or the spread of Nazi ideology. But assisting a rebellion without Security Council authorisation violates a peremptory norm of international law and cannot be justified in the absence of facts proving that a substantial number of victims were in danger of losing their lives from the Ukrainian troops sent in to keep order. In any event, the frozen conflict in Donbas could not excuse the attack on 24 February 2022, which was not on Donbas but on all of Ukraine. The fleeing Russian stooge Yanukovych had no status to speak for Ukraine, and the quislings who announced their leadership of breakaway republics in Donetsk and Luhansk were not representative of the divided people of the region.

For severely practical reasons, in any event, the prosecution should avoid the temptation (or resist any pressure from Ukraine) to include the 2014 annexation of Crimea and the stoking of the civil conflict in Donbas as elements of the charge of aggression against Putin, which should remain focused on his 2022 invasion. There is little doubt as a matter of law that Russia committed aggression by infiltrating soldiers in camouflage to fight in Crimea, and 2014 was a time of intense political conflict – the Euromaidan protests, the jailing of Tymoshenko and the expulsion of Yanukovych – and Ukraine was in no state to fight back, as it did soon enough to assert its sovereignty over the coal-rich Donbas. Putin would defend himself by claiming 'acquiescence' to the Crimea aggrandisement and self-determination for Donetsk and Luhansk, and the evidence would have to be heard for many months before these defences could be dismissed as unsustainable. It was the Ukrainian people's reactions to the annexation of Crimea and to the eastern insurgency that undoubtedly strengthened national feeling and over eight years put steel in the hearts and minds of the majority, who were determined to risk their lives for freedom from Russia when it came to the crunch for their country in 2022. It is for that aggression that Putin must be tried, because a prima facie case against him can be established beyond any reasonable doubt.

A PRIMA FACIE CASE

Whether Putin has a case to answer is a determination which must be made by the judges at the close of the prosecution case, and it indubitably will be: there is overwhelming evidence that unless refuted or justified on grounds of self-defence, the Russian leader (or former leader, if he is actually in the dock) will have to be convicted. He will be invited to give evidence in his own defence – by Zoom if he remains in Russia – but the likelihood is that he will decline. However, stranger things have happened. At Nuremberg, Hermann Göring, the most senior of the Nazi defendants, urged them at first to refuse all cooperation with the tribunal. But as preparations seemed to be fair, Göring decided (as did his co-defendants) to have his day – many days – in court. So did Charles Taylor and Milošević (who died before he could take the witness stand). If Putin is being tried *in absentia*, his court-appointed lawyers will have to put up the best case possible on his behalf. Although his supporters will claim the defence is irreparably damaged by his absence, this will not be the case at all. The facts about the invasion will not be in dispute, and the law of self-defence can be left to lawyers, assuming that Putin's legal team is first class. It should have sufficient funds to call expert evidence, where relevant, for example on the question of the likelihood of Ukraine being admitted to NATO and, more importantly, of NATO attacking Russia. But the ultimate issue – whether Russia was acting in self-defence by invading Ukraine on 24 February 2022 – is for the court alone to decide, after hearing Putin's defence.

CHAPTER 4

PUTIN'S DEFENCE

Should Vladimir Putin come to be prosecuted in person, he will have at this point a choice of how to conduct his defence. He can always take his earphones out and turn his back to the judges – the equivalent of the 'kiss my ass' approach that Göring recommended at first to the Nuremberg defendants. Or he could adopt the 'king's gambit' which worked well for Charles I's posterity, namely argue that as a matter of law, the court was improperly constituted, but avoid any entry (even by cross-examination of witnesses) into factual disputes which he is likely to lose. He could stay silent, defy the prosecution to do its worst and argue that, at the end of the day, it had not proved his guilt beyond reasonable doubt. Or else he could turn the trial into a full-blown adversary proceeding, entering the witness box and taking an oath to tell the truth – on the Bible of the Russian Orthodox Church, since he affects a belief in God, or by simple affirmation. He may (as Churchill feared that Hitler would do if he were put on trial) be tempted to use the dock as a soapbox to declaim his case for invading Ukraine so as to make Russia great again.

PUTIN'S DEFENDERS

If the trial is *in absentia*, tactical decisions will depend on the team of lawyers appointed or approved by the court to represent Putin as powerfully as possible. On their conspicuous ability will hang the credibility of this trial, and those constructing the aggression court must ensure that it has ample financial and administrative resources for them. Called amici curiae or 'friends of the court', they must have legal distinction with a reputation as outstanding advocates, to give Putin (although he may never meet them) a 'fair crack of the whip'. He must, like O. J. Simpson, have a 'dream team' (Alan Dershowitz would make himself available, but Rudy Giuliani might not be advisable).

Many advocates who accept appointments to act as amici for people credibly accused of hideous international crimes loathe the clients on whom they are imposed but nonetheless have no difficulty formulating and advancing legal arguments in their favour. The rule of law requires judges to have before them every reasonable argument about the meaning and extent of the law, and for this purpose, advocates for bad people serve the ends of justice. But full-blooded legal representation must involve decisions about tactics and strategy, how severely to cross-examine and a willingness to use the law, as far as is ethical, to effectuate the wishes, even the presumed wishes, of a client who refuses to speak with them. This will be the case if Putin remains in Russia, ignores the proceedings and declines to have any contact with the amici.

The defenders will have some guidance – Russia, at Putin's direction, filed a note to the UN secretary-general just after the invasion saying it relies on Article 51 of the charter: the right of self-defence as an answer to aggression. This will be the principal line of defence. They could also argue an unstated claim of 'humanitarian intervention', but it may be difficult to find any evidence that Ukrainian people needed liberation from genocide or Nazism. Nor could they come up with any local politician to allege that he had 'invited Russia in' – Yanukovych had long departed Ukraine and pro-Russian politicians in Donbas were unelected and unrepresentative. But as Putin would wish to use the trial, whether he participated or not, to cause as much embarrassment for Western nations as he legitimately could, he would certainly wish his lawyers to run what was known at Nuremberg as the *'tu quoque'* defence, loosely translated as 'I did it, but you did it too'.

PRE-TRIAL MOTIONS

The defence team will have been put on its mettle before the trial proper can begin, because it will try to stop it by making an application that the court is not a court at all as a matter of international law. It will also say that the court cannot try Putin, because he enjoys head-of-state immunity, or else that he has been cloaked by an amnesty from his own government or from some truce negotiated with Ukraine. This will raise legitimate legal questions and will require extensive legal arguments which could go on for months unless the judges sensibly decide that they should be advanced by written submissions, with only a few days allocated to oral advocacy. The defence counsel should try, in writing, to shake the court to its foundations – it has been set up by states hostile to Russia and is unprecedented. This is true, of course, as it was for Nuremberg (as the prosecutor will doubtless reply), but it cannot resolve the question of whether the tribunal is a valid emanation of international law.

This will depend on how it is finally established. The guiding authority – a 2002 ICJ decision known as the 'arrest warrants case' (*Congo v. Belgium*) – affirms that courts set up by the Security Council and the ICC Treaty are international courts before which immunities do not apply but leaves undecided the categorisation of a court like the proposed aggression tribunal. This gives the defence an opening to argue that the tribunal is powerless if it is merely an agreement between the UN secretary-general and Ukraine. But the Special Court for Sierra Leone was an international court, although set up without Security Council Chapter VII authority. This was decided by the SCSL itself so 'it would, wouldn't it', to quote Mandy Rice-Davies (which a Russian lawyer probably would not). The defence have a good argument, but courts must decide between arguments that are good and arguments that are better. The thirty-nine states of the 'core group' constructing the court should do enough to separate it from Ukraine's legal system and ensure that it will, like the SCSL, be entitled to apply international law to reject the immunities that would protect Putin were he to be tried in the domestic courts of Ukraine or domestic courts anywhere else.

On the coat-tails of this argument, the defence will urge that Putin cannot be tried, whether he is still the head of state or an ex-head of state, because of the immunity which in customary international law attaches to this status. If the prosecution has succeeded in showing that the tribunal is indeed an international court, it will rely on a provision in its charter invalidating immunities. The defence may be able to argue that the tribunal structure is too dependent on Ukraine and its law – if it can be characterised as a Ukrainian court transported to The Hague, this argument could succeed. But in any event, if the hostilities in the Ukraine War are ever to end, it is likely that Russia will insist on an amnesty for Putin as a condition of any armistice.

Amnesty is certainly a device which has been much used in the past – notably by President Abraham Lincoln to 're-store the tranquillity of the commonwealth' after the US Civil War. It was also the reason why the pardon for Richard Nixon, granted by his successor Gerald Ford, was upheld by a US court. But here the prosecution will rely on a run of recent cases to the effect that amnesties cannot pardon se-rious international crimes which are unforgivable. This was the conclusion of the appeals chamber of the SCSL, which struck down a notorious amnesty (brokered, incredibly, by Jesse Jackson and Charles Taylor) which gave an 'absolute and free pardon' to leaders of the faction which ordered mass mutilation and mass murder. The court decided that such-like amnesties, which might be upheld under domestic law, would not apply in international law to bestow impunity. The defence will have to argue that this case was wrongly decid-ed, although the decision was applauded by human rights groups (to such an extent that it was suggested that Amnesty International should change its name to 'No Amnesty Inter-national'). Although amnesty is certainly appropriate for sol-diers who have fought against each other, it is inappropriate for those responsible for making them fight.

THE DEFENCE CASE OPENS

Such arguments will occupy the court for some time before the trial can begin with the prosecutor setting out the case against Vladimir Putin described in the previous chapter. It will be televised and widely covered by the media, and the defence lawyers – or Putin himself, if he attends or is provided with a Zoom link – should aim to counteract it immediately by applying to make an opening defence speech. This is fair and will clarify the issues at the outset, although it is not a right and when bestowed on Milošević, he used it to rally his political support in faraway Serbia. Nonetheless, the court should in fairness grant this application, and the amici will have to do their best to reflect Putin's indignation at proceedings which can override any pardon he was given as part of the ceasefire deal.

When planning his defence, will his team be tied down to Russia's notification to the secretary-general at the outset, that it would rely upon its right to self-defence under Article 51 of the charter? That will be a matter for the court, and given the purpose of the trial – to settle the question of whether the invasion was lawful – it can be expected that any application to add other defences would be granted. In that event, the team would have to consider whether it would call evidence in support, e.g. of Putin's claim that he acted to stop genocide. This was certainly an argument he advanced at the outset of the war, and many of his people still believe it, so the court should deal with it. The court is likely to deal with it dismissively, if by this time the ICJ has not done so.

Genocide, in law, requires proof of an intention to exterminate all or part of a group because of its race or its religion. Given that there were few deaths in Donbas after 2014–15, the low casualty figures will belie Putin's claim. Sergey Lavrov has pointed to the ban on using the Russian language in schools and courts, and this would be one indicia of a determination to oppress Russian speakers, but much more evidence would be required for an intention to destroy that group. Russian speakers were living without much difficulty under Zelensky and elected him by a large majority in 2019, in an election campaign which had no trace of Russophobia on his part. The defence might find and call 'victims' from Donbas to testify to oppression from Ukrainian authorities, which would prolong the trial (and lead to the prosecution calling evidence in rebuttal), but at the end of the day, it would not amount to the kind of 'humanitarian catastrophe' that can justify armed intervention to stop it. There may well be witnesses prepared to give evidence of brutality by Ukrainian forces, but the question for the defence would be whether they could stand up to cross-examination, and whether they were in fact coached or bribed by Russia or its supporters to mislead the court (the tribunal will need to have the power to punish for perjury). At the end of the day, the question for the defence will be whether the game is worth the candle: evidence that Ukraine was a hotbed of Nazism, and its forces were committing genocide, flies against the facts and is unlikely to be available, or if it is, to be believed. It is a lie that is still echoed in Russian propaganda, from its state media and in teaching at state schools and in state textbooks, so it may be in the public interest to have an authoritative judgment demolishing it. That cannot be a reason, however, for the defence team to advance it, but it is a reason for the court to allow them to do so, if they choose to advance it.

Could they, perhaps, pull a rabbit from the hat and confound the prosecution with a defence of consent? This was always the pretence upon which Russia (and America) invaded countries in the past. The invasion of Hungary in 1956 to overthrow the moderate government of Imre Nagy was justified on the basis that the Soviet Union had been 'invited in' by the hard-line head of a local Communist party, who had no constitutional power to consent to a change of regime. Nagy was arrested and brutally executed – which at least was not the fate of Alexander Dubček, who was overthrown on a similar pretext: an invitation to Moscow from a few Communist officials to invade Czechoslovakia. He was allowed to work as a gardener for thirty years until rehabilitated by Václav Havel. Putin's defence of 'consent' could doubtless rely on requests from a few pro-Russian councillors in Donetsk and Luhansk, whom Putin and others said had begged for intervention at the televised meeting of the State Security Council on 21 February. These witnesses would be available – but would their evidence prove consent to an invasion that first headed not to Donbas but to Kyiv, to overthrow the whole government of Ukraine? Certainly not: as local councillors, they could only speak – and controversially at that – for the region and not for the nation. The defence might consider dredging up ex-President Yanukovych, who fled to Moscow in 2014 and was said to be waiting in Belarus in February 2022, to be reinstated as Ukraine's puppet President. He would certainly have asked Putin to intervene, in 2014 and thereafter, but his power to consent on Ukraine's behalf was at an end. No doubt many Ukrainians would be delighted to see him cross-examined by the prosecution, now that his massive corruption has been exposed, but the main objection to his testimony would be simply that he had no democratic warrant for inviting Putin to restore him to power. The court would be likely to rule that any claim of consent to an invasion must rest on an invitation from a constitutional authority.

ARTICLE 51

That will bring the trial back to Putin's most strongly arguable defence – that of self-defence, under Article 51 of the charter, notified to the secretary-general at the time of the invasion. It will call for the court to make a portentous legal ruling on international law: must self-defence be in response to a threat which is 'imminent', as always thought prior to 2003, or is there a right to 'pre-emptive self-defence', first advanced by President Bush's lawyers to justify the invasion of Iraq and on which Russia (which disagreed with it at the time) must rest its case for the invasion of Ukraine? The ruling will be one of law, and the court could call for arguments on that at the outset, but the defence should apply for this hearing to be held after its evidence is heard, otherwise if the court decides that 'imminence' is still the test, Putin will have no defence at all.

To understand the legal arguments, it is necessary first to set out Article 51 of the UN charter: 'Nothing in the present charter shall impair the inherent right of individual or collective self-defence if an armed attack occurs against a member of the United Nations, until the Security Council has taken measures necessary to maintain international peace and security.'

This is not a definition of self-defence but rather an assertion that it arises 'if an armed attack occurs'. If it has not already occurred, the question of proximity is all-important: at what point may force be used to thwart an expected attack? Would America, in 1941, be entitled only to sink the Japanese fleet as it prepared to sail for Pearl Harbor, or would it be entitled to attack Japan months before, when it got wind of plans that the fleet was being assembled for this purpose?

Such questions were thought to have been settled in 1837, in an exchange of diplomatic notes between the US and British governments about Britain's claim to self-defence after its soldiers had captured and burned a steamboat, the *Caroline*, being used to carry provisions to American rebels in Canada. It was attacked in an American port – two Americans were killed – and then the British set it alight and set it on a course that took it over Niagara Falls. Both governments agreed that states which claim 'self-defence' must show 'a necessity of self-defence, instant, overwhelming, leaving no choice of means, and no moment for deliberation'. The note insisted that there must be 'nothing unreasonable or excessive' in the counterattack claimed as self-defence, 'since the act, justified by the necessity of self-defence, must be limited by that necessity and kept clearly within it'. The *Caroline* rule, that self-defence could be raised only in relation to an imminent attack, was approved by the judges at Nuremberg as the yardstick for judging Nazi aggression (which generally failed it – the invaded states could not be said to pose a realistic threat to Germany).

So far as Putin was concerned, on 24 February 2022 Ukraine posed no threat that could possibly be described as 'imminent'. There had been no attack on Russia by Ukraine and no threat of such attack, whether imminent or not.

Zelensky had canvassed joining NATO, but NATO had not even discussed the proposal. So Putin's defence would fail, unless the court accepted a much wider alternative to 'imminent'. That alternative had been developed by lawyers acting for President Bush in the run-up to the invasion of Iraq to remove Saddam Hussein, and they called it 'pre-emptive self-defence'. Pursuant to this doctrine, the US was entitled to attack Saddam because it thought he might have nuclear weapons and further thought he might use them in the future against the US. This was obviously not an 'imminent' threat but one which in the future might come to pass. So was the threat to Russia from Ukraine: it might join NATO, and NATO might then invade Russia. If this kind of speculation were permissible under the rubric of pre-emptive self-defence, Putin might convince the court that Ukraine was reasonably likely to join NATO and NATO was reasonably likely to attack Russia. The defence team would have to establish, as a matter of fact, that these two developments were reasonably likely to occur, and then obtain from the court a declaration that this would amount to an 'armed attack'. It would be a difficult task, but courtesy of the Bush lawyers, the defence would have facts to build it on and some legal argument to sustain it.

The case for this defence could confidently open with evidence that promises were made to Russia in 1990, in order to obtain its assent to the reunification of Germany, that NATO would not expand eastwards. There is no doubt that such promises were made, orally and repeatedly, to Gorbachev by Western leaders such as George H. W. Bush, Margaret Thatcher and John Major. They were not binding and were not mentioned in the treaty on the final settlement, but Gorbachev certainly felt that he was duped in 1999 when Hungary, Poland and the Czech Republic were admitted as members of NATO, followed in 2004 by Bulgaria, Estonia, Latvia, Lithuania, Romania, Slovakia and Slovenia. The North Atlantic Treaty Organization had been established by the major Western states as a military organisation to confront the Soviet Union and its allies in the Warsaw Pact during the Cold War. Its 'all for one' pledge requires mutual assistance if any one member were invaded, and the more its membership expanded to include Russia's neighbours, particularly ex-members of the USSR, the more obviously it would threaten Russia – although (the prosecution will point out) only if Russia were to unlawfully invade them first.

However, the fact that Ukraine would soon apply for membership was real in 2022: Zelensky had proposed it in several speeches, and in 2019 Ukraine's constitution had been amended to make it easier for the country to join the EU and NATO. Just three months before the invasion, when Putin requested a legal guarantee that NATO would not expand further eastwards or put weapons 'that threaten us in close vicinity to Russian territory', the rude reply came from Jens Stoltenberg, NATO secretary-general: 'It's only Ukraine and thirty NATO allies that decide when Ukraine is ready to join NATO. Russia has no veto, Russia has no say and Russia has no right to establish a sphere of influence to try to control their neighbours.' So Russia went to war to prove him wrong, and to show, as Putin's defence will contend, its legal right to remove a threat to its future security.

Putin's defenders would argue that NATO's hostility to Russia is implicit in its very purpose and its armed might, last on display in Libya in 2011, cannot be doubted, nor its capacity to commit what may well be war crimes (e.g. its bombing of civilian targets in Belgrade during the war against Milošević). But they would have to concede that Ukraine had made no formal application to join NATO and leading members – the US and Germany in particular – had indicated publicly that any application by Ukraine could not be considered until it had cleaned up its corruption problems.

The defence could certainly establish that Ukraine's future membership of NATO was 'on the cards'. It would have to go further, of course, and prove the likelihood of NATO attacking Russia without legitimate reason. The defence could show that NATO went on alert over Crimea in 2014, convening a mandatory meeting of member states that can be a prelude to armed action, although it went no further. The defence would argue that once NATO rockets were stationed in Ukraine, as a result of its membership, Russia would be in danger of, and vulnerable to, attack if, for example, Russia's security concerns caused it to invade any NATO member for what it considered a just cause. The defence could readily secure 'expert' testimony from the likes of John Mearsheimer and other professors of international relations who blame the Clinton and Bush administrations for irresponsibly pushing NATO further east despite Putin's warnings that Russia would not accept more of its neighbours – Ukraine and Georgia in particular – being in league with its enemies. This may well be true, but it cannot absolve Putin from committing a heinous crime – declaring a war without justification – in order to control Ukraine's security policy. But first, the court would have to decide whether the Bush doctrine of pre-emption is a good defence under Article 51 of the charter. To do so, it would have to overrule the *Caroline* case that has stood as the law since 1837, and face up to the fact that 'pre-emptive self-defence' has only ever been embraced by the US and Israel.

So Putin's defence would have the task of showing firstly that Ukraine was likely to join NATO and secondly that NATO, with Ukraine as a member, was likely to attack Russia. The first argument would not be unreasonable; although NATO (and EU) membership was said to be out of the question at the time of the invasion, at least until Ukraine cleaned up its corruption problem, Zelensky was on track for doing just that, and it is possible to argue that he would have succeeded in a few years' time, to a degree which would have made his country acceptable to other NATO members. Indeed, by the end of 2023, Ukraine's prospects were very much brighter, although that was largely because it was fighting an unjust war – Putin was bringing about the very movement of which he claimed to be afraid at the start. NATO countries had been supplying Ukraine with weapons to fight the war, just as they would if it had been a member of NATO, under its 'all for one' policy.

The second stage of the argument will prove more difficult for Putin's defenders: was there any likelihood that NATO, with Ukraine as a member, would attack Russia? Although there were examples of NATO belligerence, these were confined to words rather than actions – it had not gone further than holding a special meeting when Crimea was annexed in 2014 and, although it had bombed Libya in 2011, that was pursuant to a Security Council resolution in which Russia had joined. The best evidence was the NATO bombing of Belgrade after Milošević had refused to halt the ethnic cleansing in Kosovo, an action taken without asking for Security Council approval because Russia had made clear it would veto any such resolution. Action against Milošević was certainly called for, but NATO action involved a number of war crimes. In apparent breach of Article 8 of the Rome Statute, it bombed civilians and civilian targets in Belgrade, like bridges, a water purification plant and a TV station (killing sixteen technicians), and the RAF used cluster bombs to kill several hundred Serbian citizens. The defence could call evidence of this unattractive episode to show that NATO was a danger, although it would really prove that NATO could fight irresponsibly rather than that it would be likely to start a war. Putin's argument, the prosecution would point out, was circular: NATO would fight a war only if Russia first invaded Ukraine or another of its members.

The legal arguments for Putin's Bush-style defence would begin by taking the court to Article 38(1) of the statute of the International Court of Justice, which sets out the four sources for deciding a dispute over international law. The first is to look at the treaty in question – here, Article 51 of the UN charter – which is silent on the proximity of the threat. The second is 'international custom' – i.e. the practice of states, what they do in the belief that there is an existing legal right or obligation for them to do it. In the majority of cases since Nuremberg, where states have invaded others, leaders have justified the attack (at least to domestic audiences) on the grounds of removing a future rather than an 'imminent' threat. Although this may be the test set down in textbooks (subsidiary sources), it relies on an old case that is not even a court decision but merely an exchange of notes between politicians about a burning ferry sent over Niagara Falls. For all the lip service paid to the *Caroline* case, states have in practice always acted on the basis that they are entitled to remove a future threat: who could say that the US was not entitled to act against Cuba in self-defence when it set up missile bases that could threaten America, or indeed when it did act to stop Russian ships on their way to deliver these missiles, which would not be shot at the US 'imminently' and probably not at all, given that Cuba would have been obliterated in response.

The Bush doctrine, asserted to justify the invasion of Iraq in 2003 to pre-empt Saddam obtaining nuclear weapons (which they thought he already possessed) and shooting them at America (a long way, but they could reach its bases in Britain), would be the central plank of Putin's defence. The doctrine held that America was entitled to go to war without Security Council approval, as self-defence against a country it intuited might put its national security at future risk. It was first enunciated in Bush's 'axis of evil' speech in 2002: 'We will not hesitate to act alone, if necessary, to exercise our right to self-defence by acting pre-emptively.' He identified 'rogue states' as the aggressor to be feared, but the fear from a nuclear-armed permanent member of the UN Security Council would be all the greater.

The prosecution will reply that the differences between Saddam, a mass-murdering dictator, and Zelensky, a former comedian fairly elected to run a democracy, are stark enough. But the defence will insist that the principle must apply to both: once Ukraine constituted a credible threat, which Stoltenberg reinforced by his refusal to give Putin the assurance he wanted, Russia was entitled to invade and to occupy the country. The same defence that is open to the American goose must be open to the Russian gander.

This irony will not go unappreciated, in the courtroom or the wider world. Did George W. Bush so refashion the law of self-defence that it now permits Vladimir Putin – and any other head of state – to order war in response to a mere possibility of a future attack? The prosecution answer must be emphatic: so-called pre-emptive self-defence is a perversion of international law, invented by US government lawyers at a 'unipolar moment' in history when America could do what it liked and say what it liked to justify it. Nothing in the wording of Article 51 presages this development: on the contrary, the phrase 'if an armed attack occurs' suggests it can be applicable only after Ukraine had attacked, and the time for this attack has been expanded by the 'imminence' test, to allow a period for legitimate self-defence just before the armed attack occurs. The notion of an armed attack or 'imminent' armed attack by Ukraine on Russia on 24 February 2022 is simply absurd, and the court should reject the Bush doctrine without further ado.

Moreover, it was effectively rejected at Nuremberg, where Hermann Göring argued that only Germany alone could decide whether to go to war in self-defence. The court replied that 'whether action taken under the claim of self-defence was in fact aggressive or defensive must ultimately be subject to investigation and adjudication if international law is ever to be enforced'.

This meant that the defence could not rest upon the subjective views of the aggressor state. Even if Putin did genuinely fear Ukraine joining NATO because this could lead to war, this could not be anticipated by any reasonable and objective observer, given NATO's record of applying force only to stop unlawful conduct by the likes of Milošević and Gaddafi. The case for war could not rest on speculation about a far-distant future, however much it might be feared.

The prosecution will point out to the court an aspect of the decision to invade Iraq that is often forgotten: on its legality, there was no Bush–Blair consensus. Indeed, the UK Attorney General said very clearly that pre-emptory self-defence 'is not a doctrine which, in my opinion, exists or is recognised in international law'. The UK and Australia relied on an entirely different argument – that a Security Council resolution from the time Saddam had attacked Kuwait had been miraculously 'revived' to entitle them to invade Iraq without waiting for a second Security Council resolution that they should do so. This was dubious enough, but it enabled them to eschew reliance on the Bush claim of any right to anticipatory action. Subsequently, the US distanced itself from the exorbitant Bush claim: Obama in his Nobel Prize lecture declared that the US would follow international law on the use of force because it could not 'insist that others follow the rules of the road if we refuse to follow them ourselves', and the US amended its national security strategy accordingly. In 2017, the UK Attorney General suggested that the 'imminence' test might be somewhat relaxed but made clear that

> the approach I am setting out ... is a very long way from supporting any notion of a doctrine of pre-emptive strikes against threats that are more remote ... It is absolutely not the position of the UK government that armed force may be used to prevent a threat from materialising in the first place.

One benefit of an aggression tribunal is that it can decide, authoritatively, on the meaning of 'self-defence' in the UN charter. If the judges are conservative, they will apply the imminence test settled by long adherence to the *Caroline* case. If realistic, they might relax the time element, to permit an armed response if the threat is judged objectively, as highly probable and there are warnings before the counterattack. But they would not give carte blanche to any state to invade on the subjective appreciation of a threat that may never materialise. As the Nuremberg court insisted, whether a war is aggressive or defensive must be decided objectively, and not by the country which starts it. So far as Putin's trial is concerned, a judicial decision that 'pre-emptive self-defence' is not a defence at all in international law would leave him without a legal leg to stand on. Even if it were deemed a defence, and Ukraine was judged likely to be made a NATO member, the court would have to decide whether it would be too far-fetched to imagine NATO going to war against Russia, unless Russia unlawfully attacked Ukraine, or another NATO member, first.

TU QUOQUE

Putin's lawyers would have one last shot in their locker, which their client, if he were to instruct them, would wish them to deploy, because it would embarrass Russia's enemies even though it would be unlikely to succeed. Lawyers are generally prepared to advance points that are 'arguable', by which they mean they will accept a fee to argue them with a grin on their face, although they have little or no hope of success. There is no reason why, at Putin's trial *in absentia* or more so if it is being held in his presence, they should not put forward what was called at Nuremberg the '*tu quoque*' defence – 'I did it, but you did it too.' The court immediately ruled that it was not a defence at all – two wrongs do not make a right – but later in the trial, it admitted evidence to show cases in which Nazi defendants were being tried for offences which Allied forces had committed. So the defence would argue that if Bush and Blair could get away with invading Iraq in 2003, so Putin should escape conviction for invading Ukraine in 2022. This is hardly an attractive defence, but advanced as an 'abuse of process' application would allow evidence to be heard about the hypocrisy of the West and the heated Security Council debates in 2003, after which the US and the UK invaded without the council's approval.

The defence would argue that the Nuremberg decision against allowing the *tu quoque* argument was predetermined by the Allies' concerns that their own war crimes would be used against them. If anyone was guilty of preparing for aggression it was Stalin, who in 1939 approved the Molotov–Ribbentrop Pact with the Nazis to invade Poland, and the war crime of indiscriminate bombing of civilian-packed cities was committed by the RAF over Dresden. As the prosecutor, Robert Jackson, confessed to Truman, the Allies had

> done or are doing some of the very things we are prosecuting the Germans for. The French are violating the Geneva Convention in the treatment of prisoners of war … We are prosecuting the Germans for plunder and our allies are practising it … We say aggressive war is a crime and one of our allies asserts sovereignty over the Baltic States based on no title except conquest.

On this basis, the defence could argue that the emphatic rejection of the *tu quoque* defence at Nuremberg was predetermined and political, and that as the trial continued, fairness required admission of evidence that Allies had behaved in the same way as defendants. The double standard was called out in the case of Admiral Karl Dönitz, accused of ordering unrestricted submarine warfare. Evidence was submitted on his behalf from Admiral Chester Nimitz, commander of the Pacific fleet, to show that American submarine orders were much the same. Dönitz was not convicted on this charge, but others accused of a war crime for bombing were not permitted to call evidence of similar Allied behaviour. Whether or not Putin is permitted to call evidence comparing his invasion of Ukraine to the unprosecuted Bush–Blair invasion of Iraq, his application to do so will allow the point to be made about the hypocrisy of certain states behind his prosecution.

The prosecutors will argue that Iraq is irrelevant and that *tu quoque* is not a defence at all. It is mitigation, certainly: if others have not been brought to account for the same crime, a defendant might receive a lighter sentence than they deserve. But otherwise, 'I did it, but you did it first' amounts to a plea of 'guilty'. Moreover, as a matter of law, Bush and Blair could not be guilty of aggression in 2003 because it was not then a crime in international law. It was in a state of suspended animation – notionally inserted in the Rome Treaty (Article 5) but expressly on a contingency basis, i.e. until it had been satisfactorily defined by ICC members. That agreed definition did not come until the Kampala conference in 2010, to be implemented in 2018. So in 2003, there was no clearly defined international crime of aggression that Bush could be accused of committing, and only since 2018 has the crime as defined (see above, Chapter 3) entered international law. In any event, the threat levels in the two cases were different, as well as the conduct of the leading victims – Saddam and Zelensky. *Tu quoque* evidence might be relevant to show that particular conduct charged as a war crime was not regarded as criminal by other armed forces, and that the trial was therefore unfair on these particular charges, but the fact that others have not been prosecuted for starting war is not a reason for abandoning prosecution of Putin for doing so.

It is likely that the aggression tribunal would follow Nuremberg and reject the *tu quoque* defence. It could not stop Putin from developing it, were he to enter the fray with his own lawyers, and the amici team, bound to take every arguable point, should give it a go, if only to obtain a definitive legal ruling. That will probably be against them, for good reason, but it will be important for the credibility of the trial *in absentia* for the defence team to be seen to make the argument, so that critics cannot accuse them of omitting to take a point embarrassing for the West. Scholars have counted no fewer than sixty-five occasions since Nuremberg on which states have invaded other states – sometimes justifiably, sometimes not. The court will have to restrict any comparative historical exegesis and deal with the question as an issue of principle, using Iraq as a comparator. The conclusion will be simple: international criminal law moves on, and for the better, and two wrongs still do not make a right.

CLOSING SPEECHES

There will be a break after the end of this evidence to enable each legal team to prepare a final presentation. They will concentrate on the issue of 'pre-emptive self-defence'. The prosecution will argue that it does not exist: 'imminence' has always been the test and still is. Even if it should be re-laxed, the attack which permits an armed response must be reasonably foreseeable, and any future attack on Russia by Ukraine acting as a member of NATO was not foreseeable – this would be sheer speculation, a consequence much too remote and hypothetical to serve as a warrant for starting a war. The defence will argue, like Göring and Bush, that it was for Putin, in his own mind, to decide subjectively whether and, if so, how seriously Russia was threatened. That he did so honestly with the good of his country as his only motive is irrelevant. The prosecution, relying on the Nuremberg judgment, would argue that to let countries decide for themselves whether they should go to war would make a mockery of international law.

The speeches need not be lengthy – a couple of days should suffice if the legal arguments are confined to written submissions. Were Putin to defend himself, of course, he must be given whatever time he needs, within reason. There will doubtless be applications by victims' representatives to make concluding addresses, but if they have not been permitted to intervene or to call evidence, this should not be allowed and even if they have, they can be directed to make the submissions very brief, or in writing, confined to legal issues. It is important for the court to avoid the impression that the dice are loaded in favour of the prosecution. It would not be a problem if some Russian legal firms or university law faculties ask to make submissions on the side of the defence, or some NGOs or academics want to offer their opinions, favourable to Putin's case, on the law. The court could invite such written submissions – the more the merrier – but is likely to confine oral speeches to the leaders of the two legal teams.

Then will come the adjournment for the judges to decide on guilt or innocence and write judgments (preferably, a joint judgment) applying the law (as they have decided that it is) to the evidence they have heard. Some international trial courts take an unconscionable time – Charles Taylor's judges retired for over a year – but Putin's case is relatively simple and a decision should be reached within three months. The judgment in Nuremberg took two days for the court president to read, but judgments in today's international criminal courts – frequently over 1,000 pages – are handed down electronically.

In Putin's case, the court should set a judgment day and agree on a shortish statement, to be made by the court president, explaining the outcome. It will be covered worldwide by television and the press, so the actual hearing must be carefully choreographed. The full judgment, with its less digestible analysis of the complex jurisprudence, should be uploaded immediately and available in regional languages, including Russian and Ukrainian. The sentencing proceedings, if any, will be described in Chapter 6.

CHAPTER 5

WAR CRIMES: AT THE ICC

On 17 March 2020, the pre-trial chamber of the International Criminal Court decided that there was 'a reasonable basis to proceed' against Vladimir Putin and his 'children's rights commissioner' Maria Lvova-Belova, for the war crime of unlawfully transporting to Russia children from occupied areas of Ukraine. It issued arrest warrants which spoiled his travel plans – he could not attend an important conference in South Africa because, like the other 123 member states of the ICC, it would be legally bound to arrest him. This single act has branded him, at least potentially, as an international criminal and has forced him to embrace as allies the likes of the North Korean dictator, Kim Jong Un. There have been many more war crimes committed by Russia under Putin's command, the evidence seen on television news around the world – residential buildings with windows blown out and ceilings collapsed with residents underneath awaiting removal in body bags. There are the ghastly remains of international crimes – mass graves, bombed hospitals and precisely targeted non-military targets like churches and museums. Russian execution squads have turned civilians into victims, without disapproval from their commanders and without their supreme commander – Putin – batting an eyelid. He is, of course, responsible for these foreseeable consequences of the war of aggression that he ordered, but the ICC cannot prosecute him for that crime. Can it hold him responsible for particular war crimes, even if he did not know about them at the time they were committed? The answer, heavily qualified, is yes, under the command responsibility theory, but even in relation to war crimes that he ordered, would he ever stand trial?

IN ABSENTIA TRIALS

Russia is not a member of the ICC and has claimed its arrest warrants 'null and void'. They are not: Ukraine has seen to it that war crimes committed on its territory are within the ICC's jurisdiction. But the court does not have power under the Rome Statute to conduct trials *in absentia*, so any proceedings against Putin must be against the man in person, surrendered by Russia after a coup or economic collapse or a defeat by Ukraine. He might be arrested on a visit to a member state and extradited to the ICC's prison at Scheveningen, on the Dutch coast near The Hague, which may then be vulnerable to any attack by the Russian fleet which may try to secure his release. The only other way to bring him to account for specific war crimes is for ICC member states to amend the Rome Statute to allow for *in absentia* trials, which they could do at a review conference or state party meeting. Foolishly, state parties decided that any amendments must be ratified by seven-eighths of them – a condition very difficult to meet for any controversial change.

There is a stubborn attachment by Anglo-American states to having the defendants present 'in the flesh', which has the consequence that many atrocities go unexamined and unaccounted for as a matter of international criminal law. As a defendant who is convicted *in absentia* may, if subsequently apprehended, be granted a retrial, there should be no objection to such proceedings, if the trial follows the basic rules of fairness and ends with a judgment that provides an authoritative application of the law to proven facts and thus gives the public an objective account of the crime and provides some solace to its victims. There should be no objection at all to a trial *in absentia* on a charge of aggression, where the facts are unchallengeable and the defendant's intentions, if relevant, are in evidence in his speeches and writings. If charged with a war crime, a close forensic examination of the facts of a particular atrocity, by lawyers acting on behalf of an absent defendant, can lead to a judgment that defies

THE TRIAL OF VLADIMIR PUTIN

Russian propagandists and their claims, for example, that pictures of dead bodies are those of paid actors and scenes of devastation are staged. Such judgments, by distinguished jurists after properly contested evidence and legal arguments, can provide an antidote to Russian propaganda. Weeks after the war began, state media had managed to convince 80 per cent of Russians that their war was 'just', an intervention to stop genocide by a Nazi–Ukrainian government. War crimes judgments help to refute such distortions and show – at least to the open-minded – that atrocities were really committed by their troops under orders from their commanders. The ICC has been set up to provide this expert adjudication, but what it can do in respect of powerful leaders charged with heinous crimes depends on whether the Anglo-American bias against trials *in absentia* can be overcome.

INTERNATIONAL HUMANITARIAN LAW

This is a ridiculous title for war law, because no war can be 'humanitarian' unless it is stopped before it starts. But the world over many centuries, starting with the Hammurabi Code and early heraldic customs, has developed rules to curb wars from descending into outright barbarity. The first modern prohibition was that prescribed by the Lateran Council of the Catholic Church in 1139 – the use of the crossbow to kill Christians (killing Muslims with a crossbow was fine). In due course, scholars like Hugo Grotius and Emmerich de Vattel rationalised war law and were at pains to identify 'just' wars and to protect non-combatants, but they were always subject to royal rulers for whom wars, like royal marriages, were necessary diplomatic activities. Nonetheless, by the seventeenth century, professional soldiers were well aware of the duty to give 'quarter' to opponents who surrendered to them on the battlefield, to respect the lives and property of civilians and to treat prisoners humanely. Shakespeare's pedantic Welsh captain, Fluellen, could at Agincourt call out conduct 'expressly against the law of arms' and by 1642 the three armies that fought the English Civil War – for the king, for Parliament and for Scotland – all had codes of conduct requiring that 'none shall kill an enemy who yields and throws down his arms, upon pain of death'. On his way to Drogheda, Cromwell hanged two of his soldiers caught stealing chickens from a local farmer.

The first modern set of war rules was compiled by Dr Franz Lieber at the direction of Abraham Lincoln, and the Lieber code – *Instructions for the Government of Armies of the United States in the Field* – remains the model for modern military law, supplemented by treaties and conventions and by principles distilled from the Nuremberg trials. The rules governing the conduct of hostilities in relation to prisoners of war and the civilian populace were expressed in the four

Geneva Conventions of 1949, and the most egregious violations of these rules are listed as war crimes in Article 8 of the Rome Statute of the ICC.

The ICC came into existence, after sixty ratifications of the Rome Treaty, in 2002, and now has 124 member states – excluding Russia, America and China. Its war crimes jurisdiction is built upon the judgment at Nuremberg and the Geneva Conventions, as developed and refined by the 'ad hoc' courts of the ICTY, the ICTR and the SCSL, and enumerated in detail by Article 8 of the Rome Statute. Among the Article 8 crimes that have been committed by Russia in the war thus far are 'wilful killing', 'wilfully causing great suffering or serious injury to body or health', 'extensive destruction and appropriation of property, not justified by military necessity and carried out unlawfully and wantonly' and, in particular:

- Intentionally directing attacks against the civilian population.
- Attacking or bombarding towns and villages or undefended buildings which are not military objectives.
- Intentionally launching attacks in the knowledge that they will cause loss of life to civilians disproportionate to any anticipated military advantage.
- Deportation or transfer of parts of the population of the occupied territory (one of the charges that Putin already faces for transporting children).

- Intentionally directing attacks against buildings dedicated to religion, arts, science or charitable purposes, historic monuments, hospitals and places where the sick and wounded are collected, provided they are not military objectives.
- Launching attacks knowing that they will result in widespread, long-term and severe damage to the natural environment excessive in relation to the overall military advantage anticipated.

All these crimes have allegedly been committed by Russia in the course of the war, and it is to be assumed that the ICC prosecutor will in due course issue indictments for individuals responsible for committing or ordering them. Could this include Putin, as supreme commander? Certainly if there is evidence of his direct involvement, as with the transporting of Ukrainian children, but not necessarily in respect of the other crimes of which he may not have heard until afterwards. In this case, he may yet be charged as bearing 'command responsibility' for them. It is necessary to look at these two different ways of approaching his accountability for a war crime, as the evidence will differ for each charge.

TRANSPORTING CHILDREN

This is the first case that the ICC prosecutor, Karim Khan KC, has chosen to bring against Vladimir Putin, convincing judges to issue an arrest warrant on the grounds that he has 'a reasonable basis to proceed' over the unlawful deportation of children (said by the UN to number 21,000) from Ukraine. Because the victims were 'kidnapped' children, the case aroused both pity and ire, but it struck home for another reason: Khan had the 'smoking gun' – evidence that irrefutably showed that Putin ordered the operation, which will be shown at the outset of his trial. It was live television coverage of a ceremony in Moscow on 16 February 2023, when his co-defendant Lvova-Belova congratulated him on enabling the transportation and subsequent Russian nationalisation of Ukrainian children – described as orphans. So grateful was this 'Mother Russia' to Putin that she said she had adopted an orphan herself!

This was a staged propaganda event to display the leader's compassion for children caught up in the war. Ironically, what Putin and Lvova-Belova and all their advisers failed to realise was that transporting people (including children) from occupied territory was an international crime, and by glorifying it they were providing the best evidence of their complicity – indeed superior responsibility – for its commission. The first charge against them therefore alleges their personal criminal responsibility for this trafficking of children. There is a second charge, based on a fall-back provision of the statute, that of 'superior responsibility', namely Putin's failure to exercise control properly over subordinates who committed crimes and were under his effective responsibility and control.

This alternative charge is brought to cater for the possibility (it seems distant) that the prosecution will not have sufficient evidence to convict him of direct responsibility. It is a lesser charge for failing to take 'all necessary and reasonable measures' to investigate and disband the operation.

The prosecutor will have no shortage of evidence. He will show the court TV footage of the co-defendants, posing as angels of mercy for Ukrainian orphans, Putin glowing in the praise and accepting the credit. The prosecutor could call Zelensky's wife, Olena, who has led efforts to trace and to return the stolen children, and should have no scruples about calling some of the teenage victims to the witness box, those who recall being separated from their parents, and parents who were told their children were being taken for a fortnight to a 'holiday camp' in order to 'keep them safe' but were taken away to Russia. The children will testify they were taught to speak Russian and to sing its patriotic songs, then told their parents had abandoned them or been killed, and that they would be taken to Russia for adoption. Evidence to this effect was featured in a UK television documentary, *Ukraine's Stolen Children*, transmitted in September 2023, and the laughter of Lvova-Belova, when allegations about Russian 're-education' were put to her, was more shocking than the plight of the children, or of their parents desperate to retrieve them.

On his side, Putin could certainly show that he did not know that transportation could be a war crime, otherwise he would not have been at the ceremony to accept all the praise. But ignorance of the law is no defence. He will have to show that he genuinely believed that the children's parents had given them consent (difficult if he believed they were orphans) or that the action was intended to remove them from immediate danger. The presence of a co-defendant may be a problem – she may accept a plea bargain and turn against him, making clear to the court that she acted under his orders. The issue of Putin's guilt might be settled by production of the government documents relating to orders for the transportation, but unless he is overthrown or out of favour, the government is unlikely to cooperate. But his conduct at the ceremony, accepting credit for the transportation plan, should be enough to convict him. If not, the second count of 'superior responsibility' will come into play.

SUPERIOR RESPONSIBILITY

This doctrine derives from the US Supreme Court decision holding the notable Japanese general Tomoyuki Yamashita guilty of war crimes – the killing of American and Australian prisoners by his troops when they ran amok in the Philippines towards the end of the war. The court ruled that a person in a position of superior authority should be held individually responsible for giving the unlawful order to commit a crime, and he should also be held responsible for failure to deter the unlawful behaviour of subordinates, if he knew they had committed or were about to commit crimes yet failed to take the necessary and reasonable steps to prevent their commission or to punish those who had committed them.

This was the test reflected by drafters of the Rome Statute when Article 28 entered the law, under the rubric 'responsibility of commanders and other superiors'. Article 28(a) provides:

A military commander ... shall be criminally responsible for crimes within the jurisdiction of the court committed by forces under his or her effective command and control ... as a result of his or her failure to exercise control properly over such forces, where:

i. That military commander or person either knew or ... should have known that the forces were committing or about to commit such crimes; and

ii. That military commander or person failed to take all necessary and reasonable measures within his or her power to prevent or repress their commission or to submit the matter to the competent authorities for investigation and prosecution.

Article 28(b) applies the same test to superiors outside the military whose subordinates commit war crimes: the duty is to repress them or to submit evidence to competent authorities for investigation and prosecution.

This provided the basis for the 'fall-back' charge that Putin 'failed to exercise control properly' over the civilian and military authorities who organised the transportation. He obviously knew about the program as he attended the ceremony to celebrate it, and it could be inferred that he had 'failed to take all necessary and reasonable measures' to have it investigated and disbanded as contrary to international law. He would have to call evidence to show that this was an autonomous programme over which he had no control: his duties as President in a war were confined to policy issues and he had no responsibility to oversee specific targeting or civilian relief programmes. Or else he could claim – as Russian television programmes do – that these children were taken over the border out of necessity, for their own safety.

This raises the more general question of whether Putin can be brought in, as supreme commander, to indictments of his subordinates for actually ordering or carrying out war crimes such as the destruction of the Mariupol theatre or the bombings of funeral services or churches. The court would have to accept that Putin, as head of state, was a 'military commander' or 'superior' within the meaning of Article 28. He would claim to be an elected political supremo but to have no close control over or responsibility for military operations. The ICC prosecutor could readily call evidence of Putin's power over the use of the armed forces – his order started the war – and would screen the televised meeting of the State Security Council on 21 February to show his complete control over commanders of the army and of the ministers responsible for it. The court could admit evidence of his 'personalised' role throughout the war, with servile ministers and a lickspittle Duma, and that nobody doubted that he could negotiate an end to the war if he wished.

Putin can be prosecuted under Article 28 if he knew about war crimes but failed to repress them or failed to submit the matter to competent authorities for investigation and prosecution. The evidence is likely to show that he knew all about them – he would have seen them on television, as his forces bombed civilian residences – and was insouciant, at least until November 2023, when nine Russian soldiers were arrested for rape and abuse of a Ukrainian family. The case was much publicised because it was the first of its kind. Putin must have seen, or been shown, pictures that shocked the world – civilians in Bucha, for example, being marched off to execution. Charles Taylor's guilt was inferred from his presidential briefings about war crimes by the troops he was sponsoring, and Putin could not have been left in ignorance by his advisers of the nature of Russian drone, warplane and tank attacks and the outrage the civilian casualties were causing throughout the world. He will claim, no doubt, that they kept the details from him – after all, they were the same advisers who had told him that his forces would be met with flowers and kisses – but any claim of ignorance about what was being viewed on television and social media around the world would be disbelieved.

Nonetheless, the prosecutor must satisfy the court that Putin was, as a matter of law, either a 'military commander' or a 'superior', and, as a matter of fact, that it was realistic to expect him to act so as to stop the atrocity or to investigate and prosecute it afterwards. Most war crimes will have been committed by individual Russian soldiers, airmen or drone controllers, usually at the direction of superiors who may in turn have been obeying orders from more senior officers, responsible to ministers who may report to the President. Where does the buck stop?

Putin may reasonably argue that he had no role in disciplining soldiers and left that to the army, but crimes that must have been drawn to his attention would, if he chose, have been made the subject of investigation at his command. By turning a blind eye, he thereby failed 'to exercise control properly'. And indeed, in some cases, he awarded medals to the culprits. If, as a commander or head of state like Charles Taylor, crimes against humanity came to Putin's attention, he had a duty to do something to stop them. Taylor's knowledge in this respect of the atrocities being committed by the RUF fighters he was sponsoring did not come to his attention at the time they were being committed, 1,000 miles away, but he read about them in newspapers and in his presidential brief-ings. Putin could always say that it was unrealistic to expect him to prosecute commanders while they were trying to fight a war – he certainly could not discipline Yevgeny Prigozhin – but he had it in mind to deal with them later. It would be for the judges to decide whether to believe him. They would not expect him to discipline his men by unlawfully killing them, as many speculate he did with Prigozhin.

Command responsibility has been the basis for the ICC's prosecution of other senior political figures – Gbagbo and Bemba, for example – and their cases have come unstuck for one reason or another. Even Yamashita, the Japanese general who led his troops on bicycles to capture Singapore, is now believed by historians to have been wrongfully convicted – he was isolated in the mountains without contact with his troops while they were running amok. So it can be a snare for prosecutors – it looks an easy crime to pin on the leader, but it pretends there can be a counsel of perfection amidst the chaos of war. A prosecution for command or superior re-sponsibility is vulnerable to the defence – 'I can't be expected to know everything that is happening in the war.' As Yamashita put it at his trial, truthfully as it turns out:

> My command was as big as MacArthur's ... How could I tell
> if some of my soldiers misbehaved themselves? It was impossible for any man in my position to control every action of his
> subordinate commanders, let alone the deeds of individual
> soldiers. The charges are completely new to me. If ... I had
> known about them, I would have punished the wrongdoers
> severely. But in war someone has to lose. What I am really
> being charged with is losing the war.

Prosecutors should also bear in mind that as crimes go, turning a blind eye to an atrocity is not as serious as ordering or committing it, and it should carry five to ten years in prison rather than a life sentence.

The catalogue of war crimes is not closed, and each conflict brings its own horrors. In Sierra Leone, there was the new crime of 'chopping' – revenge taken by anti-government forces by cutting off hands of civilians who marked their ballot paper – and 'forced marriage' (the RUF supplied its soldiers with brides forced at gunpoint to marry them) and recruitment of children for frontline fighting. Ukraine could add the carpet-bombing of towns, which was in The Hague rules of aerial warfare back in 1923 but left out of Article 8 because the UK was squeamish about Dresden. Russian terror tactics such as indiscriminate bombing of towns and multiple drone attacks on residential areas are methods that Putin must have approved, or declined to investigate, and should be charged either directly or under Article 28 as command or superior responsibility.

The 'elephant in the war room' is the threat to use nuclear weapons, made impliedly by Putin on several occasions and more directly by his former deputy, Dmitry Medvedev and by his foreign minister, Sergey Lavrov, who warned the West not to underestimate the risk because 'NATO, in essence, is engaged in a war with Russia through a proxy'. Article 8, unaccountably, contains no explicit crime of using or threatening to use nukes, and if any significant Russian leader does make that threat, he should be prosecuted so as to create a precedent. One problem is the *Legality of the Threat or Use of Nuclear Weapons* case decided by a narrow majority of ICJ judges in 1996. A narrow majority said they could not declare that the use or threat to use nuclear weapons would be unlawful in all circumstances because of 'the fundamental right of every state to survival and thus its right to resort to self-defence, in accordance with Article 51 of the charter, where its survival is at stake'. This would appear to allow Putin to nuke Kyiv if he was about to lose the war! The decision, however, does not stop the ICC prosecutor from charging the threat or incitement to use nuclear weapons as a war crime, should Putin or his associates cross this red line and make the threat clearly in the future.

Much work is going on in Ukraine to log all the war crimes, discover the mass graves and collect eyewitness testimony and evidence of Russian use of 'white phosphorus', an incendiary weapon banned by conventions that Russia has ratified. Karim Khan KC has made public visits to Ukraine but has been distracted by the conflict in Gaza and his promise to investigate war crimes committed there by both sides. His office needs a massive injection of funding to do its job in respect of both wars, and his prospect of putting Benjamin Netanyahu in the dock for indiscriminate bombing of civilians in hospitals and refugee camps may be as remote as arresting Putin for aggression. Nonetheless, Khan is right to prepare indictments against Russian and at least some Israeli ministers and commanders if his evidence warrants proceeding, against the day when they are surrendered by their own country or the state parties to the ICC sensibly agree to allow trials *in absentia*. Ukraine has itself captured a number of Russian soldiers and proposes to put them on trial for war crimes: if its prisoners of war come to include persons of high rank, it should document their crimes and send them to the ICC.

Putin himself will not be put on trial unless surrendered by a Russia that has turned against him as a result of economic collapse or military defeat. Like other indictees, he would be held in Scheveningen Prison, provided with lawyers if he did not have the money to retain some himself and afforded his rights to a fair trial before judges whom he could challenge if there was evidence of bias. He would face the dilemma of other indicted leaders – to turn his back on the court (the Charles I gambit) or to testify an oath to deny responsibility for war crimes. He could not talk about self-defence and the 'just war' he thought he was waging – this would be relevant to aggression but not the specific war crimes charges that the ICC under Article 8 and his evidence would be confined to in answering these allegations. The prosecution would be keen to show that he kept abreast of military progress in the war, so that any evidence of his attention to its detail and his 'hands-on' style would be relevant. This could come from observations by members of his staff or testimony from a servant, who had watched Putin as he was briefed about the progress of the war and been shown television news of bombings and bombardments. Documentary evidence – the memoranda and situation reports that were sent to him for scrutiny – would be as incriminating as they were for Charles Taylor and Hermann Göring, if a new Russian government were to hand them over. It would not be necessary to put Putin on trial separately from his accomplices: if convenient, the court could order overlapping cases to be joined on the one indictment, so that Putin could sit like Göring in the dock alongside Lavrov and Medvedev, a few generals (and Alexander Lukashenko, the co-conspirator from Belarus, and the aiders and abetters like Patriarch Kirill and and state media commentators) – a modern courtroom tableau of a mass-murdering criminal gang.

CHAPTER 6

AFTER THE TRIAL IS OVER

So what would happen if Vladimir Putin were convicted, either at the ICC or by the proposed aggression court? There would be an adjournment for the world to absorb the news and hopefully some of the court's reasoning for its verdict. The court will be reliant on its press office at this point, to distribute a summary in two or three pages, because the judgment itself will run to hundreds. It must be placed in full on the internet with translation into different languages – most importantly, Russian and Ukrainian. Arrangements should be made for its publication in book form as well. The lesson must be learned from the fate of the judgment of the Tokyo trial of the Japanese war leaders: it was a damning and convincing indictment, but the Americans stupidly decided not to publish it, for fear it might encourage communists and upset the emperor. So this judgment went unreported in detail, except in a book by the lone dissenting Indian judge,

On Japan Being Not Guilty, which became for decades the only account of the trial – with the argument that it should not have taken place!

If Putin is personally present, it is likely that before sentence he will be remanded for a few weeks for medical and psychiatric reports. For all that armchair experts in the West have diagnosed him with paranoia and other mental illnesses – inferred from such habits as sitting at the end of a very long table for meetings with foreign dignitaries (a sensible precaution against catching Covid) – it is likely that he will be found stark staring sane and in good physical health. If the trial has been *in absentia*, the prosecution will be invited to say something about his character and antecedents, which are also unexceptional (although his grandfather did serve as chef to both Lenin and Stalin). He is 'of good character' as the saying goes – corruption inquiries into his conduct as a bureaucrat in St Petersburg were closed as soon as he became President.

Putin was born in 1952 and graduated in business law, later obtaining a doctorate in economics with a thesis partly plagiarised from an American textbook. He seems to have worked efficiently in his first job, as a KGB agent in Dresden, rising to the rank of lieutenant colonel, but without promotion to the more important posts in Berlin and West Germany. He then took bureaucratic (and political) positions in St Petersburg and with President Yeltsin in Moscow, impressing him sufficiently to win his support in due course to become his successor. Although the constitution allowed only two consecutive terms, Putin circumvented this limit on his ambitions by leaving the office to Medvedev, in 2008–12, while he took the less powerful position of Prime Minister, returning to be elected to the presidency in the 2012 and 2018 elections and again in 2024. At a referendum in 2021, a grateful people permitted him to remain in office until 2036. But for purposes of mitigation, Putin has done the state some service, other than by embroiling it in his crime against humanity.

Much interest at this stage will focus on his finances, which can be confiscated and go to his victims – the ICC already has such a fund and the aggression tribunal doubtless will likewise. How much will be confiscated will depend on what the prosecution can establish. Navalny claimed Putin has massive wealth, some of it overseas and in the names of certain close friends. The *Washington Post* estimates that he has moved more than $100 billion out of Russia since 2006. He is said to own an estate twice the size of Monaco, based twenty miles from the Finland border, with trout ponds, helipads and even a waterfall relocated from a national park. Navalny identified a vast palace on the Black Sea coast held in trust for him by one of his friends. These trappings of corruption will doubtlessly be seized if he is overthrown, and any possessions found overseas can be confiscated by the aggression court.

Like Boris Johnson, the number of Putin's children is unknown, other than two daughters with a wife whom he divorced some years ago to take up, in private, with an athlete who may have borne him one or two more. He will doubtless already have made secret provision for them, so the court will order seizure of all the assets the prosecution can trace outside Russia.

Putin has, with the help of his state media, cultivated a superhero, machismatic image, but it is the consequence of any trial that it tends to cut a defendant down to size. Putin's height seems a state secret (some estimates say he is as short as 5ft 3in.) and he is certainly conservative, church-going and homophobic. He is intelligent, as lawyers go, but lacking in intellectual achievement or cultural interests. The court will acknowledge that in his life he has done some good, but it will sentence him on the basis that he has been the cause of 500,000 deaths and injuries – the estimated human toll so far of the war on both Ukrainians and Russians.

The court, in sentencing Putin, will probably comment on his motives for going to war. There will be no surprises: he was infuriated by the Maidan Revolution and its overthrow of his puppet Yanukovych, not only because it could bring NATO closer but because he realised that Ukraine, which he genuinely believed was historically and spiritually a part of Russia, was moving towards the EU and the decadent, hostile West. 'I will never disavow my conviction that Russians and Ukrainians are one people,' he said just after invading. Moreover, he thought he could get away with an armed assault because he had suffered only a few sanctions as a result of his annexation of Crimea: he had no notion that the West would stand firm behind Ukraine with so much money and so many arms. And he probably did believe advice from purblind courtiers, wishing to please, that his troops would be greeted with hugs and flowers. He really thought it would not be difficult to absorb Ukraine, to force his own illiberal views on that recolonised country and to put forward, as of old, the Cold War conceit of Russia as a military equal to the USA.

The court may say that the war was entirely Putin's own doing and that the support for it by the great majority of Russians was down to propaganda or state television and to the jingoistic sermons from Patriarch Kirill and the Russian Orthodox Church. The judges might say this to mollify the populace over the jailing (at least on paper) of their leader, but it would not be true. Ordinary Russians knew very well what was happening in the war – they heard about it from their children, who were fighting it. They are as responsible for Putin as ordinary Germans were politically responsible for Hitler. There is likely to be evidence which has emerged in the trial that Putin's closest advisers, such as hardliners Alexander Bortnikov (head of the FSB) and Yury Kovalchuk ('Putin's banker', massively rich and controller of much private media), urged him to invade. This may well be true, but neither man would qualify as a 'leader' for the purposes of the definition of aggressors under Article 8 of the Rome Statute. And in any event, the court will make clear that Putin had personal control of Russian policy, and he alone was responsible for ordering the invasion.

Although much is known about Vladimir Putin and there is not much that indicates the deeper criminality that lurked, for example, behind the bland official face of Adolf Eichmann, a trial may throw up clues to personality defects which, given his absolute power, made him a sociopath. According to MI6, he gave the order to kill Litvinenko, by use of radioactive polonium. This was an outrage which had no sensible justification, other than that Litvinenko had called Putin, without evidence, a paedophile. Anyone else would have let it pass, but it is said to have cut Putin to the quick and made him decree the most agonising of deaths for merely a peddler of scurrilous defamation.

Similarly, if Putin did order Yevgeny Prigozhin's assassination – according to the CIA, by having his secret police attach a bomb to the plane while it was being prepared for take-off – that was typical of a gang leader who kills a rival without care for innocents who get in the way (i.e. the pilots and the flight attendant). Putin's fury at Prigozhin's 'treason' made him a killer – it was not enough to humiliate Prigozhin and strip him of power. That Putin has a temper that drives him to criminal excesses was apparent in his reaction to Magnitsky laws promoted by Bill Browder, which led to sanctions on Russian oligarchs. First, Putin stopped Americans from adopting Russian orphans – a response even Sergey Lavrov condemned as 'heartless' – and then offered at the Helsinki summit meeting with Trump in 2018 to surrender Russian officials wanted by Special Counsel Robert Mueller if the US would hand over Bill Browder, presumably for life imprisonment in a gulag. It was, on the face of it, ridiculous behaviour, but it was suggestive of a gang leader who becomes furious when crossed and will do anything – even invade another country – to get their own way.

Putin will have to be granted every prisoner's right to address the court before it passes sentence. He may simply turn his back – a 'do your worst' signal of defiance – or he may make an impassioned plea. This is a risk that any court must take, that the defendant will justify their crime and use their last televised opportunity to appeal to their supporters. Although Putin's time can be limited by the presiding judge (at the Milošević trial, the microphone was cut off), he must be allowed his final speech – his lack of contrition should increase the sentence. Putin is not, like Milošević and Hitler, a natural demagogue – after the study of law he went straight into the

KGB and worked behind the scenes on his political advancement. Rabble-rousing was not his style once he came to power. But he has addressed crowds at length on his justification for the war, and he may well use his last words to repeat the gist of the thesis he wrote while avoiding Covid, about the ethnic and spiritual unity of Russia, Ukraine and Belarus. If he does address the court in person, he is likely to be bitter and defiant.

THE SENTENCE OF THE COURT: SHOULD PUTIN HANG?

Unlike domestic judges, who deliver to the miscreant standing before them ad hominem sentencing homilies, international judges are relatively restrained. The seriousness of the crime will be briefly explained in order to justify the length of the sentence. If convicted of aggression, Putin's sentence is likely to be the maximum possible, for the reason given in the Nuremberg judgment, in words likely to be repeated before he is dispatched to prison: 'To initiate a war of aggression, therefore, is not only an international crime; it is the supreme international crime differing only from other war crimes in that it contains within itself the accumulated evil of the whole.'

A well-read judge might even quote Emmerich de Vattel, a founder of international law, who, back in 1758, made the point more dramatically:

> The sovereign who … takes up arms without a lawful cause
> … is chargeable with all the evils, all the horrors of war: all
> the effusion of blood, the desolation of families, the rapine,
> the acts of violence, the ravages, the conflagrations, are his
> works and his crimes. He is guilty of a crime against the
> enemy … He is guilty of a crime against his people … Final-
> ly, he is guilty of a crime against mankind in general, whose
> peace he disturbs, and to whom he sets a pernicious example.

Putin will then be 'sent down' – a phrase referable to the
taking of convicted prisoners down to the cells in the bowels
of the Old Bailey. But sent where? The Netherlands is unlikely
to accommodate him, as it did the kaiser. If Putin's presence
is the result of regime change in Russia, his own country may
offer to gulag him in Siberia. But the issue of where to put a
fallen head of state, prone to be forcibly released by supporters or assassinated by opponents, is difficult. It arose with
Saddam Hussein, whom the US was determined to execute,
against the wishes of its British and European allies. At a judicial conference about setting up a court to try him, Finland
offered to provide a prison cell, but the Americans were out-
raged – 'Finland! Where he will enjoy conjugal visits from all
his wives and be able to watch 150 television channels, most
of them showing pornography!' Britain suggested he could
be treated as they did Napoleon and exiled to the South Atlantic island of St Helena. The idea was put to St Helenians

by the British Foreign Office, but they replied that they were trying to build up a tourist industry...

At American insistence, Saddam's court was not international but placed within the Iraqi legal system, which could and did impose the death sentence. That was the US purpose, weakly opposed by the UK, and it provides a precedent for executing heads of state convicted of crimes of aggression. Saddam was rushed to the gallows, denied his right to seek commutation and his last moments were captured obscenely on mobile phone pictures taken by prison guards. Crimes against humanity should be condemned by humanity – i.e. by the international community, through global justice institutions and not by local judges consumed, however understandably, by feelings for that wild justice, revenge.

The death penalty featured heavily at Nuremberg and Tokyo, as retributive punishment for those found guilty of war crimes which took many lives. It was at the time a common punishment for murder, and only much later, in the 1960s and 1970s, does capital punishment come to be abjured by states in Europe (under the influence of the European Convention on Human Rights – ECHR) and in Latin America (under the influence of the Roman Catholic Church). By the time international criminal courts came on the scene, most sponsor states were abolitionist. But it cannot be said that international law itself requires the disavowal of the death penalty. In the case of heads of state guilty of aggression, there are in fact good reasons for imposing a death sentence, and those constructing Putin's tribunal should certainly consider the advantages of taking him to a scaffold rather than to a prison cell.

One reason that was propounded by the Earl of Essex, for executing Charles I, was that 'a king who is dead renews no war'. The conviction of Putin, for a war with all the consequences so memorably described by Vattel, would be, comparatively, as serious as the crime of aggression that can be imputed to the Nazi leaders without adding the Holocaust – the mass killing and injuring of soldiers and civilians in pursuit of territory and 'Lebensraum'. But the sheer number of victims can no longer provide a warrant for a death sentence – there are special reasons for putting an end to the life of a malign but politically inspirational figure. He 'renews no war' as he might well do if he remains alive in some forbidding castle or island fortress awaiting rescue by armed supporters. Putin would be a formidable prize if sought by nuclear-backed Russian forces, and even if overthrown and discredited he would be a prize for any crime syndicate or terrorist group. The prospect of having to protect him, irrespective of the cost and threat to the lives of security forces, would be a reason for Western states to prefer an early execution. That was the thinking behind the executions at Nuremberg, where the dead bodies were quickly incinerated and the ashes spread over a fast-running river, so that their graves would not become shrines for later generations. That is why plans to put Putin in the resting place he has doubtless already reserved, in the Kremlin Wall between Stalin and his 'show trials' prosecutor Andrey Vyshinsky, will have to be resisted. If he is convicted, his punishment should include being put to rest in an unmarked grave, either after being hanged or after dying in prison.

Another precedent for a death sentence on a dictator is that which was passed on Nicolae Ceaușescu and his wife Elena by a court which convened on Christmas Day to convict them of genocide for killing protesters. It arranged for their immediate execution by an army firing squad. Their bullet-ridden bodies were displayed on television in order to convince their secret police (the Securitate) that there was no point in killing more of the populace to restore them to power. The lawyer who had presided as judge at this mock trial committed suicide some weeks later, and although the killing did certainly save lives and avoid a bloodthirsty fightback by the dictator and his police force, the public interest would have been better served had Ceaușescu been assassinated, rather than subjected to a farce dressed up as a legal proceeding.

The death penalty is of course abominated by human rights NGOs and by most of the nations which make up the 'core group' of states planning the aggression tribunal. Nonetheless, the case for hanging Putin, if he is convicted of aggression, must be seriously considered. He has done far more damage than Saddam, and he constitutes a much more serious threat if allowed to remain alive, even if subject to life imprisonment. It must be recognised that his victims – the bereaved and the injured, Ukrainians and Russians alike – would derive some satisfaction from watching him choke to death on a gibbet. It is only the need for states to teach reverence for life that will prevent the aggression tribunal from putting Vladimir Putin to death.

If Putin is tried and convicted at the ICC, he cannot face a death sentence. If the charge is based on his command or superior responsibility, it is unlikely to even carry a life sentence. Improper supervision of the transportation of children – one of the charges he now faces – could not justify a sentence of more than a few years, so he would have to be released for good behaviour not long after a trial which would not have heard evidence of the full extent of his criminality. It would provide some consolation to the victims of that offence – the transported children and their parents and relatives – but not to those whose loved ones were killed by his orders to carpet-bomb Mariupol, or all the other crimes committed in the course of his war. This is inevitable unless the court issues indictments for his responsibility for some of those other crimes, in which case he would go on trial in the ICC for the rest of his life, or at least until dementia sets in (as it did with a sponsor of the genocide in Rwanda, who had to be declared mentally unfit for trial when dragged out of hiding twenty years later).

The likelihood, however, is that after a trial *in absentia* will come a sentence *in absentia*. The defence team will be invited to address the court in mitigation, but as they have no instructions from Putin, they may well decline – if the conviction is for aggression, there will not be much to say. If it's for a command or superior responsibility offence, however, there may be some precedents from the ICC that could provide guidance as to the length of the appropriate sentence. It would be handed down, after a short break for any deliberation, and the presiding judge would refer to the main judgment and give short reasons to justify its length – a televised performance which will need to be stern and short and end with a reminder that Putin has a right to return for a retrial. Transcripts of both the judgment and sentence will go online and should be published in various languages – Russian and Ukrainian at least, as well as English and French. Although it will be subjected to a deluge of criticism from Russian trolls and propagandists, it should be detailed and powerful enough to demonstrate to any open-minded reader that Putin's guilt, although he was not present in court, has been proved beyond reasonable doubt.

This is the prime function of a war crimes trial – namely, to provide an authoritative account of a crime against humanity and to allocate responsibility for it. There will have been everything said on behalf of the defendant, and the evidence will have been challenged and appropriately cross-examined. Whatever school textbooks in Russia say about the war in years to come, teachers and students will be able to access on the internet a judicial account which is tested and true and will stand long after Putin himself is dead and buried, whether in an unmarked grave or beside Stalin in a Kremlin tomb of honour.

THE AFTERMATH

Following a conviction, the aggression tribunal will have proved its worth. The court will have to stay in operation at least until Putin's death if it has convicted him *in absentia*, because he will be entitled to return for a retrial, however unlikely it is that he would take up this option. In the meantime, it could proceed – *in absentia* or in the flesh if they have been caught – against others who satisfy the 'leadership test' for aggressors in Article 8 *bis* of the Rome Statute, namely that they have during the war been 'in a position effectively to exercise control over or to direct the political or military action of the state'. This would certainly include Lukashenko who allied his state, Belarus, to the criminal enterprise undertaken by Russia, and it would include Medvedev, Lavrov and the high-ranking generals who directed the actions of Russian forces notwithstanding that they had been ordered to do so by Putin. The trial at Nuremberg cast a much wider net – Goebbels, had he not committed suicide, would have been indicted (and doubtless hanged) for masterminding Nazi propaganda, a punishment given to the odious Julius Streicher for his antisemitic newspapers. Their equivalents are the 'commentators' on Russia Today who adopted Kremlin lies to whip up hatred against Ukrainians. The worst propaganda comes from the Russian Orthodox Church which described the crime of aggression as a 'holy war' against what Patriarch Kirill identified as the anti-Christ. He promised that any soldier killed in the fighting would have all his sins forgiven and hailed Putin as a 'miracle of God'. On Kirill's orders, any priest caught praying for peace was expelled from the church. Kirill is the vilest of hypocrites: a Christian who encourages bombing that kills children and who encourages his flock – over half the population – to vote for 'God's miracle'. If anyone deserves to be prosecuted for inciting support for the war it is Kirill, himself an alleged former KGB operative, but he does not qualify as a defendant under the Rome Statute because he had no control over political or military action. It will be important for the court to consider whether he can be prosecuted for 'aiding and abetting' or 'counselling and procuring' Putin's acts of aggression.

The court should not be an 'ad hoc' institution, designed only for Putin or only for the Ukraine War. The US is opposed to it becoming a permanent institution, quite transparently out of fear that it might one day indict an American President. The ICC will continue: it has survived US opposition, virulent at times under George W. Bush (during his first term) and Donald Trump, and has proved its worth, and there is no reason why an aggression tribunal should not do the same, in the interests of deterring this worst of all war crimes. It would, of course, be expensive and (like other international criminal courts) attract hostility from diplomats who fear its existence might interfere with their efforts to broker peace deals with amnesties and agreements to allow aggressors to keep part of their conquests. But history tends to show that peace without justice is no peace at all – only the peace of the mass grave.

The reason why a court – as distinct from a UN inquiry or some other form of official investigation – carries weight is precisely because it delivers a form of justice. There is a sense that in a true adversarial setting, with an 'equality of arms' between prosecutors and defendants, disputing each other's evidence in public, with final decisions made by impartial judges, there will emerge a verdict that is right and just (at least when confirmed on appeal). No other format can compare: put a judge as good as Erik Møse at the head of a commission of inquiry into the Ukraine War, and he will (and did) produce a report which accurately listed all the possible Russian war crimes. But he did not take evidence in public, heard no cross-examination from Russian counsel, reached no conclusive conclusions and the publication of his report was not treated as of much moment. Not because it was a trial *in absentia*, but because it was not a trial at all. The report was just another document beside the many books that detail Russian war crimes.

One such crime – the shooting down of a Malaysian airliner – was the subject of a trial in the Netherlands, where two Russian soldiers and a Ukrainian separatist were convicted of murder in their absence. But they were unrepresented. The court gave them no amici defenders and, as a consequence, may have made a wrong finding about their level of guilt, because the evidence suggested that they thought the target was a Ukrainian military aircraft and not a passenger plane. Hence the real importance of ensuring that Putin has a 'dream team' of top-class counsel with funds to explore any evidential leads that may assist in his defence.

This is additionally important to prevent allegations of a 'show trial'. The phase derives from Stalin's frame-up of old Bolsheviks who confessed to absurd conspiracies with Trotsky under examination by the prosecutor Vyshinsky, who supervised their scripts which were rehearsed in torture chambers and spoken in fear of reprisals against their families if they failed to confess. The purpose, of course, was to publicly show the guilt of Stalin's enemies, and the technique was regularly used at political trials in communist countries after the Second World War.

'Kangaroo court' is another phrase used for unfair trials, although it has no sensible meaning and no clear derivation (Australians cannot understand why their beloved marsupial has become a synonym for injustice). Both epithets were used to describe the Rwandan court which convicted Paul Rusesabagina, hero of the movie *Hotel Rwanda*, in 2021, after its judges did not allow his counsel to cross-examine the main prosecution witness. Most unfair courts in the world are 'no-show courts', which hear cases in secret. The aggression court must avoid any taint of unfairness, even when trying absent defendants, by sitting in public, hearing arguments from evenly matched advocates, before impartial and distinguished judges. That is generally the case at the ICC, and every effort must be made to ensure that the aggression tribunal maintains the same standards.

In that event, the tribunal, whatever its cost, would be of value to the world, even after the end of this unforgivable war which will have caused so much loss of life and so many crippling injuries to soldiers on both sides and so much grief to their bereaved families, and so much suffering to the innocent citizens of Ukraine. Assigning responsibility to Vladimir Putin will provide some consolation, and some basis in courts of other countries to allow compensation claims against Russian property. Even if a negotiated truce leaves Russia with Crimea, or a part of its conquered territory, its responsibility for the death and destruction resulting from the war will be clear and will dog that country, its diplomats and businesspeople, its lawyers and artists and athletes, wherever they go, certainly as long as they owe any allegiance to Putin as their head of state. His act of aggression has opened a Pandora's box of troubles for his country, which only his removal can diminish. The judgment of the tribunal, if it convicts, will help to underline his guilt as a matter of history, whatever spin is put upon it by the Russian media and educational institutions.

Ultimately, the establishment of an aggression tribunal is necessary to vindicate international criminal law, to show the world, and to show potential criminals, that this law is not found only in textbooks and university classrooms. Unless law-breaking has consequences in the real world, it is not law at all – merely pious precepts to which any political leader or general can turn a blind eye when military conquest beckons. Laws must by definition have courts which can declare if they have been broken, even if enforcement of the judgment is beyond their grasp. It is for that reason that Vladimir

Putin should be brought to whatever justice can be done on a leader who has nuclear weapons and a permanent seat on the Security Council but who has killed or crippled half a million people: if no one is above international law, there must be a court to take his measure.

Otherwise, in the words of an old, pre-war Japanese song:

> There is a law of nations, it is true,
> But when the moment comes, remember,
> The strong eat up the weak.

CHAPTER 7

A WORLD SAFE FOR DEMOCRACY?

Ukraine's battle in its war with Russia has, essential-
ly, been for its right to democracy – what Winston
Churchill once described as 'the worst form of government,
except for all the others'. Its hallmarks – fair elections, free
speech and an independent judiciary – were enjoyed by a
populace of 44 million, who were threatened by a Russian
military occupation and an unelected puppet government.
Other democratic governments in Europe, America, Canada,
Japan and Australia came to its aid – not, as Sergey Lavrov
alleged, for a proxy war against Russia but to vindicate an
international rules-based order so badly damaged by Russia's
use of force. That order, however, did not include protection
for democratic government.

There is no protection for democracy in international law. The UN charter is silent – 'democracy' is not even

mentioned. It proclaims its purpose: to save the world from 'the scourge of war' and its very first objective, in Article 1, is the 'suppression of acts of aggression'. But even for that purpose, whether the aggression is directed against a democracy or not, it is unfit. The General Assembly is just a debating chamber, and the Security Council, in which all UN power is vested, is pole-axed by the veto given to each of its five permanent members. So Russia will veto any resolution calling for a ceasefire in Ukraine, just as America has vetoed three resolutions calling for a ceasefire in Gaza. And a permanent member is permanent – it cannot be expelled, except on a recommendation by the Security Council, which that permanent member will of course veto. So if Russia were to drop a nuclear bomb on Kyiv, it could not be expelled from the United Nations.

This is a consequence of the way the UN was constructed in 1945. At the time when the League of Nations collapsed, in 1938, there was much discussion about its replacement, and while Stalin was in bed with Hitler (working out how they could carve up Poland), there was support for a world organisation of democracies – 'parliamentary peoples' as H. G. Wells described them – which would exclude authoritarian regimes and endorse an international charter of rights for all its member states. Once Stalin became an ally, this vision had to be abandoned. The Yalta Agreement even provided UN membership for states already part of the USSR, including

Ukraine and Belarus. When it comes to aggression, democracies that fall victim have no special protection – as Ukraine has discovered, as will Taiwan if China carries out its threat to invade.

That threat has no legal basis. Taiwan has no wish or capacity to attack China, and history – Mao's defeat of the democratic Chinese forces in 1949, which fled to Taiwan – gives no right for the People's Republic to resume and to win again that seventy-year-old war. Beijing's right to China's UN seat was blocked by the US until 1971, but by the time the People's Republic was permitted to occupy it, Taiwan was a sovereign and independent state, despite the numerous times China blocked its sovereignty from being recognised by other countries. A verdict that Putin was guilty of aggression would make it clear that his historical claim about Russians and Ukrainians being 'one people' gave him no right to invade, just as Chinese history does not entitle Xi to reclaim Taiwan by force of arms. A judgment by any court with power to apply (if not to enforce) international law would at least provide a legal basis for resisting future acts of aggression.

There are other examples: the elected leader of Myanmar, Aung San Suu Kyi, languishes in prison after an army coup, and in Hong Kong even talk of democracy is a criminal offence. Democracy was destroyed in the little enclave of Nagorno-Karabakh in September 2023 without the Security Council even noticing, by criminal aggression from

Azerbaijan. At much the same time, three fragile democracies that were relics of French colonialism – Mali, Burkina Faso and Niger – collapsed in military coups. In February 2024, *The Economist* calculated that only 8 per cent of the world's population live in fully fledged democracies, against 39 per cent who suffer strict authoritarian rule.

Meanwhile, China is behaving as though it were minded to commit the crime of aggression, by massing its formidable army on a coast only 100 miles from Taipei and from time to time blockading its skies and straits with warships and warplanes. The casualties of an invasion would be massive. China, doubtless backed by Russia, would need to destroy American communication systems and troops in Australia, and probably Japan and South Korea as well. Taiwan is a settled democracy of 24 million people – it is not, as Xi pretends, a 'breakaway' province which requires 'reverification'; it has been independent ever since Japanese occupation ended and the Republic of China government, on the run from Mao's army, set up its permanent base there. Today its people – 95 per cent of them – want to remain independent, learning from the brutal repression of democratic protests in Hong Kong just what Chinese rule entails. An invasion would be a crime against humanity, but the Security Council, hamstrung by great power vetoes, would be worthless as interlocutor or mediator. In 2023, as the bodies of several thousand children were being dug up from rubble in Gaza, it could not even manage to pass a ceasefire resolution.

THE FALLEN DEMOCRACIES

Joseph Goebbels thought that the best joke about democracy is that it gives its enemies the means to destroy it. That may be so with the enemy within – populist politicians and power-crazed colonels – but also the enemy without: hostile neighbours with long-standing racial and political hatreds. Democracies have fallen recently without UN action or concern by relevant regional organisations like the Association of Southeast Asian Nations (ASEAN) or the Council of Europe. Three examples illustrate this point.

Myanmar

ASEAN is a powerful trading and political bloc of ten Asian nations, including major democracies such as Malaysia and Indonesia, half of them Muslim and the others Buddhist. When one of their number, Myanmar, fell to an army coup, its freshly re-elected President, Aung San Suu Kyi, was jailed along with her government ministers and many supporters. There was a popular revolt which the army generals who overthrew her have fought with bloody reprisals. ASEAN has not expelled Myanmar – its only action has been to refuse to allow the junta president to attend its annual conference, or to vote on its call for a ceasefire in Gaza. Its democratic Muslim members are critical of Myanmar, but the Buddhist countries tend to support the generals. With members as authoritarian as Laos, Cambodia, Brunei and Thailand, loss of democracy to a junta of corrupt and cruel soldiers does not incur much pushback from ASEAN, or from the UN.

Sudan

The military dictator Omar al-Bashir seized power in Sudan in 1989 and brutally held it for thirty years, until he was overthrown by a popular revolution in 2019 which led to a transitional government to prepare for democracy. Bashir had been indicted by the ICC for approving genocide in the western province of Darfur in 2004, carried out by his shock troops, the Janjaweed (known to their many thousands of victims as 'the devils on horseback'). In the intervening years, Bashir strutted around African countries that were ICC members, and which should have arrested him, although he beat a hasty retreat from South Africa when a court action required the government to comply with its ICC obligations. (This decision dissuaded Putin from attending a BRICS conference in August 2023 after his own ICC arrest warrant.)

In 2023, as Bashir was in prison awaiting transfer to The Hague and the transition to civilian rule was proceeding, a vicious and deadly dispute arose in the capital Khartoum between the head of the army and his deputy, the head of a paramilitary group called the Rapid Support Forces (RSF), which had been formed from the old Janjaweed militia. More than 10,000 civilians have so far been killed, with the UN rapporteur reporting that Sudan is 'verging on pure evil', with sexual and gender-based violence, enforced disappearances, arbitrary detention and killing of children. All progress to democracy has stopped, and the UN and the African Union have done nothing to start it again. It was a classic case for the Security Council to use its Chapter VII powers to intervene, with armed forces from the African Union, but it did nothing other than to issue a despairing declaration that it could not choose between the two disputing forces. It had a short memory, given that the RSF had transmogrified from the genocidal Janjaweed while the army, on the other hand, had been assisting the transition.

The fighting inevitably spread to Darfur and in August 2023, the ICC prosecutor came to visit and re-opened the mandate from the UN in 2004 to investigate war crimes in Darfur, but he explained that regrettably the Security Council had given him no warrant to investigate in Khartoum where most of the crimes against humanity have occurred. The killings continue, and both sides seem motivated by greed for power and money, rather than by ideology: neither the African Union nor the Security Council have acted effectively to save imperilled civilians or to put democracy back on track.

Nagorno-Karabakh

This is (or was) a country in the clouds, covering the mountainous enclave between Armenia and Azerbaijan, both members of the Council of Europe, which sponsors the ECHR and is dedicated to 'democracy and the rule of law'. Neither was extended to Nagorno-Karabakh when its democracy was obliterated by Azeri aggression in September 2023, when over 120,000 people were forced to surrender at gunpoint and to suffer ethnic cleansing, leaving their ancestral homes and trudging as refugees to Armenia. Nagorno-Karabakh had always been Armenian – as its thousand-year-old Christian churches attest. Russia annexed it and an 1825 census showed it was populated by Armenians, who made up 95 per cent of the population in 1920 when Lenin, fatefully and wrongly, allocated it to Azerbaijan. That was still the case when the Soviet Union broke apart in 1990: the Karabakh council voted for independence and fought a war in order to win it. The Azeris had been conducting pogroms against Armenians in Sumgait and Baku, and went on to commit major war crimes, notably during their siege of the Karabakh capital, Stepanakert, in 1992. This was *Guernica* writ small, as they bombed schools and hospitals, killed several thousand citizens and tried to starve the rest into submission. But in 1994, Karabakh won the war and thereafter for almost thirty years developed a genuine democracy, with fair elections, a free press and an independent judiciary. It deserved the status of a self-determined territory, accorded by the UN to Kosovo and East Timor, but the Azerbaijan President, Ilham Aliyev, was determined to extinguish it. He whipped up long-standing race and religious hatreds and attacked the Christian enclave in a war in 2020, in which 6,000 died. The Security Council, with fatal ignorance, appointed Russia to keep the peace, which was like nominating a fox to guard the henhouse.

In 2023, after Armenia angered Putin by voting against Russia at the UN over its criminal invasion of Ukraine, his revenge was to tip off Aliyev that he would not stand in the way of an invasion of Karabakh. So on 19 September 2023, a massive army arrived at the border and threatened a shooting war: the Karabakh government had no alternative but to surrender to save the lives of its citizens, who all fled to Armenia. This was not only ethnic cleansing but the crime of aggression, which the Security Council should have referred to the ICC prosecutor. It did nothing, and nor hypocritically did the Council of Europe, despite its proclaimed dedication to democracy. The council's president, after the ethnic cleansing, sought talks which Aliyev, already the victor, refused to attend. Although the European Parliament condemned him, the council never sought to expel Azerbaijan for aggression (as it had Russia when it invaded Ukraine) or even to sanction this malevolent (but very rich) state.

● ● ●

These three disparate examples demonstrate the lack of principled support for democracy from the UN and from regional organisations. There is no support, either, in international law. There is one case – *Prasad* (2001)– in which a court comprising judges from Australia, New Guinea, New Zealand and Tonga declared a presumption in favour of democracy, after an army coup in Fiji removed the elected government and replaced it with an appointed parliament 'ethnically cleansed' of Indian MPs. The court ruled that a usurping regime must prove that it has popular support, as well as power, and evidence from civil society (churches, women's groups, business, trade unions and human rights organisations) was admitted to prove that it did not. This ruling would not have come from a UN court where some judges represent authoritarian countries, although it is the kind of decision which could be expected from a court established by an organisation of democracies.

AN ORGANISATION OF DEMOCRACIES?

It cannot be foretold how Putin's war will end, but at some point, the killing will have to stop. There may be a ceasefire agreement, or an armistice or the war may diminish into a frozen conflict. But it will stand as the textbook example of the crime of aggression – the most serious of war crimes and one which amounts to a crime against humanity – committed by a permanent member of the Security Council. If it ends with any advantage won by the aggressor, it will be a setback for world peace, because it will carry the message that states can profit from violent breaches of international law. Putin had no right to invade Ukraine, and that will have to be the verdict of any honest court. His war has shown, dramatically, that the United Nations is no protector of democracy, and those who wish this form of government to have more security must come up with an alternative to the UN, and certainly to the Security Council.

There are 193 member states of the UN, but ninety-two of them are authoritarian or totalitarian, ruled by military or theocratic dictatorships or directly – by kings or hereditary princes and sheiks. So the UN cannot represent, let alone favour, just one political system. It remains useful as a venue where states can come together to negotiate international treaties on matters that affect them all, like climate change, refugees and the laws of sea and space, and to fund bodies like UNICEF, UNESCO and the World Health Organization. The Human Rights Committee inevitably has a significant number of members from non-democratic countries: it sometimes orders reports that explain conflict situations, but it does not try to resolve conflicts. It should be possible for governments of all kinds to continue to support and fund these bodies with creditable objectives, but democratic governments must look to a new organisation to promote their values. The Security Council would not be missed – by raising expectations that it can stop aggression, it does more harm than good.

A body committed to the protection of democracy might be half the size of the UN. It could set up a court of outstanding jurists applying international law under a charter of rights which would include the rights of peoples to democracy and of course to freedom from aggression. Its members would be obliged to join the ICC and to enforce its judgments. The body could impose severe economic sanctions on non-members, most heavily on those which threaten aggression or host terrorists. It would not primarily be a military alliance, although provision for the use of force should be made for cases when sanctions prove inadequate. There would be an associate status available for sheikdoms and monarchies which generally wish for the economic and security advantages of alliance with the West – they could be expelled for repressive conduct (such as Saudi Arabia's murder of journalists like Jamal Khashoggi).

There are already associations of democratic states that could draw together for such a purpose. Some thirty-five have 'Magnitsky Acts' – domestic legislation which enables them to sanction, by visa bans and seizure of assets, foreigners involved in human rights abuses (for which reason, as accomplices to his aggression, most of Putin's oligarch friends have been sanctioned, but not, curiously, Putin himself).

There are 124 states, mostly democracies, which have ratified the ICC, a sign in most cases of their good intentions and respect for international law. And there is the 'core group' of thirty-nine countries that are meeting to construct an aggression court to try Putin. A similar conference will need to be held if the 'parliamentary peoples' of the world decide that democracy and the rule of law are worth protecting – by an organisation other than the UN.

Magnitsky laws have been passed by many liberal democracies to close their borders, their banks, their hospitals, schools and other sought-after institutions to outsiders suspected of human rights abuses, including the support of aggression (hence the targeting of Putin's oligarchs) and the overthrow of democracy (the Myanmar generals). These states should be willing to ratify a new convention that embodies the right to democracy and enables the targeting of regimes which threaten it, denying their leaders access to the free world and its banks and financial institutions. The US would have to be a member because of the power of the dollar as the basic currency of global business and the difficulty of doing it in the face of sanctions from the US Treasury. There is, however, always a concern about the steadfastness of the US when it elects a (like Trump) as President: there is a loss of the political empathy that democracies normally extend to each other as a result of their shared values.

Putin, in 2019, described liberal democracy as 'obsolete'

and Xi Jinping is wedded to Lenin's policy of absolute control by the party through its politburo. The Chinese President wields real influence at the UN as its second-highest contributor, and with his representatives heading four of its specialised agencies. China's influence over beneficiaries of its Belt and Road Initiative is such that even if they are members of the Commonwealth, they have voted down UK resolutions critical of the clampdown on democracy protests in Hong Kong. Xi has called upon the UN to redefine human rights as 'the right to national development', without respect for individual freedoms. China, Russia and their satellites lack each of the three basic pillars of democracy. Elections and referenda are rigged. The media is censored and the judges are state lickspittles with impossibly high conviction rates – 99 per cent in China and 99.75 per cent in Russia, where judges and prosecution in political cases lack both independence and integrity. Democracies do not need to sit down with states like this to talk about human rights.

Would the Security Council be missed? In 2020, it could not even agree on a simple resolution requesting member states to stop all wars during the Covid pandemic. The Security Council was deadlocked, because China wanted to make a reference to the World Health Organization but America did not. There is no hope that the Security Council can serve its purpose of securing world peace or, *a fortiori*, of protecting democracies against aggression, and Putin's war on Ukraine has at least served to destroy that illusion.

● ● ●

On 7 October 2023 and thereafter, the war in Ukraine was wiped off the front pages by Israel's response to the attack by Hamas which killed a thousand of its citizens and 400 of its soldiers and took 240 hostages. These were serious war crimes and Israel was entitled to respond, although it was accused of doing so disproportionally, by indiscriminately carpet-bombing parts of Gaza, hitting hospitals, schools and refugee camps and killing many thousands of Palestinians, nearly half of whom were children. The main difference between Russia's war on Ukraine and Israel's war on Gaza was that the latter had some justification whereas Putin had none. Many human rights organisations accused Israel of genocide, and certainly some of its leaders made statements evincing genocidal intent (the minister of defence claiming that the Israel Defense Forces (IDF) were 'fighting human animals' and would fight accordingly), but the government proclaimed its intention to 'destroy Hamas' rather than to destroy a racial or religious group as such.

Hamas is a political organisation with a military wing, and Israel was to that extent committing not genocide but what might be termed 'politicide', but it was imposing a form of collective punishment on Gaza's 2 million citizens, by way of bombings and missile attacks on civilians, just as Putin did by attacking Ukraine. If prosecuted for war crimes, the defendant must show that its self-defence measures are 'proportionate', but when Israel bombs a refugee camp to kill one Hamas fighter and kills fifty refugees as well, neither a philosopher nor a war crimes judge would consider that 'proportionate'. Israel, as the *de facto* occupier of Gaza, had a duty to treat its people humanely – it was entitled to order them to leave the north for their own safety, but it then kept bombing the south, where they had been directed to move. The threatened starvation of residents by minimising food, medicine and fuel deliveries was at least an incipient war crime of starvation, and a precursor of the genocide allegation that it so vehemently denied.

In early November, Karim Khan, his hands full with Putin's prosecution and the investigation of war crimes in Ukraine, stood at the Rafah border in Egypt (he was not allowed to enter Gaza) and promised investigations and indictments for war crimes. Quite how he is to proceed is unclear. He should certainly prosecute the leaders of Hamas for their crimes on 7 October, and Israel should be urged to capture rather than kill them if the opportunity arises – e.g. if they are found in the Gaza tunnels. As for Israeli Cabinet ministers and commanders, the prosecutor must proceed as best he can with evidence connecting them with particular war crimes. Any trials of the Israeli Army will face diplomatic sabotage by the US, which does not even accept that the ICC has jurisdiction over Palestinian territory, despite the fact that the court in 2021 ruled that it did. Were Israeli soldiers, in years to come, to travel to Europe, however, they might be arrested and put on trial under a 'universal jurisdiction' law, as happened recently in Sweden to an Iranian executioner. But this is a long shot.

Nevertheless, a hopeful precedent emerged early in 2024, with a hearing at the ICJ – the World Court – about whether it was plausible to argue that Israel was committing genocide in Gaza. A case was brought by South Africa and followed by another case brought against Myanmar, also pursuant to the Genocide Convention, by Gambia. These third-party actions have been rare – dog does not eat dog on the diplomatic circuit – but they show a new determination on the part of middle-ranking powers to put up no longer with blatant human rights violations by great powers or other allies. The ICJ is not a criminal or a human rights court – its judges are appointed by governments and are generally concerned with interstate property disputes, but some have high qualifications in international law. Israel appeared in the court because it thought it would win: genocide means the destruction of a religious or racial group as such, and Israel was hell-bent on destroying a political entity, namely Hamas, with its programme of abolishing Israel. South Africa's lawyers cleverly began their submissions with bloodthirsty rhetoric from speeches by Israel's President and its defence minister describing all Gazans as 'animals' and promising their extermination, thus betraying a genocidal intention. The court ordered, as a preliminary measure, vital supplies of food and medicine to be brought into the besieged areas and an end to indiscriminate bombing. Hamas was ordered to give up its hostages as well, but the judgment was perceived as a warning to Israel that it was in breach (or about to breach) international law. Israel's most emphatic supporters – the US, the UK and France – redoubled efforts to discourage it from a projected onslaught on Rafah.

• • •

The war between Russia and Ukraine has entered its third year. Casualty figures are opaque, but estimates agree on over half a million deaths and disfigurements of battlefield soldiers on both sides and tens of thousands of innocent Ukrainian civilians – men, women and children – mostly killed by recklessly targeted Russian missiles and drones but some by age-old war crimes of rape, torture, arbitrary execution and murder. Russia marked the new year, 2024, by unleashing its biggest drone and missile attack yet, killing forty-one civilians and seriously wounding a further 160, including children, in hospitals and homes. Russian forces continue to attack non-military targets like schools, restaurants and shops and cities of great historical interest like Lviv. These are all war crimes which continue daily and of which Putin cannot be unaware. On 23 July 2023, for example, Odesa Cathedral was deliberately hit – on a Sunday morning. It was at the centre of the UNESCO-listed old town and its priests chanted 'Lord have mercy' but Putin did not and his friend, the warmongering patriarch, offered no prayers as missiles blew holes in its cupola, triggering its collapse and destroying a part of Russia's own heritage.

For all this death and destruction, Putin refuses to take responsibility. He accepts no blame and simply lies, his falsehoods now undeniable by anyone but himself. He lied before the invasion, pretending that the troops massing on the border were not preparing for an invasion. He lied before then when he solemnly and personally signed the Bucharest Agreement, promising to safeguard Ukraine's borders after it gave up its nuclear weapons. He lied about the Nazification of Ukraine and the genocide he alleged it to be perpetrating. Tucker Carlson is the only Western correspondent who has been allowed to question him, but he was so ingratiating that he proved an embarrassment to other practitioners of his trade. Nailing Putin's lies is not a job for a journalist but for a court, whether Putin turns up or not. Those who can best confound his lies are dead – like Prigozhin, who had begun to expose them, and Navalny, who spent his last days in an Arctic gulag, sewing tambourine covers from deer skin in temperatures of -28°C.

Navalny's fate, and that of Zelensky too, if he falls, is shared by those who defy a dictator, and this will continue until international human rights law is given more force and focus. That is one overriding reason why a prosecution of Putin and his henchpeople should go ahead. He has breached the red line of the civilised world by invading a peaceful country, slaughtering its soldiers and civilians and killing or kidnapping its children. Others, of course, share in his guilt, like the patriarch who praises him as a gift from God and the idiots in the media who applaud him, as well as most of the Russian people, as guilty as Germans who supported Hitler and shared political responsibility for the Second World War. I would add to this list the academic voices in the West that have lent support to Putin on the grounds that NATO's expansion eastwards was sure to provoke him. Professors they may be, but it is hard to credit them with intelligence or morality, in leaving out of their equation the right of Ukrainians to life and to liberty.

At this early stage of constructing international justice mechanisms to build on the legacy of Nuremberg, there is an international law duty to proceed against perpetrators of the most wicked crimes against humanity. The worst crime of all is that of aggression, because it carries responsibility for all that follows. Putin is the last in a long line of perpetrators, beginning with Genghis Khan. So there should be a recognition of the possibility of prosecuting him, and others like Aliyev, and Netanyahu and his ministers and IDF commanders if the evidence warrants, and Xi if he invades Taiwan. To empower global justice at this comparatively early stage, we must proceed by using whatever tools are available. If that means setting up a free-standing aggression tribunal, then we should do so whether Russia cooperates or not and irrespective of the cowardly failure of ICC members to include major aggressors within its jurisdiction. There should be trials *in absentia* if the alternative is to have no trials at all. They offer some comfort to victims, some embarrassment to perpetrators, a real prospect that 'pre-emptive self-defence' will be eradicated and some insight for the public to know how Vladimir Putin was able to set in motion a war machine that took so many lives for so little reason.

ACKNOWLEDGEMENTS

In writing this book, I have drawn on my experience in setting up the UN war crimes court in Sierra Leone to deal with atrocious offences committed by rival factions during the war in that country, and I acknowledge with gratitude the work of the late Sir Robin Vincent, the most capable of registrars, and that of prosecutor David Crane and defence office counsel Steven Powles. In relevant advocacy in international courtrooms I have been notably assisted by Amal Clooney, Jen Robinson and Lionel Nichols, and I have benefited from discussions with Dr Carrie McDougall and Aarif Abraham. I express my gratitude to Olivia Beattie, James Stephens and Ella Boardman for their enthusiasm and editorship at Biteback, to Richard Walsh and to Kathy Bail at UNSW Press, who assisted me with arranging Australian publication, as did Alexandra Bone-Morato. There are others who have assisted me and are well aware of my gratitude: I have respected their wish for confidentiality.

Geoffrey Robertson KC
Doughty Street Chambers
March 2024

INDEX

Herbert Somplatzki

Traumpferde

Die schönsten Pferdegeschichten

Ravensburger Buchverlag

Als Ravensburger Taschenbuch
Band 54176,
erschienen 2001

Erstmals erschienen 1995
beim Franz Schneider Verlag GmbH,
München, für diese Ausgabe ergänzt
um die Geschichten „Ein Pferd aus
purem Gold", „Prinz Ludwig und die
Prinzessin mit der schönen schwarzen
Haut", „Das sprechende Pferd des
Teufels", „Das Gespensterpferd",
„Die mutigen Frauen von Lyk" und
„Der Frosch auf dem Seidensattel"
© 1995 by Herbert Somplatzki

Umschlagillustration: Gertraud Funke

Konzeption Innenlayout:
Heinrich Paravicini, Jens Schmidt

5 4 3 2 1   05 04 03 02 01

ISBN 3-473-54176-1

www.ravensburger.de

Geschichten aus alten Tagen

Zeiten der Begegnung

Zwischen gestern und heute

Geschichten von heute und morgen

Sagen- und Märchenpferde

Geschichten aus alten Tagen

Jokans Traum

Schon vor der Morgendämmerung waren sie aufgebrochen. In einer langen Reihe waren sie durch das beginnende Dämmerlicht in die freie Steppe hineingezogen, lange vor Aufgang der Sonne. Als dann der rote Glutball langsam am Horizont zu steigen begann und das Land allmählich ins Licht des Tages tauchte, da hatten sie in der Weite der Steppe eine grasende Pferdeherde entdeckt.

Sie waren ausgeschwärmt, immer dem Wind entgegen und jeden Vorteil des Geländes nutzend. Langsam waren sie den Tieren näher gekommen, dieser Herde aus Hengsten und Stuten, Jungpferden und Fohlen.

Die Nacht hatte Raureif über die Gräser gebreitet und auch die herbstfarbenen Blätter der Büsche und Sträucher besetzt. Ein wunderschönes silbernes Schimmern lag über dem Land und ließ das Licht der Morgensonne in Reflexen tanzen.

Die Männer schlichen durch die Morgenkühle und

das feuchte Gras unter ihren nackten Sohlen erinnerte sie bei jedem Schritt an die Kälte der Nacht.

Jokan war heute zum ersten Mal mit auf die Jagd gegangen. Lange schon hatte er davon geträumt; seit jeher war es sein größter Wunsch, mit den Jägern im Dämmerlicht in die Steppe hinauszuziehen.

Nun hatten sie ihn mitgenommen, er ging zum allerersten Mal durch die Kühle des Frühtaus mit den Männern zur Jagd. Er schlich so leise, wie es ihm nur möglich war, hinter ihnen her und ahmte nach, was er bei ihnen sah.

Inzwischen waren sie der Herde schon sehr nahe gekommen. Immer langsamer und tief gebückt bewegten sie sich zwischen den spärlichen Büschen auf die grasenden Pferde zu.

Der Leithengst war größer und kräftiger als alle anderen Pferde, aufmerksam wachte er über seine Herde. Ab und zu hielt er im Grasen inne und hob den Kopf; er sog den Wind durch die Nüstern ein, lauschte im Spiel seiner Ohren auf jedes Geräusch.

Noch behutsamer als bisher – es schien, als hielten die Männer den Atem an, so tasteten sich ihre nackten Füße über den Boden der Steppe – schlichen sie immer näher an die grasende Herde heran.

Dann hob der Älteste langsam die Hand. Die Reihe der Männer erstarrte. Und auf einmal wusste Jokan, dass nun die Jagd begann. In den nächsten Augenblicken würde sich alles entscheiden, das fühlte er. Und plötzlich hörte er sein Blut in den Ohren rauschen, hörte den dumpfen Schlag seines Herzens so laut, dass ihn Angst überfiel, er könne sich und die anderen an die grasenden Pferde verraten.

Da aber gab der Älteste schon das verabredete Zeichen. Wie von der Sehne eines riesigen Bogens geschnellt, so stürmten die Männer nun auf die Herde zu. Die Speere zum Wurf bereit, so schnell ihre Füße sie trugen, liefen sie durch das vom Raureif knisternde Gras der Steppe auf die Pferdeherde zu.

Jokan lief so schnell wie nie in seinem Leben. In der rechten Hand trug er den Speer. Er hielt ihn in geübter Jagdhaltung neben seinem Kopf und rannte hinter den Männern her.

Das Wiehern des Leithengstes hatte die Herde gewarnt. Schon stürmten die Pferde in wildem Galopp über das nachtfeuchte Gras der Steppe.

Die Männer hatten ein Tier zum Ziel genommen; ein junges Pferd, das seine Flucht einen Augenblick später als die anderen begann. Nun versuchten sie das Tier immer weiter von der schützenden Herde abzudrängen und in die freie Steppe hineinzujagen. Doch das junge Pferd war sehr schnell.

Da warf einer der Männer seinen Speer, er warf ihn aus vollem Lauf. Es war der Mann, der dem Tier am nächsten war.

In einem flachen Bogen raste die Jagdwaffe auf den Morgenhimmel zu, senkte sich dann der Erde entgegen und folgte in schnellem Flug dem galoppierenden jungen Pferd.

Und während das todbringende Geschoss sich seinem Rücken näherte, verstärkte das gehetzte Tier noch seine rasende Flucht. Doch trotz des wirbelnden Schlags seiner Hufe schien es keine Chance zu haben, der fliegenden Unausweichlichkeit des Speers zu entkommen.

Jokan war stehen geblieben, so abrupt, dass er beinahe zu Boden gestürzt wäre. Wie gebannt stand er da und schaute dem Flug des Wurfspeers zu, sah die sich neigende Flugbahn dem galoppierenden Pferd entgegensausen. Und für einen Augenblick hatte er das Gefühl, selber jenes Pferd dort zu sein; ein junges Tier auf der Flucht über den taufeuchten Boden der Steppe.

Doch der Speer verfehlte sein Ziel. Im allerletzten Augenblick hatte das flüchtende Pferd kaum merklich die Richtung gewechselt, war trotz des rasenden Galopps noch einem Strauch ausgewichen. Es nützte den Männern nichts mehr, dass sie jetzt alle ihre Speere warfen. Zu schnell war der Lauf des Tieres durch die Weite der Steppe. Dann, einige Atemzüge später, war das fliehende Pferd nur noch ein springender Schatten, der sich in rasendem Galopp dem Horizont näherte.

Noch dreimal an diesem Tage jagten sie eine Herde, aber immer vergeblich. Und von Mal zu Mal wurden ihre Bewegungen langsamer und schwerer, verwandelte sich die hellwache Spannkraft der ersten Jagd in immer größere Müdigkeit.

Nun saßen sie um das Feuer, sahen in die Flammen und schwiegen. Prasselnd schlugen Funken gegen das trockene Holz, züngelten empor und ließen ihre Schatten tanzen. Fast unbeweglich saßen die Männer im Kreis, regungslos, hungrig und müde.

Irgendwann hob der Älteste den Kopf und sah in die Runde. Einige Männer hatten die Augen geschlossen. Der helle Widerschein der Flammen zuckte über ihre vollkommen unbeweglichen Gesichter und gab ihnen scheinbar Bewegung.

In der Ferne heulte ein Wolf.

Der Älteste wandte langsam sein Gesicht in die Richtung, aus der das Heulen zu hören war.

Der Wolf heulte ausdauernd und lange.

Mehrere Männer erwachten. Mit angespannten Mienen horchten sie in die Nacht hinein.

Ein zweiter Wolf gab Antwort, dann ein dritter.

Die Körper der Männer am Feuer strafften sich, ihre Müdigkeit schien verflogen. Aufmerksam und sehr gespannt lauschte der Kreis der Jäger in die Dunkelheit hinein.

Dann wurde das Heulen leiser, begann sich zu entfernen.

Die Spannung der Männer am Feuer ließ nach.

Der Älteste warf eine trockene Wurzel in die Flammen. Sie umspielten das Holz, züngelten und fraßen sich dann an ihm fest. Knisternd flammte die große Wurzel auf.

Nun war das Heulen der Wölfe so weit entfernt, dass das Prasseln und Knistern der Flamme es übertönte.

Der Älteste verteilte die Wachen.

Die Jäger rückten zusammen und wärmten sich aneinander. Dann senkten sich die Köpfe der Männer und ihre Augen schlossen sich wieder. Einer nach dem anderen sank in sich zusammen, übermannt von großer Müdigkeit, die den Hunger im Schlaf vergessen machte. Nur vereinzelte Rufe von Nachtvögeln schwebten über der Stille der Nacht.

Jokan hatte das Pferd mit seinen bloßen Händen gefangen. Er war seinen Spuren durch das feuchte Gras gefolgt und stand auf einmal dem Tier gegenüber: ganz ruhig, Auge in Auge mit einem jungen schnaubenden Pferd.

Und auf einmal, er wusste nicht, wie es geschehen war, hatte er auf dem Rücken des Tieres gesessen. Ehe er noch nachdenken konnte, galoppierte der junge Hengst schon mit Jokan über die Weite, sprang mit federnden Sprüngen über das glitzernde Steppengras.

Jokan hatte das Gefühl zu fliegen. Er hielt sich mit beiden Händen an der wehenden Mähne fest und flog auf dem Rücken des Pferdes über die Weite der Steppe. Er spürte ein unbeschreibliches Glücksgefühl, fühlte sich für Augenblicke von der Schwerkraft befreit, sah sich und das junge Pferd dem Horizont entgegenfliegen. Er war so schnell, wie es eines Menschen Fuß niemals sein konnte. *Ich bin schneller als alle jagenden Männer!,* dachte Jokan und flog auf dem Rücken des jungen Hengstes dem Grashorizont entgegen.

Als Jokan erwachte, war er noch ganz benommen von seinem Traum. Und dieser Traum blieb Wirklichkeit, bis die anderen erwachten.

Der Morgen kam mit schimmerndem Grau, das sich über die Glut des Feuers breitete.

Steif von der Kühle der Nacht rissen sich die Männer aus dem Schlaf. Sie trommelten ihre Glieder wach in einen neuen Tag hinein.

Die Jäger entfachten die Glut zum Feuer. Sie öffneten ihre Fellbeutel und tranken das nachtkalte Wasser; mehr hatten sie nicht. Hungrig begannen sie den neuen Tag.

Als Erster begann der Älteste zu singen, da stimmten die anderen mit ein. Es war eine einfache Melodie, die immer stärker wurde und bald ganz ihre Körper erfasste. Sie begannen zu tanzen.

Dann stieß der Alte seinen Speer in den Boden und zelebrierte den großen Jagdzauber. Es war der mächtige Zauber, der ihnen an diesem Tage Jagdglück bringen sollte.

Jokan sang und tanzte inbrünstig mit. Hell stießen seine Lungen die Töne der Jagdbeschwörung in die raue Luft des Frühherbstes hinaus; diesen Gesang der erfolgreichen Jagd, der ihren Hunger beenden sollte.

14 Dann brachen die Jäger auf. Sie suchten die Spur einer Herde zwischen dem Raureif der Nacht.

Als Jokan zwischen den Jägern ging, dachte er wieder

an seinen Traum, der so lebendig war, als sei er noch nicht zu Ende. Jokan spürte immer noch, wie er im Flug die Steppe bezwang, wie er beim rasenden Trommeln der Pferdehufe dem weiten Horizont entgegenflog.

Und je länger er zwischen den Jägern ging, desto klarer wurde ihm, dass er über seinen Traum schweigen musste. Niemandem durfte er ihn erzählen, denn niemand würde diesen Traum verstehen.

„Ein Pferd musst du jagen", hatte der Älteste einmal zu ihm gesagt, „denn ein Pferd ist dazu geboren, gejagt zu werden. Es ist unser Jagdtier hier in der Steppe. Lerne deinen Speer genau zu werfen und triff das Pferd im Galopp! Wirf ihn genau, denn wir alle brauchen das Fleisch um zu leben!"

Nachdenklich folgte der Junge den Jägern, die langsam jenem Lichtstreifen entgegengingen, der den Aufgang der Sonne verkündete.

Eines Tages, dachte er, *eines Tages werden wir keine Pferde mehr töten. Dann werde ich in schnellem Galopp über das Gras der Steppe fliegen, auf dem Rücken eines Hengstes, der schneller ist, als je ein Mensch zu laufen vermag!*

Und während die Reihe der Männer immer vorsichtiger durch das Ende der Dämmerung ging, dem purpurnen Glanz der Morgensonne entgegen, dachte Jokan an seinen geträumten Hengst. Ganz deutlich sah er ihn im dunkelroten Glutball der Sonne vorüberfliegen. Und da wusste er auf einmal ganz sicher, dass er diesen Traum auch erleben würde. *Irgendwann*, dachte er, *irgendwann werde ich auf dem Rücken eines Pferdes sitzen; und ich werde größer und schneller sein als alle anderen neben mir!*

Die Quadriga

Pagondas' vier Stuten jagten durch das Hippodrom. In rasender Fahrt näherten sie sich der Wendemarke. Der Mann aus Theben sah die Marmorsäule näher kommen, er sah sie im Staub der gleißenden Hitze vor seinen Augen auftauchen und zog heftig an den Leinen. Seine Pferde warfen die Köpfe auf.

Als die Quadriga in Höhe der Wendemarke war, riss Pagondas sein Gespann scharf herum. Für einen Augenblick schien sein Wagen nur auf einem Rad zu stehen, schien an der Grenze zwischen Sturz und rasender Fahrt. Aber schon hatte der Zug der vier Pferde gewonnen; der Wagen umrundete in einer engen Kurve die Wendesäule und jagte in die lange Gerade.

Jetzt gab Pagondas den Stuten die Leinen frei. Mit weit ausholenden Sätzen jagten sie über den Sand. Sie waren zu viert nebeneinander vor den Wagen gespannt; ihre Hufe flogen die Gerade entlang und ließen den Boden dröhnen.

Der Abstand zwischen den beiden Wendesäulen betrug genau eine Spina, das waren zwei Stadienmaße. Und auf diesen 384,5 Metern, die in der Geraden verliefen, konnten die Vierergespanne ungeheuer schnell fahren.

Als Pagondas im Staublicht die Umrisse der anderen Quadriga erblickte, feuerte er seine Stuten an. Breitbeinig stand der Mann aus Theben auf seinem zweirädrigen Gefährt. Er hielt die Leinen fest in den Händen und sah auf den Rücken des anderen Wagenlenkers.

Sie waren schon neun Runden gefahren, jede vier Stadien lang. Und in jeder Runde war die Zahl der Wagen kleiner geworden, denn sie hatten sich in wilden Jagden erschöpft oder waren durch Stürze nicht mehr fähig weiterzufahren.

Nun waren sie noch mit drei Wagen im Rennen: die beiden Hengstgespanne und seine vier Stuten. Doch mit jeder Runde, die sie weiterrasten, war Pagondas den beiden anderen näher gekommen.

Sie hatten ihn spöttisch angesehen, als er mit den Stuten zum Rennen kam. Einige hatten auch gelacht und ihn gefragt, ob das hier ein Weiberrennen wäre.

Pagondas war ruhig geblieben; er hatte erwidert, dass es das Olympische Gesetz nicht verbiete, im Stutengespann gegen Hengste zu fahren. Dann hatte er seine Konkurrenten gefragt, ob ihre Hengste sich vielleicht vor seinen Stuten fürchteten. Da hatte man ihn zwar in Ruhe gelassen, doch heimlich wurde er belächelt.

Man schrieb das Jahr 680 vor Christus. Bis zu diesen

25. Olympischen Spielen waren nur Hengste die Rennen im Hippodrom gelaufen. Und nun wagte es ausgerechnet ein Mann aus dem siebentorigen Theben, hier in Athen eine Stutenquadriga über den kampferprobten Boden des Hippodroms zu lenken!

Pagondas war dem Wagen vor ihm nicht näher gekommen, als sie in die Wendekurve bogen. Doch als das Hengstgespann, seine rasende Fahrt kaum vermindernd, um die Wendesäule jagte, zogen Pagondas' vier Stuten einen geschmeidigen Bogen nach innen. Und als sie wieder in die Gerade kamen, galoppierten sie schon eine halbe Wagenlänge vor den vier Hengsten.

Pagondas ließ seinen Stuten wieder freien Lauf. Mit weit ausholenden Sätzen jagten sie über den wirbelnden Sand der Geraden. Ihre Hufe schlugen dröhnend den Boden und rissen das zweirädrige Gefährt durch die Wolken aus Staub der Wendemarke aus Marmor entgegen. Als sie die Wendesäule zur elften Runde umfuhren, hatte Pagondas das letzte Hengstgespann direkt vor sich. Es war an der Wendemarke zu schnell gewesen und der Athener hatte die Fahrt so sehr verringern müssen, dass die vier Stuten die andere Quadriga schon erreichten, als die ihre Fahrt auf der langen Geraden soeben begann.

Der Athener Wagenlenker war so überrascht gewesen, dass er für Augenblicke zur Seite sah. Nur winzige Augenblicke, aber in ihnen hatte seine Aufmerksamkeit nicht den Hengsten gegolten. Zwar zögerten die Pferde nur kaum merklich in ihrem rasenden Lauf, aber dieses geringe Zögern hatte genügt. Schon waren Pagondas' vier Stuten vorbeigejagt, hatten in donnerndem Galopp die Quadriga vorbeigezogen.

Pagondas ließ seinen Stuten freien Lauf. Und als sie nach rasender Fahrt an der Marmorsäule ankamen, wendeten sie dort schon ganz allein.

Pagondas feuerte seine Stuten noch einmal an. In gestrecktem Galopp preschten sie über die lange Gerade. Breitbeinig und die Zügel in beide Hände gefasst, so stand Pagondas aus Theben auf seinem Wagen, der mit rasend schnell drehenden Rädern über den staubigen Boden des Hippodroms jagte.

Erst als seine Stuten die Wendesäule umrundet hatten und schon ein gutes Stück über die Gerade fuhren, kamen ihnen die zwei Hengstgespanne entgegen. Sie waren so dicht aneinander geraten, dass sie nun Rad an Rad dahinjagten.

Beide Fahrer versuchten die Wildheit ihrer Hengste noch anzustacheln. Mit heftigen Peitschenschlägen hofften sie die letzten Kräfte aus ihren Tieren herauszuholen. Aber die Pferde waren schon zu erschöpft, um in der nun beginnenden letzten Runde noch schneller werden zu können.

Pagondas lenkte seine vier Stuten in die letzte Gerade. Er wusste genau, dass er fast eine Stadienlänge vor den zwei Hengstgespannen fuhr. Er sah die Reihe seiner vier Stuten vor sich und war sich seines Sieges sicher. Hoch aufgerichtet stand der Mann aus Theben auf seinem schnellen Gefährt und sah das Ziel näher kommen. Er hörte das Trommeln der sechzehn Hufe vor seinem Wagen und es kam ihm vor wie eine wilde Musik, die selbst die Begeisterungsschreie der Zuschauer übertönte.

Als sich nach Ende der zwölften Stadionrunde die Räder seines Wagens über das Ziel drehten, spürte Pagondas einen wilden Triumph. Er spürte ihn im schnellen Schlag seines Herzens und im heftigen Keuchen der Stuten, die zum ersten Male auf olympischem Boden gelaufen und schneller als alle Hengste gewesen waren.

Mitternachtssonne

Die Mitternachtssonne warf lange Schatten über das Land. Sie gaben den dunkelbraunen Felsen bedrohliche Gestalt.

Einar sah diese steinernen Gestalten näher kommen, sah zwischen ihnen unbekannte Wesen huschen. Ein- oder zweimal meinte er sogar das grinsende Gesicht eines Trolls zu sehen.

Er ritt ganz dicht hinter dem Vater her.

Der Kopf seines Ponys berührte fast den Schweif des Pferdes vor ihm. Dicht gefolgt von seinem Bruder und den Packpferden, so näherten sie sich jetzt den für Einar unheimlichen Felsengebilden.

Sie waren gerade erst in Island angekommen. Als sie um die Südspitze der Insel gesegelt waren, hatte Einar gestaunt, wie grün dieses Land ganz oben im Norden doch war. Sie hatten die Segel fallen gelassen, dann waren sie aus der großen Bucht im Südwesten in eine kleinere gerudert. Dort hatten sie Anker geworfen und waren mit ihren Pferden an Land gegangen. Sie hatten noch mit den anderen im großen Lager übernachtet, ehe sie aufgebrochen waren, um ins Land zu reiten.

Es war das erste Mal, dass sie nach Island gesegelt waren. Sie wollten zu Vaters Bruder, der vor einiger Zeit die Heimat verlassen hatte um hier eine neue zu finden: auf dieser Insel im Norden, die sie noch nicht kannten. Einar war der Jüngste unter den Männern und es war seine erste Reise.

Im Morgengrauen eines warmen Sommertages des Jahres 978 hatten sie im Norden Dänemarks den Anker gelichtet. Sie waren aufs offene Meer gerudert und hatten dort die Segel gesetzt.

Mit Südwestwind fuhren sie nach Norden. Als sie vor die norwegische Küste kamen, drehte sich der Wind. Er wehte jetzt von Osten und erleichterte ihre Fahrt, die sie immer weiter nach Nordwesten brachte.

Der Wind war ihnen günstig. Er wehte stetig und brachte das Wikingerschiff gut voran.

Tag um Tag waren sie nach Nordwesten gesegelt. Nur einmal hatten sie eine kleine Insel angelaufen und dort frisches Wasser gefunden. Der günstige Wind schob sie immer weiter über das Meer, dessen grünlich blaue Wellen sie gleichmäßig wiegten.

Da hatten die Männer von langen Fahrten erzählt, von Abenteuern und heftigen Stürmen. Und obwohl Einar schon viele dieser Geschichten von langen Winterabenden kannte, kamen sie ihm hier auf dem offenen Meer

23

doch anders und auch viel wilder vor. Er spürte den Wind, das Schlagen der Wellen gegen die Schiffsplanken, und ihm war, als wollten ihm Wasser und Wind die alten Geschichten noch einmal erzählen.

Die Überfahrt verlief ohne einen einzigen Sturm. Das war besonders gut für die Pferde. Und obwohl Einar einen der gefährlichen Stürme, die er aus den alten Geschichten kannte, gern selbst erlebt hätte, war er über das gute Wetter doch froh, weil es die Ponys schonte.

Nun ritten sie zwischen den Felsen entlang. Noch enger waren die steinernen Gestalten zusammengerückt und ließen kaum Platz für ein Pferd. Einar ritt jetzt dicht hinter seinem Vater und hinter sich wusste er den Bruder.

Im Schatten des nächsten Felsens hockte ein Troll. Einar versuchte nicht hinzusehen, doch der Troll wich seinen Blicken nicht aus, unentwegt sah er Einar an. Dann streckte er seine lange Zunge heraus und verzog das Gesicht zu einer abscheulichen Fratze. Der Kobold sprang, als Einar den Felsen erreichte. Er hatte die langen, spitzen Krallen weit vorgestreckt und stürzte sich auf den Jungen.

Einars Schrei riss den Vater herum und ließ die Pferde fast scheuen. Doch ehe der Vater noch fragen konnte, hörte man Leif schon lachen.

„Schreckhafter Krieger!" Der ältere Bruder deutete lachend in die Höhe. „Eine Krähe hat zwar dunkles Gefieder, doch ist sie kein Grund Angst zu haben."

Einars Gesicht hatte sich rot gefärbt, denn auch der

Vater lachte, und Einar senkte den Kopf. Er war sicher, dass sich der Kobold in diesen Raben verwandelt hatte, kurz bevor er ihn beinahe berührte. *Ich muss auf der Hut sein*, dachte der Junge, und ritt noch näher zum Vater. *Denn wenn sich der Troll verwandeln kann, kommt er in einer anderen Gestalt vielleicht bald zu mir zurück!*

Einar machte sich selbst Mut. Er dachte an den Vater der Götter. Er sah in Gedanken die gewaltige Gestalt Odins auf seinem riesigen Pferd Sleipnir reiten. Der gigantische achtbeinige Hengst flog schneller als der Sturmwind über den Wolken dahin. Odins Auge leuchtete über dem Land und seine beiden Raben Hugin und Mumin kreisten um das mächtige Haupt des Gottes.

Sie waren ins Grasland hinausgekommen und sahen den Horizont wieder. Weit vor den jetzt freien Blicken stiegen kleine Hügel empor. Sie ritten jetzt nicht mehr so dicht, aber trotzdem fühlte sich Einar nun sicherer.

Die Ponys gingen im Tölt. Diese in unwegsamem Gelände günstige Gangart ließ sie unbekannten Boden auch bei schnellerem Tempo gut überwinden. Wo Trab oder Galopp zu hart oder zu schnell waren, kamen die Pferde im Tölt geschickt über Geröll, Krüppelholz, Abhänge und schlüpfrigen Grund, selbst über verharschte Schneeflächen. Bei dieser Gangart übertrug sich das Auf- und Abfußen kaum auf den Pferderücken und schonte Pferd und Reiter.

25

Plötzlich sah Einar den Wasserstrahl. Wie von einer Riesenhand hochgeschleudert stieg er zum Himmel empor. Für Augenblicke hob er sich über einen sanften Hügel des Graslands hinaus, zitterte in der Luft und war schon wieder verschwunden.

Einar sagte kein Wort, er sah sich um. Sein Bruder hatte scheinbar nichts gesehen. In sich versunken saß er auf seinem Pony und ritt hinter ihnen her. Und auch sein Vater schien nichts bemerkt zu haben.

Vielleicht habe ich ein Trugbild gesehen, dachte Einar, *vielleicht hat mich wieder ein Gespenst genarrt.*

Dieses fremde Land machte ihm Angst. Gerade eben der Troll, der sich blitzschnell in einen Vogel verwandelte, und nun dieser riesige Wasserstrahl, der sich vor seinen Augen zum Himmel hob und den nur er gesehen hatte.

Trotz der aufkeimenden Angst sah er weiter zum Horizont. Er achtete genau auf jene Stelle hinter dem sanften Hügel, von der sich die riesige Wassersäule hoch zum Himmel gehoben hatte.

Als er den Geysir zum zweiten Mal erblickte, waren sie ihm schon sehr nahe gekommen. Auch Vater und Leif sahen jetzt den mächtigen Strahl emporsteigen und wieder in sich zusammenfallen. Und Einar war froh darüber, dass er diesmal kein Trugbild gesehen hatte.

Sie kamen zu der Stelle, an der sich der riesige Wasserstrahl erhoben hatte. In seiner Nähe befanden sich mehrere Wasserlöcher, die glasklar waren und bläulich leuchteten.

26

Sie hielten ihre Pferde an, die Ponys wollten trinken.

Doch kaum hatten sie das Wasser berührt, als ihre Köpfe erschrocken zurückzuckten.

Als Leif dann die Hand flüchtig ins klare Wasser hielt, schrie er auf und riss sie schnell zurück.

„Du musst schon den Pferden glauben", sagte der Vater lächelnd, „sonst wirst du für deinen Unglauben bestraft werden!"

Leif blies kühlenden Atem auf die Fingerspitzen. Er sah auf die hellblaue Wasserfläche, dann wieder auf seine Hand.

„Ich wusste ja nicht", sagte er verlegen, „dass es hier draußen so heißes Wasser gibt."

Da hörten sie irgendwo unter sich ein dumpfes Grollen. Es wurde lauter, schwoll weiter an und verwandelte sich dann in ein gewaltiges Brausen, das immer mächtiger wurde und näher kam.

Die bösen Geister kommen aus der Erde gefahren!, konnte Einar noch denken, da schoss schon unter gewaltigem Pfeifen vor ihren Augen ein riesiger Wasserstrahl zum Himmel empor. Er schleuderte sich so hoch hinauf, dass Einar glaubte, er müsse den Himmel berühren.

Zum Glück war der Vater bei den Ponys geblieben und hatte die scheuenden Pferde halten können, aber es dauerte eine ganze Weile, bis sich die Tiere wieder beruhigt hatten.

27

Die Männer hatten beschlossen, an dieser Stelle zu rasten. Es wären noch zwei gute Tagesritte, hatte der

Vater gesagt, und sie mussten die Ponys schonen. Sie lagerten sich in vorsichtigem Abstand vom Geysir ins Gras, machten ein Feuer und stellten aus ihren Vorräten ein Mahl zusammen. Sie aßen und sahen schweigend zum leuchtenden Horizont. Dann breiteten sie ihre Schlaffelle aus.

Der Himmel glühte in orangerotem Licht, als sie sich zur Ruhe legten. Der junge Wikinger Einar wickelte sich in sein Schlaffell ein. Dann rollte er sich nahe an sein Pony heran, das sich ebenfalls niedergelegt hatte. Als Einar den ruhigen Atem und die Wärme des Tieres spürte, fiel alle Angst und Unruhe wie eine schwere Last von ihm ab. Er lag mit offenen Augen da und sah zum Himmel empor, unbeweglich neben dem warmen Körper des Ponys.

Einar sah in das mächtige Glühen über dem Horizont. Er spürte den Atem des Pferdes an seiner Seite und fühlte sich sicher in seinem Schutz. Auf einmal war alle Angst von ihm gewichen – die Angst vor den Kobolden, Trollen und bösen Geistern aus den alten Geschichten.

Bote der goldenen Horde

Timur jagte dahin. Die Hufe seines Rosses berührten den Boden kaum. Rasend schnell galoppierte sein Pony über das dürre Gras, hetzte zwischen den Büschen entlang, preschte einen Hügel hinauf, pfeilschnell und sicher.

Als Timur die Hochfläche erreicht hatte, sah er noch Spuren von Schnee; zu kleinen weißen Inseln zusammengeschmolzen, lag er zwischen den Büschen.

Das Pony galoppierte vorwärts. Wirbelnd schlugen seine Hufe durch Gras und Schnee, nahmen manchen niedrigen Busch im Sprung.

Timur hatte sich vorgeneigt, so weit es die Bandagen erlaubten. Er lag über den Hals des Pferdes gebeugt und ließ es laufen.

Der Ostwind pfiff eisig über das Land, hier auf der Hochebene war er besonders zu spüren. Timur neigte sich noch tiefer über den Hals des Pferdes und ließ die Zügel noch länger.

Das Pony war das sechste Pferd dieses Tages und Timur fühlte sich noch frisch. Er spürte die Bewegung des fahlgelben kleinen Pferdes unter sich im Galopp und fühlte sich gut dabei.

Sein Körper war mit festen Bandagen umwickelt, die eng seine Haut umgaben. Sie waren um Beine und Schenkel geschlungen, wanden sich weiter den Rumpf hinauf und gaben dem Körper Halt. Als der andere Reiter ihm im Ritt die Botschaft übergeben hatte, war Timur in die Morgendämmerung hineingejagt. Und er würde den ganzen Tag und die Nacht weiterreiten, bis sich die Sterne in der Dämmerung des Morgens wieder verloren hatten.

Jetzt hatte sein Pferd die Hochebene verlassen und näherte sich dem Fluss. Timur lenkte das Tier in die eiskalte Flut und das Pony querte, den Kopf erhoben, schwimmend die Strömung des Wassers.

Timur spürte die kalten, nassen Bandagen auf seiner Haut und trieb das Pony wieder in Galopp. Er schmiegte sich ganz dicht an das Pferd und fühlte die Wärme des Fells allmählich in die Bandagen eindringen, bis sie seine Haut berührte.

Er war etwa eine halbe Stunde weiter so geritten, als er die Pferdestation erblickte. Ein Reiter und zwei Pferde standen vor der Hütte bereit und warteten auf sein Kommen.

Als er näher gekommen war, preschte ein Reiter von dort los, an seiner linken Seite hielt er ein braunes Pferd am Zügel.

Timurs Pony jagte heran, schon war es fast neben den beiden. Und als es auf gleicher Höhe war, sammelte sich Timur zum Springen.

Der Sprung war gewagt, in vollem Galopp, auch die Bandagen störten. Und für einen winzigen Augenblick schwebte er zwischen den Pferden, während sie galoppierten.

Doch dann schlug sein Körper schon auf dem anderen Pferd auf. Er griff mit beiden Händen in die Mähne, nahm im Galopp die Zügel auf und jagte mit einem lauten Schrei weiter. Hinter sich hörte er den anderen Reiter rufen. Und ohne sich umzuwenden wusste Timur, dass der andere dem fahlgelben Pony folgte um es einzufangen.

Timur passte sich rasch den Bewegungen des siebten Pferdes an. Es wurde noch schneller. Es preschte in die weite Ebene hinaus und seine wirbelnden Hufe warfen Gras und Sand in die Höhe.

Timur war Pfeilbote im Dienste von Batu Khan, dem Enkel des großen Dschingis Khan, der um das Jahr 1200 die mongolischen Stämme Innerasiens mit Gewalt geeinigt und das mächtige China erobert hatte. Sein Enkel Batu Khan gründete das riesige Tatarische Reich der Goldenen Horde.

Pfeilboten waren die wichtigsten Nachrichtenträger dieses großen Reiches, das sich von Peking über Samarkand bis nach Osteuropa erstreckte. Sie ritten bei Tag und Nacht und trotzten jedem Wetter.

Gute Reiter legten bis zu dreihundertfünfzig Kilometer an einem einzigen Tag zurück. Es soll Reiter gegeben haben, die bis zu fünfhundert Kilometer schafften.

Pfeilboten waren zu heiligen Personen erklärt worden und dem besonderen Schutz ihres obersten Herrschers unterstellt. Sie waren aus tausenden der besten Reiter des Landes ausgewählt worden. Sie aßen im Sattel und wechselten ihre Pferde im Galopp. Ihre Beine sowie der ganze Körper waren mit Bandagen umwickelt, damit sie die Strapazen der Gewaltritte überstanden.

Dreihunderttausend Pferde standen im Reich der Goldenen Horde für die Pfeilboten bereit. In vielen tausend Stationen, die etwa fünfundzwanzig Kilometer weit voneinander entfernt waren, standen sie für die Reiterstafetten zum Wechseln bereit, um eine Nachricht über weite Entfernungen von einem Ort des riesigen Tatarischen Reiches ins Zentrum der Macht zu bringen – oder von dort zurück.

Das Licht der Sterne kam vom Himmel über die Steppe, als Timur im Galopp auf den Rücken des einundzwanzigsten Pferdes hinübersprang. Und während das zähe Pony über die Hügellandschaft lief, fühlte sich sein Reiter mit dem Pferd schon wie verwachsen. Er spürte seinen eigenen Körper kaum mehr und fühlte auch keine Schmerzen; er bemerkte den Schweiß nicht und auch nicht den Druck der Bandagen, die eng und sehr fest um seinen Körper gebunden waren.

Und während das Pony durch die Steppennacht eilte,

32

sah Timur zum Nachthimmel auf, an dem die Milchstraße ihr funkelndes Sternenband breitete.

„Sieh dir die Venus an, mein Sohn", hatte sein Mon-
golenvater zu ihm gesagt, als er noch ein Kind war. „Sie
ist die strahlende Hüterin der Himmelspferde; jener goldenen Herde herrlicher Pferde, die in Sterne verwandelt
im Dunkel der Nacht über die Steppe wachen!"

Timur sah im Galopp zum nächtlichen Himmel empor, zu seiner goldenen Herde. Und er spürte im Funkeln
der Sterne jene Kraft, die ihn weitertragen würde über
den Boden der Steppe; weiter und immer weiter bis ans
Ende der Nacht.

Der Sohn des Kreuzritters

Was ist die erste der sieben körperlichen Tüchtigkeiten?"

Walter antwortete: „Die erste der sieben körperlichen
Tüchtigkeiten besagt: Der vollkommene Rittersmann
muss reiten und schnell auf- und absitzen können. Er
muss mit dem Ross traben, rennen und es im schnellsten
Laufe wenden können. Auch muss er im Stande sein,
während des Rittes etwas vom Boden aufzunehmen!"

„Richtig!" Der Zuchtmeister nickte.

Sie ritten vom Inneren der Burg eine enge Gasse entlang, die zum Burgtor führte. Der Zuchtmeister ritt vor
Walter, er trug eine Lanze in seiner Rechten.

„Wenn Ihr älter seid", sagte er zu dem Jungen, „dann
dürft auch Ihr eine Lanze tragen; Ihr werdet sie im großen Turnier und auch im Kampf führen!"

34   Sie waren am Burgtor angekommen. Der Zuchtmeister senkte grüßend die Lanze und die Wachen ließen die
Zugbrücke hinab.

Als sie dann auf der Brücke über den Wassergraben ritten, sah Walter im Dunst des Morgens das weite Land vor sich liegen.

Ganz in der Ferne, wie ein gezackter Scherenschnitt auf der Spitze eines Berges, lag die Burg seines Großvaters. Wenn er nicht gewusst hätte, wie mächtig ihre Mauern und wie hoch die Zinnen waren, hätte er sie hier aus der Ferne für eine der kleineren Burgen des Landes gehalten.

Das Tal vor ihnen war von weißem Nebel erfüllt. Nur ab und zu, wenn ein Windstoß ihn zerriss, konnten sie die dunklen Wipfel des Waldes erkennen, dessen Bäume sich zwischen den beiden Burgen breiteten.

Sie ritten an dem großen umzäumten Platz vorüber, auf dem die Turniere stattfanden. Besonders der Buhurt, der Massenkampf zweier Reitermannschaften, war faszinierend für den Jungen. Dieser Kampf wurde mit stumpfen Waffen geführt, und wenn ein Ritter einen Gegner vom Pferd gestoßen hatte, musste er selbst absteigen um vom Boden aus weiterzukämpfen.

Sie verhielten einen Augenblick am Rande des großen leeren Platzes.

„Im Namen Gottes, des heiligen Georg und des heiligen Michael schlage ich dich zum Ritter; sei tapfer, frei und fromm", sagte der Zuchtmeister feierlich. „Diese Worte wird man zu Euch sagen, junger Herr, wenn Ihr ein Mann geworden seid. Und wenn Ihr dann in den Ritterstand aufgenommen seid, werdet Ihr Gott und Eurem

Kaiser des Heiligen Römischen Reiches Deutscher Nation in Treue dienen. Ihr werdet wie Euer Vater ins Heilige Land aufbrechen, um unter dem Zeichen des Kreuzes zum Lobe des Allmächtigen Herrn Eurer Ritterpflicht nachzukommen!"

Walter dachte an seinen Vater, der vor zwei Jahren fortgeritten war, um sich dem Heer der Kreuzritter anzuschließen. Seit diesem Tage beteten sie für ihn.

„Der Weg deines Vaters ist ehrenvoll und Gott dem Herrn gefällig, mein Sohn", hatte der Priester gesagt, als Walter ihn damals fragte, warum sein Vater so lange fortbleiben würde. „Er ist unter dem Zeichen des Kreuzes ins Heilige Land gezogen und er wird unter diesem Zeichen zurückkommen!"

Ehrenvoll und Gott dem Herrn gefällig, dachte der Junge, als er hinter dem Zuchtmeister des Weges ritt. Und als sie zu den Kornfeldern kamen, blickte er noch einmal zu der Burg zurück. Er sah zum Turm hinauf, dort über der Mauerkrone, und es schien ihm für einen Augenblick, als stehe dort oben die schmale Gestalt seiner Mutter. Sie war eine gute Mutter, er wusste es; sie ging jeden Tag in die Burgkapelle um für den Vater zu beten. Doch immer, wenn sie glaubte allein zu sein, sah er die Mutter weinen.

„Sie brauchen nicht zu weinen, liebe Frau Mutter", hatte Walter einmal tröstend zu ihr gesagt, „mir hat der Priester erzählt, des Vaters Weg unter dem Kreuz sei ehrenvoll und Gott dem Herrn gefällig!"

36

Sie hatte sein Haar gestreichelt und ihn unter Tränen angesehen. „Verzeih mir, mein Kind", hatte sie leise gesagt, „dass ich zweifelte. Du sagst mit Recht, dein Vater sei in sicherer Hand. Auch dort in jenem fremden Land steht er unter dem Schutz unseres allmächtigen Herrn." Noch während sie diese Worte sprach, flossen ihre Tränen wieder.

Die Felder begannen nicht weit hinter dem Turnierplatz. Als die beiden Reiter einigen ärmlich gekleideten Bauern begegneten, zogen die ihre zerschlissene Kopfbedeckung und verneigten sich tief.

„Seid streng, aber gerecht gegen das gemeine Volk", sagte der Zuchtmeister und deutete über das Land. „Sie sind unfrei und beackern unseren Boden. Es ist ihnen untersagt, Waffen zu tragen wie der edle Ritter, dem sie ihren Schutz verdanken. Und wenn man einen Bauern entdeckt, der heimlich an einem Buhurt teilnimmt, wird ihm die Hand abgehackt!"

Der Junge nickte und schwieg. Er sah noch einmal zur Burg zurück. Der Schein der Morgensonne lag auf ihren Mauern, das Licht spielte auf den mächtigen Steinquadern.

„Ihr habt mir in der Burg die erste der sieben körperlichen Tüchtigkeiten eines Ritters genannt", fuhr der Zuchtmeister fort, „nennt mir jetzt die anderen!"

Walter zögerte nicht einen Augenblick. „Der vollkommene Rittersmann soll schwimmen und tauchen können", antwortete er. „Er muss drittens mit Armbrust und

37

Bogen vertraut sein, viertens an Leitern, Stangen und Seilen gut klettern, fünftens turnieren und stechen können. Er hat sechstens zu ringen, zu fechten und weit zu springen. Und siebtens muss er bei Tisch aufwarten können und tanzen und Brett spielen."

„Das prägt Euch gut ein, junger Herr", der Zuchtmeister sah dem Jungen ernst ins Gesicht. „Ihr werdet dies alles können müssen, wollt Ihr ein guter Rittersmann werden!"

Walter, der Sohn des Kreuzritters, hörte aufmerksam zu und nickte.

Sie waren an den Feldern vorübergeritten und näherten sich nun dem Wald. Der Zuchtmeister deutete nach oben. Walter sah in der Höhe die graue Spitze des Felsens aufragen. Wie ein Wachtturm stand er über dem dunklen Grün des Waldes.

Ein Adler war von dem Felsen aufgestiegen. Mit mächtigen Flügelschlägen hatte er sich von seinem Horst in die Lüfte geschwungen und schnell an Höhe gewonnen. Nun ließ er sich in weiten Kreisen vom Aufwind immer weiter nach oben tragen.

„Er ist der König der Lüfte", sagte der Zuchtmeister, „ihm ist kein Vogel an Kräften gleich. Er herrscht in der Luft, doch der Mensch beherrscht Land und Wasser. Die Menschen haben ihr Reich hier auf Erden! Die Lüfte sind für die Vögel geschaffen und für die Engel des Herrn. Der Platz für Menschenkinder ist, solange sie leben, hier unten auf Erden."

Der Junge nickte wieder. Er klopfte den Hals seines Pferdes. Er liebte den Schimmel.

Walter sah den Adler immer kleiner werden. Und als sie die ersten Bäume erreichten, war der mächtige Vogel zu einem winzigen Punkt im rötlichen Blau des Morgenhimmels geschrumpft.

Nun ritten sie zwischen den Bäumen. Das dichte Blätterdach dämpfte das Licht und färbte es zu grünem Gold.

Wenn ich wie ein Adler wäre, dachte Walter, *dann flöge ich mit meinem Pferd über Land und Meer, so weit wir nur könnten. Und wenn ich meinen Vater sähe, dort unten im Heiligen Land, dann würde ich ihm zurufen, dass meine Mutter oft weint. Dann würde mein Vater seinen Rappen umkehren heißen um schnell nach Hause zu reiten. Er weiß ja dort weit im Heiligen Land nichts von den Tränen der Mutter.*

Zeiten der Begegnung

Das Anthrazitpferd

Es war kurz vor fünf, als die Mutter ihn weckte. Schlaftrunken war er in die Küche getaumelt und wäre am liebsten wieder in die Wärme des Bettes zurückgekrochen, das er mit seinem jüngeren Bruder teilte. Aber ein strenger Blick seines Vaters trieb ihm diesen heimlichen Wunsch sofort wieder aus.

Franz setzte sich an den Küchentisch und biss hastig ins Brot. Er kaute schweigend und schnell, und es war, als kaute er mit dem Vater und dem Großvater um die Wette.

Neun Menschen lebten in dieser kleinen Wohnung, hier in der Zechenkolonie. Drei winzige Räume, in denen Großeltern, Eltern und Kinder zu Hause waren.

Franz war gerade elf geworden, er war das älteste der fünf Kinder. Mit seinem Vater und dem Großvater arbeitete er auf der gleichen Zeche. Franz als Pferdejunge, sein Vater als Kohlenhauer; beide im Bergwerk tief unter der Erde. Nur der Großvater war nach Jahrzehnten schwerster Arbeit der Anstrengung nicht mehr gewachsen; er hatte die Grube verlassen müssen. Jetzt suchte er am Schacht Steine heraus, die zwischen den Kohlen lagen.

Es war dunkel und kalt, als die drei zum Bergwerk gingen, an diesem Januarmorgen des Jahres 1889. Nur der schmutzige knirschende Schnee unter ihren Füßen verbreitete einen Schimmer von Helligkeit.

Großvater ging als Letzter, er atmete schwer. Seine Lungen, die vom Staub zahlloser Steine in vielen, vielen Arbeitstagen zerfressen waren, ließen keine schnellen Bewegungen mehr zu. Wenn ihn ein besonders heftiger Hustenanfall schüttelte, blieb er keuchend stehen.

„Lass dir Zeit", sagte der Vater schließlich zu ihm. „Wir laufen schon mal vor."

Der alte Mann nickte.

„Wir müssen uns beeilen", sagte der Vater dann zu Franz. „Der Förderkorb wartet nicht auf uns!"

Sie ließen den Alten zurück und eilten weiter. Und der Junge war froh darüber, weil er beim schnelleren Gehen die eisige Luft nicht so spürte. Zitternd vor Kälte beschleunigte er seine Schritte noch mehr. Und wenn ihn die unförmigen Holzschuhe nicht daran gehindert hätten, wäre er, nur um etwas wärmer zu werden, auch durch den Schnee gerannt.

Sie gingen zur Lampenstube und holten ihr Grubenlicht ab. Als Franz dann über den Zechenplatz ging, sah er im flackernden Schein seiner Grubenlampe, dass der Schnee hier von dicken Rußflocken bedeckt war.

Am Schacht angekommen, stellten sie sich in die lange Reihe der frierenden Kumpels. Wild heulte der Ostwind zwischen den Eisenstreben des Förderturms und ließ die wartenden Bergleute in der Kälte zittern.

Als sie dann den schwankenden Boden des Förderkorbes betraten, verkündete der schrille Schrei der Dampfmaschine gerade den Beginn der Schicht. Sechs Uhr morgens.

Dicht gedrängt in dem Käfig aus Eisen, so standen die Bergarbeiter im Förderkorb. Und als das Signal dreier Glockenschläge ertönte, begann ihre rasende Fahrt in die Erde.

Schneller und immer schneller jagte der Förderkorb nach unten. Schüttelnd und dröhnend in senkrechter Fahrt, vom Wind gepackt, nur gehalten von einem Stahlseil, so raste er mit seiner lebenden Last der finsteren Tiefe entgegen.

Sie waren am Ende des Schachts angekommen, mehrere hundert Meter tief. Und während der Förderkorb hart aufkam, verließen die Bergleute schon ihren Käfig.

Sie gingen in verschiedene Richtungen auseinander. Und je weiter sie sich vom Schacht entfernten, desto beschwerlicher wurde ihr Weg.

Hitze und Staub drangen Franz entgegen, als er durch verwinkelte Tunnel und Gänge eilte. Bald schon war es um ihn her so heiß geworden, dass ihm der Schweiß den Rücken hinunterlief und von der Stirn in die Augen.

Obwohl der Weg immer mühsamer wurde, die Gänge

immer niedriger, hatte Franz bald alle Bergleute überholt; war er doch der kleinste und schmalste von allen. So konnte er auch überall dort aufrecht gehen, wo sich die anderen tief bücken mussten.

So schnell es ihm seine großen Holzschuhe und der holprige Weg erlaubten, eilte der Junge weiter. Und nur sein Schatten, den das flackernde Licht seiner Lampe gegen die staubigen Wände warf, lief unruhig neben ihm mit.

Franz hörte das leise Wiehern, noch bevor er die Holztür erreichte. Als er die raue Brettertür dann einen Spaltbreit öffnete, schlug ihm Stallgeruch entgegen.

„Glückauf!", rief der Junge. Und aus der Dunkelheit kam ein Wiehern als Antwort.

Franz machte die Tür weit auf. Im trüben Flackern der Grubenlampe stand er vor einem alten Pferd.

Der Junge trat ein und hängte die Lampe an den Ausbau über dem Eingang des Verschlages. Das Pferd schnaubte und griff mit den Zähnen nach seiner Jacke.

„Sei nicht so ungeduldig, Sultan!" Franz entzog den Stoff seiner Jacke dem Pferdemaul.

Der alte Graue schnaubte noch einmal und zupfte am rechten Ärmel des Jungen.

„Lass das!" Franz schob den Kopf des alten Wallachs mit der linken Hand ein wenig von sich fort. „Sonst kriegst du gar nichts, hast du gehört?"

Als habe es die Worte verstanden, ließ das Pferd den Jackenärmel los. Dann wandte es den Kopf geradeaus.

Franz tätschelte den Hals des Pferdes und schleppte in einem Holzeimer Wasser heran.

Der alte Wallach senkte den Kopf tief hinab und trank in durstigen Zügen. Lächelnd sah ihm der Junge zu, er streichelte sanft das Fell des Grauen.

Das waren die schönsten Minuten seines langen Arbeitstages, seitdem er als Pferdejunge hier unten arbeitete. Deshalb auch eilte er, trotz des beschwerlichen Weges durch Hitze und Staub, den anderen immer als Erster voraus. Er wollte wenigstens ein paar Minuten lang ganz allein sein mit dem alten Pferd.

Franz war jeden Tag zwölf anstrengende Arbeitsstunden mit dem alten Grubenpferd zusammen. Aber nur während dieser wenigen Minuten am Morgen konnte er gut zu ihm sein und mit ihm reden.

Sultan war alt und schon lange unter Tage. Er war sogar länger hier unten, als Franz an Jahren zählte.

Der Wallach sei in das Bergwerk gebracht worden, als er noch ein junges Pferd gewesen sei, hatten sie Franz gesagt. In dieser Zeit hatte er nicht ein einziges Mal wieder das Licht des Tages gesehen. Und der Junge wusste, dass der alte Graue für immer hier in der Tiefe bleiben würde; so lange, bis er vor Erschöpfung starb.

Wenn Franz daran dachte, tat ihm der alte Wallach unendlich Leid. *Es muss schrecklich sein, nie mehr die* *warmen Sonnenstrahlen zu spüren und niemals wieder das silberne Licht des Mondes oder die blinkenden Sterne zu sehen*, dachte er.

Behutsam strich er dem alten Pferd über das graue Fell. Sultan hob den Kopf und schnupperte an seiner Hand. Franz griff mit beiden Armen um Sultans Hals. Er legte sein Gesicht an das warme Fell des Pferdes und hörte den ruhigen Schlag seines Herzens.

Ob Pferde wohl träumen können?, dachte der Junge. *Und wenn sie es können, was träumen sie dann? Von grünen Wiesen mit saftigem Gras? Von Kräutern und Blumen auf Frühlingsweiden? Vom goldenen Mittagslicht und einem Sommerhimmel, in dessen Blau kleine Wolken schwimmen?*

Die langen Jahre im Dunkel der Erde hatten dem alten Wallach das Augenlicht genommen. Sultan konnte nur noch Umrisse erkennen, er war fast blind. Aber er kannte jeden Weg in der Grube so genau, dass er sich hier unten ohne Licht besser zurechtfand als alle Menschen. Die jedenfalls brauchten hier in der Tiefe das Licht ihrer Lampen, das ihnen mit seinem trübe flackernden Schein bei ihrer Arbeit leuchtete.

Als die anderen Kumpel gekommen waren, hatte Franz dem grauen Wallach schon sein kärgliches Futter gegeben. Bald standen sie beide bereit für ihren langen Arbeitstag.

Es war irgendwann am Nachmittag. Sultan hatte wieder einen Zug mit schwer beladenen Kohlenwagen zum Schacht geschleppt. Die Wagen waren so voll geladen, dass der alte Wallach an der letzten Steigung keuchend stehen blieb.

47

Zitternd und schweißnass, mit aufgerissenen Augen, stemmte sich das alte Pferd mühsam ins Zuggeschirr.

Doch der Kohlenzug rührte sich nicht. Verzweifelt und voller Angst schlug Franz das Pferd. Doch auch die härtesten Schläge nützten nichts: Die Wagen kamen nicht eine Handbreit mehr von der Stelle.

Franz hörte auf, das Pferd zu schlagen. Er weinte. Dann riss er sich das verschwitzte Hemd vom Leib. Er kroch auf allen vieren seitwärts an den voll beladenen Wagen vorbei, bis er das Ende des Kohlenzuges erreichte.

Hinter dem letzten Wagen richtete er sich auf. Er stellte sich breitbeinig zwischen die Schienen, stemmte die Fußsohlen gegen die hölzernen Schwellen und drückte mit all seiner Kraft. Er schrie vor Anstrengung, als er zu schieben begann.

Seine dünnen Kinderarme drückten, so sehr sie konnten, gegen die Kohlenwagen. Er presste mit solcher Anstrengung gegen den Wagen, dass seine Adern am Hals und an den Schläfen anschwollen. So sehr strengte er sich an, dass ihm schwarz vor Augen wurde. Sein Puls schlug rasend schnell.

Das alte Pferd zog keuchend vorn am Kopf des Kohlenzuges, Franz drückte mit all seiner Kraft gegen den letzten Wagen. Beide versuchten gemeinsam die gewaltige Last wieder in Bewegung zu setzen.

48 Unendlich langsam, Handbreit um Handbreit und Schritt für Schritt, so wuchteten sie endlich den schwer beladenen Kohlenzug gemeinsam die Steigung hinauf.

Am Schacht angekommen sah sich ein Steiger die beladenen Kohlenwagen an. Dann schrieb er mit Kreide auf einen Wagen eine große Null. Das hieß, dass sie für die Kohlen dieses Wagens keinen Lohn bekommen würden.

Vergeblich also hatten die Kohlenhauer das harte Anthrazit aus dem Felsen geschlagen; vergeblich und bis zur Erschöpfung hatten Sultan und Franz diesen Wagen zum Schacht geschleppt. Den Lohn dieser Mühe und Plackerei würden nicht sie, sondern die Besitzer des Bergwerks bekommen.

Der Vorgesetzte hatte ihnen diesen Kohlenwagen *genullt*, wie sie es nannten, weil darin angeblich zu viele Steine lagen. Und so etwas geschah mehrmals am Tage.

Mit einem einzigen Kreidekreis hat uns der Steiger die Arbeit von Stunden gestohlen!, dachte der Junge verbittert. Noch vor Erschöpfung zitternd, hatte er in stummer Wut die Fäuste geballt. Er presste die Finger so fest zusammen, dass seine Nägel ins Fleisch der Hände drangen. Aber es gab keine Möglichkeit, sich gegen diese Ungerechtigkeit zu wehren. „Steh hier nicht rum", hatte der Steiger nur gebrüllt. „Fürs Rumstehen wirst du nicht bezahlt!"

Da nahm Franz das alte Pferd schnell am Halfter und zog es mit den leeren Förderwagen wieder vom Schacht fort.

Nun waren sie auf dem Rückweg zum Flöz. Franz führte Sultan neben sich her. Und beide spürten die große

Anstrengung des Weges noch immer im Zittern ihrer Muskeln.

Es war kurz vor der letzten Abzweigung, als Sultan plötzlich stehen blieb.

Franz zog ihn am Halfter, doch der alte Wallach rührte sich nicht. Da riss ihn der Junge heftig nach vorn, doch auch das nützte nichts, selbst als Franz noch einmal zog.

Sultan schnaubte, er begann schrill zu wiehern, aber er tat keinen einzigen Schritt.

Sie mussten weiter, denn vor Ort warteten die Hauer schon ungeduldig auf die leeren Kohlenwagen.

Da schlug der Junge das Pferd.

Aus angstgeweiteten Augen blickte ihn der alte Wallach an, rührte sich aber auch jetzt nicht von der Stelle.

In seiner Verzweiflung schlug Franz den grauen Wallach wieder.

Da begann sich das alte Pferd zurückzuziehen. Je mehr sich der Junge mühte ihn zu halten, desto weiter schob sich das Tier zurück. Es wurde immer unruhiger, wie wild drängte es zurück.

Verzweifelt versuchte der schmächtige Junge den Grauen zu halten.

Das Pferd trat gegen den ersten Wagen. Die Hufschläge dröhnten, sie klangen wie donnernde Trommelschläge. Schrill wiehernd und in Panik, mit Schaum vor dem Maul, schlug der alte Wallach seine Hufe gegen den leeren Kohlenwagen.

Ein schrecklicher Donnerschlag übertönte plötzlich den Lärm. Die Erde erzitterte. Von so einer Urgewalt war dieses Geräusch, dass es das Gehör des Jungen betäubte. Zu Tode erschrocken stand er da, regungslos, und starrte vor sich ins Dunkel.

Dort, wo soeben noch der Zugang zu seinen Kumpels gewesen war, war nichts mehr zu sehen. Eine undurchdringliche Wolke aus schwarzem Staub drang ihnen entgegen und deckte das trübe, flackernde Licht seiner Lampe zu.

Das alte Pferd hatte ihm das Leben gerettet! Denn wären sie auch nur ein paar Schritte weitergegangen, hätte der herabstürzende Felsen sie unter sich begraben. So gewaltig war diese Steinlawine, dass sie den Gang in einer Länge von mehr als zwanzig Metern zugeschüttet hatte.

Franz rannte zum Schacht und schrie um Hilfe. Bald arbeiteten die Kumpel in fieberhafter Eile, denn es ging um das Leben der Eingeschlossenen. Auch Franz' Vater war unter den Verschütteten.

Der Junge half mit, so gut er konnte. Er schleppte Holz heran, mit dem sie die Felsen stützten, und er weinte aus Angst um den Vater.

Sie arbeiteten, so schnell sie nur arbeiten konnten, wussten sie doch, dass den Verschütteten bald die Atemluft ausgehen würde.

51

Franz warf die scharfkantigen Steine zur Seite und riss sich die Finger blutig. Schließlich schaufelte er mit bloßen

Händen, achtete nicht auf seinen Schmerz, dachte nur immer an den Vater.

Es dauerte Stunden, bis sie zur anderen Seite durchkamen. Einige der Verschütteten waren so schwach, dass sie getragen werden mussten. Aber alle hatten den Steinschlag überlebt.

Dann sah Franz die Augen seines Vaters. Es waren die einzigen hellen Flecken im tiefschwarzen Kohlengesicht. Für einen Moment standen sie sich regungslos gegenüber. Dann schlang der Mann die Arme um seinen Sohn und weinte. Und so lange Franz zurückdenken konnte, hatte ihn sein Vater noch niemals zuvor umarmt.

Erschöpft standen sie da, aneinander gelehnt, bis sie keine Tränen mehr hatten.

„Sultan", sagte der Junge endlich stockend, „er hat uns gerettet!"

Der Vater sah seinen Sohn an, dann nickte er langsam. „Sultan weiß mehr als wir", sagte er müde. „Er kann viel mehr sehen als wir alle."

Aber er ist doch blind, wollte Franz sagen.

Doch der Vater sprach schon weiter. „Er sieht viel mehr als wir, mein Junge, weil er blind ist."

Der Durst des Kosaken

Eine Staubwolke wirbelte die Dorfstraße entlang.
„Die Russen kommen!", hatte die Großmutter gerufen, doch da war es schon zu spät.

Ehe sie und die Kinder ins Haus laufen konnten, waren die Reiter herangesprengt. Einer von ihnen löste sich aus der Formation, bog von der Dorfstraße ab und preschte auf den Hof.

Er galoppierte einmal im Hof herum und hielt vor dem Brunnen. Es war ein Offizier; ein Kosak, wie die Großmutter später erzählte. Hoch aufgerichtet saß er auf seinem Pferd, das unruhig tänzelte. Er sah zu der alten Frau und den Kindern hinüber. Dann zog er den Degen aus der Scheide. Er hielt die blanke Waffe in der rechten Hand, hob sie über den Kopf und winkte.

Die drei Kinder drängten sich angstvoll an die alte Frau. Das kleinste Kind begann zu weinen. Die Großmutter legte ihre Arme schützend um die kleinen Köpfe, ängstlich blickte sie dem Reiter entgegen.

Da winkte der fremde Soldat noch einmal mit seinem Degen. Er rief ein paar Worte in einer fremden Sprache. Es klang wie ein Befehl.

Langsam und unsicher ging die Großmutter mit ihren drei Enkeln auf den fremden Soldaten zu. Sie hielt die Kinder schützend umfangen.

Es war im Sommer des Jahres 1914, der Erste Weltkrieg hatte gerade begonnen. In kurzer Zeit waren die Soldaten des russischen Zaren in Ostpreußen eingedrungen ohne auf Widerstand zu stoßen, denn der deutsche Kaiser Wilhelm II. hatte seiner Armee befohlen, das westliche Nachbarland Frankreich anzugreifen. So war die Grenze zu Russland nur wenig geschützt. Und hier, so nahe der Grenze, waren die ostpreußischen Bauern auf eine Flucht nicht vorbereitet worden.

Nun waren die ersten russischen Reiter ins Dorf galoppiert. So schnell es nur ging, hatten sich die überraschten Menschen versteckt. Der alten Frau und den drei Kindern war das nicht mehr gelungen.

Als die Großmutter und die Kleinen vor dem fremden Reiter standen, sah die alte Frau zu ihm empor. Seine Uniform war mit Staub bedeckt, auf dem Fell des Pferdes klebte der Schweiß. Der fremde Offizier senkte den Degen und zeigte damit auf den Brunnen.

Die Großmutter verstand, was er meinte. Sie ließ die Kinder los, nahm den Wassereimer aus Holz und hängte ihn an die Brunnenstange. Dann ließ sie den Eimer in den Brunnen sinken. Als sie ihn herauszog und auf den Brunnenrand stellte, war er bis zum Rand gefüllt. Die alte Frau nahm den Eimer vom Haken und stellte ihn vor den Reiter hin.

Der Mann schob seinen Degen in die Scheide zurück. Er legte die Hände zu einer Schale zusammen und machte die Geste des Trinkens. Dann deutete er mit der rechten Hand auf die alte Frau.

Die Großmutter zögerte keinen Augenblick. Sie hatte begriffen, was der fremde Soldat meinte. Er wollte prüfen, ob sie den Brunnen vergiftet hatten: Sie selbst sollte zuerst trinken. Sie tauchte die Hände in das kalte Wasser, schöpfte etwas heraus und trank. Das tat sie noch zweimal.

Der Offizier nickte und zeigte auf sein Pferd.

Die Großmutter stellte den Wassereimer vor das Pferd. Es senkte den Kopf, dann trank es mit langen, durstigen Zügen den Wassereimer leer.

Noch einmal musste die alte Frau den Holzeimer füllen. Das Pferd trank auch den zweiten Eimer leer. Und während es trank, sah ihm der russische Reiter stumm zu. Erst als das Pferd genug hatte, trank auch der Reiter. Er hatte zuerst den Durst seines Pferdes gelöscht, ehe er an seinen eigenen dachte.

Die Großmutter hob den Wassereimer zu ihm hinauf. Der Offizier nahm den Eimer mit beiden Händen, setzte den Holzrand an seine Lippen und trank lange. Er war sehr durstig.

Als er schließlich der alten Frau den Wassereimer zurückgab, sagte er etwas, das in seiner Sprache ein Dank sein mochte. Er blickte prüfend über den Hof, dann sah er die Kinder an und lächelte. Und es war das erste Lächeln auf seinem harten Gesicht, seitdem er auf den Hof geritten war. Dann nahm der Mann in der Uniform eines russischen Offiziers die Zügel seines Pferdes auf. Gehorsam stand es vor dem Brunnen bereit. Ein Kosakenpferd. Der Reiter legte die rechte Hand grüßend an die hohe Mütze, dann presste er die Schenkel an den Leib des Pferdes und gab dem Rappen die Sporen.

Wie von der Sehne eines Bogens geschnellt, so preschte der Hengst davon. Er sprang durch das Hoftor und jagte auf die Dorfstraße hinaus. In eine Staubwolke gehüllt, schneller und immer schneller, so galoppierte der fremde Reiter auf dem schwarzen Pferd davon. Und als die alte Frau mit den Kindern zum Hoftor ging, waren sie nicht mehr zu sehen.

Heimweh

Karl kam in die Küche gelaufen. ‚Liese ist wieder da!‘, rief er aufgeregt. ‚Ich hab sie gerade zum Zaun kommen sehen!‘

Wir gingen alle nach draußen. Von der Tür aus konnten wir die alte Stute sehen. Sie stand am Hofzaun, hatte den Kopf über die Bretter gelegt und sah zu uns herüber.

‚Ihr seid wohl zu faul gewesen, das Pferd weit genug wegzutreiben‘, sagte mein Vater vorwurfsvoll und sah uns der Reihe nach an.

‚Aber wir haben sie über eine Stunde getrieben‘, sagte Hermann jetzt, ‚bis weit über Groß-Dankheim hinaus!‘

Wir nickten alle heftig.

‚Ich werde sie nachher selbst wegbringen!‘, sagte Vater. ‚Dann weiß ich wenigstens, dass sie da bleibt, wo ich sie lasse!‘

Nach dem Frühstück holte er die junge Fuchsstute aus dem Stall.

‚Und du nimmst die Liese!‘, sagte er zu mir.

Ich kletterte auf den Hofzaun und von dort auf den blanken Rücken des Pferdes. Dann ritten wir in Richtung Grenze. Wir waren fast eine Stunde unterwegs, ehe wir den Grenzfluss Orzyc durchquerten. Als wir auf der anderen Seite waren, sahen wir eine Pferdeherde weiden.

Wir ritten heran. Kein Mensch war in der Nähe.

,Steig jetzt ab und lass die Liese laufen', sagte mein Vater zu mir. ,Und du bleibst hier!', sagte er dann zu dem alten Pferd. ,Lass dich nicht mehr zu Hause blicken!'

Er zog mich auf die junge Fuchsstute hinauf und dann galoppierten wir wieder zum Hof zurück …"

„Ihr habt das alte Pferd einfach ausgesetzt?", fragte Silke empört. „Hattest du denn überhaupt kein Mitleid mit der armen Stute?"

„Doch." Urgroßvater nickte. „Aber wenn mein Vater etwas bestimmte, dann durfte man nicht widersprechen! Das war damals eben anders als heute."

„Trotzdem war es gemein!", sagte Silke.

„Du darfst nicht vergessen, es war auch Krieg, damals im August 1914. Die russische Armee war über die Grenze nach Ostpreußen einmarschiert. Und in der Gegend von Tannenberg, das war bei uns ganz in der Nähe, war es zur großen Schlacht gekommen. Die deutschen Soldaten, angeführt von Generalfeldmarschall Hindenburg, nahmen über hunderttausend russische Soldaten gefangen. Die anderen flohen, als sich die Nachricht verbreitete, der russische Fürst Samsanow, Oberbefehlshaber der Narew-Armee, habe sich selbst erschossen.

Eine wilde Flucht begann. Die russischen Soldaten ließen ihre Kanonen und Pferdewagen stehen, warfen ihre Gewehre und alles Gepäck von sich, viele sogar ihre Stiefel, nur um schneller laufen zu können. Viele Pferde blieben zurück und niemand kümmerte sich um sie. Die verlassenen Tiere irrten tagelang in den Wäldern und auf dem Land umher."

„Schrecklich", sagte Silke. „Das war ja schrecklich."

„Später schlossen sich viele Pferde zu großen Herden zusammen und zogen grasend über das Land. Mein Vater hatte unsere alte Fuchsstute gegen ein junges russisches Pferd eingetauscht. Es hatte die gleiche Farbe wie Liese und auch einen ähnlichen Stern auf der Stirn, nur war es viele Jahre jünger. Es sah der jungen Liese zum Verwechseln ähnlich.

Unser Vater wusste, wenn die Schlacht beendet war, dann mussten alle fremden Pferde an die deutschen Soldaten abgegeben werden. Da aber die junge Stute unserer alten so ähnlich war, glaubte er, sie an ihrer Stelle behalten zu können. Und deshalb brachten wir das alte Pferd auch über den Grenzfluss zu der fremden Herde, damit es nicht mehr bei uns war.

Doch am nächsten Tag war Liese wieder da! Leise wiehernd umkreiste sie unseren Hof. Sie blieb am Zaun stehen, lief weiter, blieb wieder stehen. Es war ein jämmerliches Bild.

Vater befahl uns Jungen, das alte Pferd erneut fortzubringen. Hermann und ich brachten es jetzt in eine andere Richtung. Wie trieben die Stute fast zwei Stunden weit.

Doch am nächsten Morgen stand Liese wieder am Zaun. Sie schien müde zu sein und rieb ihren Hals an den Brettern des Zaunes. Sie wieherte leise, es klang furchtbar traurig.

Unser Hof lag am Waldrand, etwas außerhalb des Dorfes. Vater versuchte das Pferd fortzujagen. Die alte Stute lief ein Stück in den Wald hinein, aber bald kam sie wieder zurück. Es nützte nichts, wir mussten das Pferd wieder zu einer neuen Herde bringen. Diesmal noch weiter."

„Das ist ja grausam!", rief Silke. „Was hatte euch das Pferd denn getan?"

„Es hatte uns nichts getan, wir befolgten nur Vaters Befehle. Nun, die Liese kam wieder zurück. Als sie dann am nächsten Morgen wieder vor dem verschlossenen Hoftor stand und leise wiehernd wartete, spannte unser Vater entschlossen den Wagen an. Er band die alte Stute hinten am Wagen fest und fuhr mit ihr davon. Als er nach stundenlanger Fahrt erst spät am Nachmittag wieder zurückkam, da war er sicher, dass die Liese den Weg nicht mehr finden würde. Und wirklich, am nächsten Morgen stand sie nicht am Zaun.

,Dort wo ich sie jetzt hingebracht habe', sagte unser Vater, ,von dort findet kein Pferd der Welt zu uns zurück!' Wir Jungen waren traurig, aber wir wagten nichts zu sagen."

„Feige seid ihr gewesen!" Silke war ganz rot im Gesicht. „Ihr wart richtige Feiglinge!"

Urgroßvater lächelte, als er weitererzählte: „Die Nacht war fast vorbei, als mich das Wiehern weckte. Ich glaubte, dass ich geträumt hatte, dann aber war ich hellwach. Ohne die anderen zu wecken schlich ich mich nach draußen. Im hellen Mondlicht sah ich die alte Liese am Hofzaun stehen. Als sie mich sah, wieherte sie wieder. Sie hatte den großen Kopf durch die Bretter des Zauns geschoben und sah mit traurigen Augen auf unseren Hof.

Auf einmal stand der Vater neben mir auf der Schwelle. ‚Verdammt noch mal, was soll ich denn noch machen', rief er ratlos. ‚Ich kann sie doch nicht bis nach Königsberg bringen!'

‚Wer weiß', sagte da meine Mutter, die mit den anderen Geschwistern nun auch aus dem Haus kam. ‚Wer weiß, ob sie nicht auch von Königsberg den Weg nach Hause findet.'

Vater sah lange auf das alte Pferd. Dann ging er mit schweren Schritten zu ihm hin. Unschlüssig stand er vor der alten Stute.

Die Liese wieherte leise, als er ihren Hals berührte. Langsam strich ihr der Vater über die Stirn. ‚Komm, Liese', sagte er schließlich und ging zum Hoftor. Er hatte das Holztor gerade einen Spaltbreit geöffnet, als Liese schon vor ihm stand. ‚Komm rein', sagte Vater und wischte sich verstohlen mit dem Handrücken über die

Augen. ‚Du bist zwar ein alter Gaul, aber ich glaube, du gehörst zu uns!‘

Dann gab er der Stute einen Klaps auf die Kruppe. Liese wieherte hell, dann sprang sie wie ein junges Fohlen auf unseren Hof zurück."

Hafermotoren oder
Das Rosswerk

*T*olle Kiste!", erklärte Andreas. „Und dann dieser Spoiler! Total super!" Er blätterte eine Seite weiter. „Wow! Ein V8-Cabriolet mit Stereo-Kassetten-Radio, Ledersportlenkrad, Chromfelgen, Alurädern und Hochgeschwindigkeitsreifen – das ist echt stark!"

„Guck mal da: eine 8-Rohr-Edelstahl-Auspuffanlage", Michael deutete auf das Blatt, „das gibt 'nen voll satten Sound!"

Andreas und Michael lagen am Boden, vor ihnen der Autoprospekt.

„In Hellrot-Metallic mit schwarzen Ledersitzen und Weißwandreifen müsste er klasse aussehen!"

„Mit Rallyestreifen gefällt er mir am besten", Michael deutete auf das Hochglanzfoto. „Und da: Kompressor und modifizierte Einspritzanlage mit hochglanzpoliertem Alu-Ventildeckel, da geht vielleicht die Post ab, das kannst du glauben!"

„Servolenkung, Klimaanlage und elektrische Fensterheber – und dann noch in sieben Sekunden von null auf hundert!"

„Das packt er doch spielend", bemerkte Michael, „bei zweihundertfünfundsechzig PS!"

„In sieben Sekunden von null auf hundert", Großvater ließ die Zeitung sinken. „Und dann zweihundertfünfundsechzig PS. Ihr scheint beide richtig in Fahrt zu kommen!" Die Jungen blickten auf.

„Zweihundertfünfundsechzig PS", der Großvater hatte die Zeitung beiseite gelegt und sah lächelnd zu ihnen hinüber. „Als ich so alt war wie ihr, da waren wir froh, wenn wir ein einziges PS hatten."

„Das müssen ziemlich lahme Kisten gewesen sein", meinte Andreas. „Was waren denn das überhaupt für Autos mit einem einzigen PS?"

Großvater lächelte. „PS heißt Pferdestärke, aber das brauche ich euch wohl nicht zu erklären."

„Ach, so meinst du das", sagte Andreas. „Du denkst an den Hafermotor!"

Großvater lachte. „Stimmt", sagte er nach einer kleinen Pause. Er war nachdenklich geworden. „Damals in Masuren waren die Pferde die Motoren, du hast Recht!"

Er drehte seinen Sessel in Richtung der beiden Jungen.

Andreas und Michael streckten sich auf dem Teppich aus. Sie lagerten sich vor Großvater, stützten die Köpfe in die Hände und sahen zu ihm empor.

64

„Zu meiner Zeit waren wir auf diese ein oder zwei PS unserer Hafermotoren angewiesen. Ohne sie ging nichts bei uns auf dem Hof. Angefangen vom Pflügen und dem Ziehen der Erntewagen bis hin zum Rosswerk ... ohne unsere Pferde hätten wir die Arbeit überhaupt nicht machen können."

„Rosswerk?", fragte Michael. „War das so was wie 'ne Pferdefabrik?"

„Nicht ganz." Großvater lächelte. „Es sei denn, dir würden ein oder zwei, in Ausnahmefällen vier PS für eine Fabrik genügen. Aber damals waren unsere Pferde ganz einfach Pferde. Nach PS wurden sie nicht gemessen!"

„Was machten die Pferde im Rosswerk?", wollte Michael nun wissen. Er war neugierig geworden.

„Sie gingen einfach im Kreis, wirklich. Manchmal mussten sie das allerdings ziemlich lange machen, besonders dann, wenn Korn gedroschen wurde."

Der Großvater sah die fragenden Gesichter der beiden Jungen.

„Wir hatten ja schon eine eigene Dreschmaschine damals, es muss so im Jahr 1930 gewesen sein. Bis dahin mussten wir Roggen und Weizen noch mit Dreschflegeln dreschen. Das war eine schwere Arbeit, die auch sehr lange dauerte. Mit der Dreschmaschine ging dann alles leichter und auch viel schneller. Das Rosswerk war ein großer Fortschritt und eine rechte Erleichterung für die schwere Arbeit bei uns auf dem Lande. Jetzt konnten die stärkeren Pferde viele Arbeiten machen, die bis dahin von Menschen getan werden mussten."

„Du sagtest vorhin, die Pferde gingen dabei im Kreis."

Michael wollte es genauer wissen. „War das wie so ein Pferdekarussell?"

„Kein schlechter Vergleich." Großvater nickte. „Doch bei einem Karussell fährt man im Kreis mit. Beim Rosswerk musste ich mitgehen, stundenlang hinter den Pferden her, immer im Kreis herum. Ich bin als Junge oft dabei gewesen, da war ich noch jünger als ihr, vielleicht so sieben oder acht Jahre alt. Damals musste ich auf die Pferde Acht geben. Und wenn gedroschen wurde, lief ich manchmal den ganzen Tag mit ihnen im Kreis herum."

„Stundenlang immer im Kreis, davon wird man doch rammdösig! Furchtbar!", meinte Andreas.

„Die Arbeit musste gemacht werden, da wurde jeder gebraucht, auch wir Kinder. Wir mussten schon sehr früh mitarbeiten, damals bei uns auf dem Bauernhof. Wenn Erntezeit war, wurde von Sonnenaufgang bis Sonnenuntergang gearbeitet; und das waren ungefähr fünfzehn Stunden am Tag."

„Auch die Pferde?", fragte Michael entsetzt.

„Wenn sie im Rosswerk gingen", sagte Großvater ernst, „dann hatten sie zwei Stunden Mittagspause. Sie wurden getränkt und gefüttert und konnten sich wieder etwas erholen. Sie gingen ja ziemlich langsam im Kreis. Es gab für Pferde andere Arbeiten, die anstrengender waren als das Rosswerk."

66   „Trotzdem", meinte Michael jetzt, „von so was kriegt doch auch ein Pferd glatt 'nen Föhn im Kopf, zumindest aber ein Karussell!"

„Und du bist immer hinter den Pferden her?", fragte Andreas. „Gingen die denn nicht von selbst?"

„Ein Pferd ist ein Pferd, es geht nicht von selbst. Pferde sind kluge Tiere. Wenn man sie ohne Aufsicht ließ, wurden sie langsamer und immer langsamer. Schließlich blieben sie stehen. Sie hatten ja Recht. Warum sollten sie auch freiwillig immer im Kreis herumlaufen?"

„Mir ist nicht ganz klar, wie euer Rosswerk funktionierte", Michael sah so nachdenklich auf den Teppich, als wären im Muster die Konstruktionspläne des Rosswerks verborgen. „Es drehte sich also im Kreis und trieb irgendeine Maschine an?"

„Ihr müsst euch ein großes, massives Holzkreuz vorstellen", sagte der Großvater zu den beiden Jungen, „ungefähr so zehn Meter im Durchmesser. An dessen äußeren Enden waren die Pferde angespannt. Dieses Holzkreuz konnte von einem Pferd bewegt werden, aber auch von mehreren Pferden, je nachdem, welche Maschine genommen wurde. Manchmal zogen vier Pferde das Kreuz.

In der Mitte des Rosswerks, dort, wo sich die Stangen kreuzten, befand sich ein großes Zahnrad, das wiederum ein kleineres Zahnrad antrieb. Das kleinere setzte dann über eine Spindel eine mehrere Meter lange Eisenstange in Bewegung, die eine Maschine antrieb, etwa ein Mahlwerk um Roggen und Weizen zu mahlen oder eine Kreissäge. Und natürlich wurde auch die Dreschmaschine so angetrieben.

Am Anfang war alles am schwersten, besonders dann,

wenn sich das Rosswerk in Bewegung setzte. Dann mussten sich die Pferde sehr anstrengen und stark ziehen. Nur langsam und ganz allmählich begann sich das Rosswerk zu drehen. War es aber erst einmal in Schwung gebracht, dann lief es stundenlang."

„Und du immer hinterher", sagte Andreas. „Die armen Pferde. Ich kann mir etwas Besseres vorstellen als stundenlang im Kreis zu gehen!"

„Du denkst wohl an unseren Videorekorder", sagte Großvater lächelnd. „Übrigens läuft die Kassette da auch im Kreis!"

„Das ist nicht die Kassette, Opa", bemerkte Michael, „das ist nur das Videoband!"

„Donnerwetter", rief der Großvater. „Du weißt aber Bescheid, Junge!"

„Klar." Michael bemerkte den leisen Spott des Großvaters nicht. „Da kenne ich mich aus!"

„Und jetzt weißt du natürlich auch, was ein Rosswerk ist!"

„Na ja, so einigermaßen schon", sagte Michael vorsichtig. „Das war doch früher so eine klitzekleine Fabrik mit Hafermotor-Antrieb!"

„So zwischen einem und vier PS stark", ergänzte Andreas.

„Natürlich nicht zu vergleichen mit eurem Cabriolet aus dem Prospekt, mit Hochgeschwindigkeitsradio, Lederfelgen, Chromreifen; in Hellgrün-Metallic mit roten Rallyestreifen auf der Stereo-Kassetten-Auspuffanlage.

Von null auf hundert in satten sieben Minuten – und das bei zweihundertsechsundachtzig PS!"

„Zweihundertfünfundsechzig." Michael starrte den Großvater an.

„Mit PS wisst ihr ja mächtig Bescheid", sagte Opa lächelnd. „Übrigens: Seid ihr beide wirklich schon so altersschwach, dass ihr unbedingt einen elektrischen Fensterheber braucht?"

Die Jungen sahen sich an.

„Weißt du, Opa", Andreas grinste, „Pferde brauchen keinen elektrischen Fensterheber …"

„… und natürlich auch keine Servolenkung und keine Klimaanlage", ergänzte Michael lachend.

Zwischen gestern und heute

Schlittenspuren

Über Nacht war Schnee gefallen. Das blendende Weiß hatte die Erde verwandelt, hatte Felder und Wiesen zugedeckt und sich über die Bäume gebreitet. Weiß dehnte sich das Land bis zum Horizont, der im Frühdunst Himmel und Erde zu verbinden schien.

Am späten Vormittag dann hatten sich die ersten Sonnenstrahlen durch die Wolkendecke geschoben. Und als die Sonne mittags am höchsten stand, hatten ihre wärmenden Strahlen den Dunst von der Erde und die Wolken vom Himmel geschmolzen.

Wie blaues Glas wölbte sich der Februarhimmel über dem weißen Sonntagsland und ließ auf dem unberührten Weiß die Schneekristalle blitzen.

Gleich nach dem Mittagessen hatte der Vater den Schlitten herausgeholt und die beiden Pferde angespannt.

Erwartungsvoll standen sie vor dem Schlitten, bewegungshungrig nach der langen Ruhezeit im Stall. Links der Rappe, rechts die braune Stute.

Noch einmal ging der Vater in den Schuppen zurück. Als er mit den beiden Glöckchen wiederkam, wendeten die Pferde ihre Köpfe nach dem Klang um.

Der Vater schnallte die Glocken an den Außenseiten der Sielen fest. Und bei jeder Bewegung der beiden Pferde ertönte jetzt das feine Klingeln an ihrem Geschirr.

Mit Fellen beladen kamen die Kinder aus dem Haus. Sie waren so warm angezogen, dass sie wie lebendige Kugeln aussahen.

Umständlich kletterten sie auf die hintere Sitzbank des Schlittens und wickelten sich in die Felle ein. Im Licht des trüben Nachmittags hingen kleine weiße Atemwölkchen vor ihren Gesichtern.

Eng aneinander gerückt saßen sie da und sahen erwartungsvoll auf ihren Vater, der die letzten Vorbereitungen zur Abfahrt traf.

Noch einmal ging er nach vorn zu den Pferden. Er fasste zum Brustblatt, zum Halsriemen und prüfte den Sitz. Sein Blick glitt über das Pferdegeschirr und über die Gruppe der Kinder hinten im Schlitten, dann stieg er auf den Vordersitz. Er nahm die Leine in die Hand und knallte zweimal mit der Peitsche.

Beim doppelten Klang ihrer Glocken setzten sich die beiden Pferde in Bewegung. Schon glitt der dunkelbraune Schlitten mit seiner Last vom Hof hinaus auf den Schnee der Dorfstraße.

Als der Vater die Pferde aus dem Windschutz des Dorfes ins Freie lenkte, zog er seine Fellmütze tief über die

Ohren. Bald fuhren sie zwischen den Birken entlang, die hinter dem Dorf die Straße säumten. Wie silberne Filigrane im Sonnenlicht, so reckten die Bäume ihre schneestaubgeschmückten Zweige ins wolkenlose Blau. Und die Äste der Fichten am Waldrand, unter ihrer weißen Last der Erde entgegengeneigt, glitzerten im hellen Schein der Wintersonne.

Endlich lenkte der Vater den Schlitten von der Straße fort ins unberührte Weiß hinein. Vor ihnen lag das schimmernde Weißland unter einem eisklaren Himmelsblau. Leise knirschend zogen die Schlittenkufen ihre Spur durch den Schnee und bahnten sich ihren Weg durch das unberührte weite Land.

Als sie hinter dem ersten Hügel waren, sahen sie einen Schwarm Krähen im Schnee; große schwarze Flecken im blendenden Weiß.

Das Klingeln der Glöckchen brachte die schwarzen Vögel in Bewegung. Krächzend erhoben sie sich in die Winterluft, kreisten neugierig über dem Schlitten, dann wandten sie sich der Sonne zu und flogen ins tiefe Himmelsblau davon.

Weit ausgebreitet unter frostklarem Nachmittagslicht, so dehnte sich jetzt das weiße Land bis zum fernen blauen Horizont. Die beiden Pferde gingen im Trab. Rhythmisch klingelten die Glöckchen. Die Kinder saßen eng beieinander und sahen über die weite Schneelandschaft.

Am Waldrand standen zwei Rehe zwischen den Tannen. Sie hatten die Köpfe erhoben, sahen dem Schlitten entgegen und witterten aufmerksam. Dann waren sie plötzlich mit drei, vier schnellen Sprüngen zwischen den Tannen verschwunden. Nur ein feiner Staubschleier aus Schnee, der von den Bäumen fiel, verriet ein paar Augenblicke lang, dass dort eben noch die Rehe gewesen waren.

Das Fell der Pferde glänzte im Sonnenlicht. Wie ein dunkler Spiegel der Rappe, auf dessen Fell bei jeder Bewegung Lichtflecke tanzten. Auf dem hellen Braun der Stute lag ein leichter Kupferschimmer, der in der Sonne aufglänzte.

Eine Wolke aus Pulverschnee stob hinter dem Schlitten auf. Der feine Schneestaub tanzte im Licht, wirbelte noch als durchsichtig weiße Fahne eine Zeit lang umher, ehe er sich allmählich auf die Schlittenspur senkte.

Dampfender Atem kam aus den Nüstern der Pferde. Weich federten die Hufe auf dem Schnee, die Schlittenkufen knirschten. Der helle Klang der Glöckchen trug seinen Rhythmus über die weiße Weite. Glitzernd im Silberstaub der Schneekristalle, die im Licht hell aufblitzten, lag das Land vor ihnen wie ein gefrorener Traum.

Die Gesichter der Kinder waren rot von der Kälte, doch sie fühlten sich warm unter den schützenden Fellen.

Nun glitten sie zwischen den Bäumen entlang, und ab und zu, wenn sie einen tief hängenden Ast streiften, fiel dichter Schneestaub wie Puderzucker über Pferde und Menschen.

Sie waren bereits auf der Rückfahrt zum Dorf, als die Sonne unterging. Wie eine riesige dunkelrote Scheibe näherte sie sich dem Horizont und ließ den Schnee im Widerschein rosa leuchten.

Die Pferde zogen den Schlitten dem roten Glühen entgegen und ihre Köpfe, dunkle Scherenschnitte im rötlichen Gegenlicht, tanzten über dem Horizont. Später, als der letzte Streifen der Sonnenglut über dem Hügel verblasst war, schien aus dem wolkenlosen Himmel das breite Sternenband der Milchstraße über das Land zu fallen. Schon spannte sich über ihren Köpfen ein gewaltiges Diamantennetz, dessen zahllose Sterne in der klaren Luft funkelten.

Im Licht der Sterne glitten die Schlittenkufen über den knirschenden Schnee. Die beiden Pferde, langsamer jetzt, kannten den Weg nach Hause.

Als sie in die Reihe der Birken zu beiden Seiten der Straße einbogen, stieg die Mondsichel über dem Wald auf. Ihr silbergrünes Licht floss über den Schnee und machte die Sterne blasser.

Sie fuhren im Klang der Schlittenglocken die Dorfstraße entlang und sahen im Mondlicht Rauch aus den Schornsteinen steigen. Und während die Pferde durchs Hoftor gingen, glaubten die Kinder schon den Geruch von Bratäpfeln wahrzunehmen. Erwartungsvoll rutschten sie auf der Rückbank hin und her und freuten sich auf die Wärme des Kachelofens, den sie hinter den hell erleuchteten Fenstern des Hauses wussten.

Die Hochzeitskutsche

D as kann ich mir gar nicht vorstellen." Sandra
lachte. „Du auf einem Pferd!"

Oma schmunzelte. „Da bist du nicht die Einzige.
Selbst deine Mutter kann sich das nicht vorstellen, und
die ist achtundzwanzig Jahre älter als du!"

„Mit wie viel Jahren hast du angefangen zu reiten?",
fragte die Enkelin.

„Das kann ich sehr schwer sagen. Weißt du, damals
ist man irgendwann auf ein Pferd gestiegen – nein, man
wurde da einfach draufgesetzt." Die Großmutter überlegte. „Wahrscheinlich hat mich mein Vater, es könnte
aber auch Opa Wilhelm gewesen sein, irgendwann einfach aufs Pferd gehoben."

„Und dann?", fragte Sandra.

„Dann hat er dem Pferd mit der flachen Hand einen
Klaps auf die Kruppe gegeben – und ab ging die Post!"

„Du bist einfach losgeritten?"

„Was blieb mir schon übrig? Ich hatte ja keine Zeit zu

langem Überlegen. Da hieß es mit beiden Händen in die Mähne gefasst und erst mal auf dem Pferd bleiben, selbst wenn es über Stock und Stein ging."

„Das waren aber raue Sitten." Sandra sah Oma mitfühlend an. „Und es ist nie was passiert?"

„Ach, weißt du", die Großmutter sah ihre Enkelin lächelnd an, „wenn man auf einem Bauernhof geboren wird, wächst man mit all den Tieren auf. Das ist nicht so, als wenn ein Kind in der Großstadt in eine Reitschule geht. Bei uns saß man eben früher oder später auf einem Pferderücken, einfach so und ohne große Vorbereitung – und eigentlich auch ohne Angst zu haben."

„Du hattest also nie Angst vor Pferden?", fragte Sandra ungläubig.

Großmutter schüttelte den Kopf. Doch dann rief sie plötzlich: „Halt, das stimmt nicht ganz. Ein einziges Mal hatte ich Angst, daran kann ich mich noch erinnern. Das weiß ich noch ganz genau! Da saß ich zwar nicht auf einem Pferderücken, sondern in einer Kutsche, aber meine Angst war riesengroß!"

„Erzähl!" Sandra hatte die Reitstiefel ausgezogen und setzte sich der Großmutter gegenüber. „Los, Oma, erzähl!"

„Es war auf der Hochzeit meiner Schwester Elfriede, das war Pfingsten 1931 oder 1932. Lass mal überlegen, ja, es war 1932. Bei uns auf dem Dorf war eine Hochzeit das schönste aller Feste. Schon ein paar Wochen vor diesem großen Ereignis wurden die Gäste durch einen Mann eingeladen, den wir den Hochzeitsbitter nannten. Er zog von Haus zu Haus und sagte seinen Hochzeitsbittspruch. Und wer so eingeladen war, dessen Teilnahme wurde zur Pflicht. Nur Tod oder Aufenthalt hinter Kerkermauern, so sagte man damals, wurden als Entschuldigung zugelassen."

„Seltsame Entschuldigung!" Sandra lachte.

Oma erzählte weiter: „Da es Sitte war, alle die Leute einzuladen, bei denen man selbst auf einer Hochzeit eingeladen worden war, wurde daraus eine Art Schneeballsystem, an dessen Ende eine richtige Einladungslawine rollte, die fast das ganze Dorf zur Hochzeit brachte!

Die Hochzeit von Elfriede war für Pfingsten festgelegt worden. In den Monaten zuvor wurden die wichtigsten Dinge vorbereitet: Die Aussteuer für die Braut wurde vereinbart, auf welchem der beiden Bauernhöfe das junge Paar wohnen würde, und so weiter."

„Was war denn bitte die Aussteuer?", wollte Sandra wissen.

„Das waren die Dinge, die von der Braut mit in die Ehe gebracht wurden. Das waren Wäsche, Geschirr und Federbetten; Sachen, die zum Haushalt gehörten und die von den Brauteltern angeschafft werden mussten. Ja, bei uns auf dem Dorf war damals manches anders als heute. So hatten auch Großvater Wilhelm und Vater ein schönes fettes Vierzentnerschwein und ein Kalb geschlachtet und dunkles, säuerlich süffiges Bier gebraut. Die Frauen backten eine große Menge Mohn- und Streuselkuchen,

79

die Nachbarinnen halfen ihnen dabei. Dann war es so weit.

Am Nachmittag kamen die jungen Leute aus dem Dorf zusammen. Sie brachten Blumen und Tannengrün mit. Sie sangen Volkslieder und flochten drei große Bögen aus dem Tannengrün, schmückten sie mit vielen Blumen. Einen Bogen stellten sie über das Hoftor. Den zweiten legten sie um die Eingangstür des Hauses. Und den dritten stellten sie an einer besonderen Stelle im Hof auf. Endlich begann der Polterabend. Er war sehr scherbenreich und dauerte bis tief in die Nacht hinein.

Am Morgen des nächsten Tages herrschte große Aufregung im Hause. Alles, was in den Wochen seit dem Osterfest vorbereitet worden war, musste noch einmal geordnet und für die Feier entsprechend hergerichtet werden.

Meine Schwester Elfriede hatte ihr weißes Brautkleid angezogen. Von Nachbarinnen und Freundinnen wurde ihr der Brautschleier umgelegt und dann der Myrtenkranz aufgesetzt. Das dauerte ziemlich lange, und für mich, ich war damals etwa so alt wie du, war alles sehr spannend. Sie waren gerade fertig geworden, als die vier Kutschen ankamen, die den Bräutigam und die Gäste aus seinem Dorf brachten.

Schon vor Tagen war das Festtagsgeschirr der Pferde, das reich mit Zinn beschlagen war, blank geputzt worden. Die Hochzeitskutsche, gewaschen und auf Hochglanz poliert, stand im Hof bereit.

Als Elfriede und ihr Johann die Kutsche bestiegen hatten, ein Prachtexemplar in glänzendem Anthrazitgrau, das von zwei lebhaft tänzelnden Hengsten gezogen wurde, setzte sich der Hochzeitszug in Bewegung.

Inzwischen hatten sich die anderen Kutschen auf der Dorfstraße aufgereiht. Nun rollten vierzehn Kutschen auf die Chaussee, die zur Stadt führte.

In jeder Kutsche saßen vier Hochzeitsgäste, die Männer in schwarzen Anzügen, die Frauen in frühlingsbunten Kleidern. Die Brautkutsche bildete den Schluss, doch nicht das Ende des Zuges. Denn ihr folgten ein paar Dutzend Reiter, die den langen Hochzeitszug noch prächtiger machten. Es war schon ein außergewöhnlicher Zug, der sich in Richtung auf die Stadt zubewegte.

Weiße Birken unter einem klarblauen Pfingsthimmel säumten die Straße, ein leichter Wind bewegte das helle Grün der Blätter. Und auf der Straße, zwischen der endlosen Doppelreihe der Birken, fuhren vierzehn geschmückte Hochzeitskutschen, gezogen von festlich geputzten Pferden, deren blankes Geschirr im Licht der Mittagssonne glänzte. Gefolgt von einer langen Reihe Reiter, die in leichtem Trab den Hochzeitskutschen hinterherritten."

„Mensch, Oma, wie im Kino!", rief Sandra. „Echt wahr!"

Die Großmutter lächelte. Für einen Augenblick war sie tief in ihre Erinnerung versunken, schweigend saß sie da.

„Es war wirklich ein wunderschöner Anblick, besonders für uns Kinder", erzählte sie weiter. „Ich und die Maria von gegenüber, die ein Jahr älter war, saßen mit in der Brautkutsche. Wir trugen schneeweiße Kleider und waren furchtbar stolz, denn wir sollten vor dem Brautpaar zur Kirche gehen und Blumen streuen.

Die Kreisstadt mit der Kirche war etwa sieben Kilometer vom Dorf entfernt. Von Süden kommend, die Mittagssonne im Rücken, fuhren wir in leichtem Trab die Birkenallee entlang und waren bereits eine halbe Stunde vor der festgesetzten Zeit da.

Die Trauung war sehr schön und stimmungsvoll. Meine Schwester Elfriede weinte, weil sie so aufgeregt war, und alle anderen Frauen weinten aus Sympathie ein bisschen mit.

Schließlich schritten die Braut und der Bräutigam, die jetzt Eheleute geworden waren, gefolgt von den Hochzeitsgästen, feierlich zum Ausgang. Sie hatten kaum durch das Portal die Kirche verlassen, als Elfriede ihr langes Brautkleid raffte und Ehemann Johann seinen Zylinder vom Kopf nahm. Sie fassten sich an den Händen, und dann liefen sie, so schnell es die Festkleidung erlaubte, auf ihre Kutsche zu.

‚Los, hinterher!‘, rief mir Maria zu. Sie hatte mehr Hochzeitserfahrung als ich, war sie doch letztes Jahr bei der Hochzeit ihrer Cousine dabei gewesen. Und deshalb fragte ich nicht, sondern lief ihnen nach.

Als wir ankamen, hob Johann gerade seine junge Ehefrau auf die Kutsche und sprang ihr nach. Schnell kletterten wir hinterher. Da knallte auch schon die Peitsche, die beiden hellbraunen Hengste liefen los.

Der Brautwerber, Gustav Karweina, hatte es sich nicht nehmen lassen, das Brautpaar in seiner Kutsche zur Kirche zu fahren. Seine Hengste standen gut im Futter, sie waren kräftig und schnell und liefen jetzt im gestreckten Galopp zum südlichen Ausgang der Stadt.

Die eisenbeschlagenen Räder drehten sich auf dem Kopfsteinpflaster, dass sie Funken schlugen. Gustav Karweina, vorn auf dem Kutschersitz, ließ die Leinen locker und knallte mit der Bogenpeitsche über seinen Braunen.

Wir waren keinen Augenblick zu früh gestartet, denn schon war Wilhelm Broska in seiner Kutsche dicht hinter uns; gefolgt von Emil Kowallecks Kutsche, die von zwei Apfelschimmeln gezogen wurde.

Als wir die Stadt verlassen hatten, das Kopfsteinpflaster in Asphalt überging, ließ Gustav Karweina noch einmal die Peitsche tanzen.

Die beiden Braunen griffen weit aus, ihre Hufe trommelten über den Asphalt. Die Wagenräder drehten sich wirbelnd und Elfriede klammerte sich noch fester an ihren Ehemann.

Maria und ich saßen den beiden gegenüber. Wir hielten uns mit den Händen an der Kutsche fest, aber wir hatten keine Angst. Noch nicht.

Gleich nach dem Sprung auf die Kutsche hatte mein Schwager Johann seinen zusammengeklappten Zylinder unter die Jacke geschoben. Er umfasste mit dem rechten

Arm die Taille seiner jungen Ehefrau und hielt sich mit seiner freien Hand am Wagen fest.

So jagten wir die birkengesäumte Straße zurück, die wir auf der Hinfahrt ganz gemächlich gekommen waren. Wir waren wohl so einen Kilometer gefahren – uns Kindern machte die rasend schnelle Fahrt richtigen Spaß –, als Emil Kowalleck seinen ersten Angriff gegen unsere Kutsche unternahm.

Er hatte die hellbraune Kutsche von Wilhelm Broska überholt und war bis auf eine halbe Wagenlänge an uns herangekommen. Die Straße war hier schnurgerade und Emil gab seinen Apfelschimmeln die Peitsche. So rasten sie bis zur nächsten Kurve, in der es Gustav gelang, als Erster einzubiegen.

Doch Kowalleck ließ nicht nach, besonders auch deshalb nicht, weil Wilhelm Broska, von Ehrgeiz gepackt, ganz dicht zu ihnen aufgeschlossen war. Kaum begann die Straße wieder gerade zu werden, da trieb er seine Apfelschimmel wieder heran. Sie kamen näher und näher. Schon waren ihre Köpfe neben unserer Kutsche zu sehen, da kam die nächste Kurve.

Für ein paar Augenblicke sah es aus, als wollte Emil Kowalleck es darauf ankommen lassen, doch dann entschied ein Peitschenknallen unseres Kutschers die Einfahrt in die Kurve. Wir lagen wieder vorn.

Inzwischen hatte Wilhelm Broska in halsbrecherischem Manöver seine hellbraune Kutsche an Kowallecks Apfelschimmeln vorbeigelenkt. Broska ließ die Leinen locker und jagte, die Peitsche schwingend, an unserer rechten Seite heran.

Die beiden Fuchsstuten preschten über den Asphalt. Sie schoben sich immer dichter heran, waren schon mit uns auf gleicher Höhe. Und dann liefen sie Rad neben Rad die lange Gerade der Straße entlang, Kopf an Kopf die Pferde, Leinen an Leinen die Kutscher.

So galoppierten wir fast einen Kilometer nebeneinander her, ohne dass es einem der beiden Kutscher gelang, seinen Wagen vom anderen zu lösen.

Als wir auf die letzte Kurve zujagten, bekamen wir beiden Mädchen Angst. Das wilde Rennen warf uns von einer Seite auf die andere und ließ uns auf- und niederhüpfen. Mit beiden Händen klammerten wir uns an der Sitzbank fest und Maria begann zu schreien.

Mir fiel wieder ein, dass vor zwei Jahren die Hochzeitskutsche von Anna und August Barbulla beim Wettrennen von der Straße abgekommen war und sich überschlagen hatte, mitten in den Graben.

Zwar war dem Brautpaar und dem Kutscher damals nichts Ernstes passiert – sie hatten ein paar Hautabschürfungen, Blutergüsse und ein paar Knochenbrüche –, aber die beiden Pferde wurden dabei so schwer verletzt, dass man sie töten musste.

Doch auch dieses tragische Ereignis hielt niemanden davon ab, das Wettrennen der Hochzeitskutschen fortzusetzen.

Meine Schwester hatte die Augen fest geschlossen und

bewegte die Lippen wie im Gebet, als wir in wahnsinnigem Tempo zwischen der langen Baumreihe dahinjagten. Und ich hatte in meiner Angst das Gefühl, dass wir jeden Augenblick aus der Kutsche geschleudert werden konnten!

Die beiden Kutschen jagten jetzt gemeinsam in die letzte Kurve. Und dort geschah es. Während die Pferde unserer Hochzeitskutsche dem Bogen der Straße folgten, galoppierten die beiden Fuchsstuten von Wilhelm Broska einfach geradeaus weiter.

Um Gottes willen, konnte ich noch denken, *jetzt ist es passiert!* Da zogen die Fuchsstuten schon ihre Kutsche von der Straße. Doch es passierte nichts, denn an dieser Stelle zweigte ein Feldweg ab. Ein Weg, der geradeaus verlief und den die beiden Pferde gut kannten.

Als Wilhelm Broska seine Fuchsstuten schließlich fluchend anhalten konnte und seinen Wagen nach langem, umständlichem Wendemanöver wieder zur Straße zurückgefahren hatte, da waren die anderen Kutschen, ja auch alle Reiter, längst vorüber.

Die jungen Eheleute Elfriede und Johann, gefahren vom Kutscher Gustav Karweina, rollten als Sieger die Dorfstraße entlang. Als sie dann in gemäßigtem Tempo unter dem blumengeschmückten Bogen hindurch langsam auf unseren Hof fuhren, sagte meine Schwester Elfriede zu mir: ‚Du hast doch nicht etwa Angst gehabt?‘

Sie lächelte zwar bei dieser Frage, aber ihr Gesicht war sehr blass.

Bevor ich antworten konnte, sagte Maria schnell: ‚Angst? Wovor denn Angst?‘

Meine Schwester sah sie erstaunt an.

Ich wollte antworten, aber da stieß mir Maria ihren rechten Ellbogen kräftig in die Rippen und zischte: ‚Du bist ganz still!‘

Mein Schwager grinste und zwinkerte uns zu. Dann wandte er sich an seine Frau und fragte: ‚Wovor sollen die beiden denn Angst gehabt haben? Die Pferde sind doch gut gelaufen! Und Gustav ist sehr gut gefahren. Wir hatten überhaupt keinen Grund, Angst zu haben!‘

Gustav Karweina drehte sich zu uns um. Er lachte. ‚Wir fuhren so schnell‘, sagte er, ‚dass uns überhaupt keine Zeit blieb, Angst zu haben!‘

Ich schüttelte langsam den Kopf und dachte an meine große Angst während der Fahrt. Da aber waren wir schon vor der Tür unseres Hauses angekommen.

Als dann der Johann meine Schwester von der Kutsche hob und über die Schwelle des Hauses trug, sagte Maria leise zu mir: ‚Klar hatte ich Schiss, Angst dürfen Kinder doch haben! Aber wenn eine so fragt wie deine Schwester vorhin, die ja selbst bald vor Angst gestorben ist, dann hab ich natürlich auch meinen Stolz!‘

‚Ich nicht‘, sagte ich. ‚Ich bin nur froh, dass ich endlich von der Kutsche auf festen Boden komme!‘“

Sandra lächelte ein wenig, als Oma geendet hatte. „Das war das einzige Mal, dass du Angst vor Pferden hattest?“, fragte sie.

Großmutter nickte: „Ja, das einzige Mal. Bei allen anderen Hochzeiten konnte ich es so einrichten, dass ich immer in einer Kutsche saß, die für ein Wettrennen nicht in Frage kam."

„Und bei deiner eigenen Hochzeit?", fragte Sandra nach einer Weile.

„Bei meiner Hochzeit waren wir nicht mehr zu Hause", sagte die Großmutter leise. „Und hier in der Stadt legte man auf solche Rennen keinen Wert. Ja, wir hatten gute Pferde damals. Und unsere Kutscher, die konnten fahren!"

Sandra stand auf. „Ich putz mal eben meine Stiefel", sagte sie und ging zur Tür, „sonst behauptet deine Tochter wieder, es stänke hier nach Pferdestall!"

„Mit ihrem empfindlichen Näschen hätte sie bei uns auf dem Hof Schwierigkeiten bekommen", bemerkte die Großmutter lächelnd. „Nur gut, dass sie keine Bäuerin geworden ist."

Lotte, Hans und Lene

Ein sonniger Sonntagnachmittag breitete sich über das Land. Kleine weiße Wölkchen zogen vereinzelt über das Himmelsblau. Sie milderten für Augenblicke das helle Licht des warmen Junitages und gaben ihm einen leichten Schimmer von dunstigem Blau, das sich zum Horizont hin verdichtete.

Horst war den Sandweg entlanggegangen, barfuß, die Wärme der Sommererde unter den Fußsohlen. Nun stand er auf der Wiese. Sie hatte sich am Rande des Kiefernwaldes ausgebreitet, umgeben von Büschen und Laubbäumen, die ausreichend Schatten boten. Später würden im Kiefernwald die großen saftigen Blaubeeren reifen; dicht an dicht gedrängt zwischen den hohen braunen Stämmen der alten Nadelbäume.

Am Rand der Wiese stand eine Weide. Sie hatte einen krummen Stamm mit weit ausladenden Ästen, auf die der Junge schon oft geklettert war. Hoch hinauf, bis in die schwankende Krone.

Drei Pferde weideten auf der Wiese: Lotte, Hans und Lene. Lotte war eine junge Stute, etwas über zwei Jahre alt.

Horst konnte sich noch an den Morgen erinnern, an dem Lotte geboren wurde. Es war noch einmal Schnee gefallen und hatte das beginnende Frühjahr wieder mit einem weißen Schleier bedeckt. Im Halbschlaf spürte Horst Unruhe im Haus. Dann hörte er Großvater Jakobs halblautes Rufen und Mutters Antwort, sie werde gleich in den Pferdestall kommen. Ein wenig später vernahm er, wie sie eilig das Haus verließ.

Plötzlich war Horst hellwach. Im Dunkeln zog er sich an und lief nach draußen. Der Wind heulte ums Haus und trieb ihm feinen Schneestaub ins Gesicht. Horst rannte durch die Schneedämmerung über den Hof bis zum Pferdestall und er hörte, noch bevor er den Stall betrat, die Stimmen von Großvater, Boleslaw und Mutter.

Horst schlüpfte leise in den Stall und blieb, um nicht bemerkt zu werden, gleich neben der Eingangstür stehen. Wärme und Stallgeruch hüllten ihn ein.

Eine Petroleumlampe verbreitete flackerndes Licht. Horst sah, wie sich hinter der Stute Lene, die in der letzten Zeit einen so dicken Bauch gehabt hatte, etwas Unförmiges auf dem Stroh bewegte. Nun drehte sich Lene um, fasste mit ihren Zähnen zu und riss eine schleimige Haut auseinander. Und da sah er schon, was darunter zum Vorschein kam: ein winziges Fohlen. Feucht und wie zusammengefaltet lag es auf dem Stroh und Lene begann schon mit ihrer hellen Zunge über das Fell ihres Pferdekindes zu lecken.

Horst huschte eilig aus dem Stall, er lief durch die Morgendämmerung über den verschneiten Hof ins Haus. Er zog sich hastig aus und war gerade wieder im Bett, als die Mutter zurückkam. Er stellte sich schlaftrunken und die Mutter erzählte ihm, dass Lene gerade ein Fohlen bekommen habe, das er sich nach dem Frühstück anschauen könne.

So schnell hatte Horst noch nie gefrühstückt! Und als er dann in den Stall kam, da versuchte das Fohlen bereits auf die dünnen Beinchen zu kommen. Es sah seltsam aus, wie sie immer wieder einknickten, wenn es sich auf dem Stroh aufzurichten versuchte, und wie es mit staksigen, unbeholfenen Bewegungen bemüht war stehen zu bleiben.

Es stand kaum, da schob es auch schon seinen kleinen Kopf unter den Bauch der Stute und suchte nach jener Stelle, an der es die Milch seiner Pferdemutter finden würde.

Das alles war vor zwei Jahren gewesen. Sie hatten das Fohlen Lotte genannt und Lotte war zu einer jungen Stute mit schön glänzendem Fell herangewachsen, dessen helles Braun nur von einem weißen Stern auf der Stirn unterbrochen wurde.

Horst kletterte über das Gattertor und ging über die Wiese auf Lotte zu. Sie schnaubte freundlich und beschnupperte ihn. Dann senkte sie den Kopf wieder und

91

graste weiter. Genau in diesem Augenblick hatte er den Einfall; ganz plötzlich und wie aus heiterem Himmel war er gekommen. Und mit der ungestümen Begeisterung eines achtjährigen Jungen setzte er seine Idee auch sofort in die Tat um: Er hatte gerade beschlossen, auf Lottes Rücken einen Ritt zu wagen. Auf dieser einsamen Wiese, von keinem beobachtet, wollte er auf diesem jungen Pferd als Erster die Wiese umrunden. Und es wäre auch das erste Mal, dass Lotte geritten würde.

Aber um reiten zu können, muss man bekanntlich erst auf dem Rücken eines Pferdes sitzen. Und das war das entscheidende Hindernis, denn im gleichen Augenblick wurde Horst klar, dass dieses Pferd für ihn zu hoch war. Selbst wenn er sich auf die Zehenspitzen stellte, es reichte nicht, um sich an dem runden, glatten Pferdeleib bis zum Rücken hinaufzuziehen.

Verschiedene völlig wahnwitzige Ideen, in Abenteuerbüchern gelesen, schossen ihm durch den Kopf. Aber so schnell sie aufgetaucht waren, so schnell verwarf er sie auch wieder. Und es wurde ihm immer klarer, dass er für diesen Pferderücken entschieden zu klein war!

So eine einmalige Gelegenheit, dachte Horst verzweifelt, *da steht ein rassiger Mustang bereit, die ganze wilde Prärie mit hunderttausend Abenteuern wartet – und der Indianer kommt nicht aufs Pferd! Beim großen Manitu, was würde Winnetou dazu sagen?*

Gesenkten Hauptes ging Horst zum Rand der Wiese und hockte sich im Indianersitz ins Gras. *Irgendeine*

Kriegslist muss es doch geben, grübelte er niedergeschlagen, *irgendeine Möglichkeit, diesen friedlich grasenden Mustang zu besteigen!*

Tief in Gedanken versunken lehnte er sich ein wenig nach hinten – und spürte plötzlich etwas Hartes im Rücken.

Horst stutzte, dann blickte er nach oben und sah im gleichen Augenblick die Lösung seines Problems: den Weidenbaum! Ungefähr in anderthalb Metern Höhe war der Stamm der Weide in einem Bogen zur Seite geschwungen, um dann nach einem knappen Meter wieder gerade nach oben zu wachsen. Es war nicht schwer, dort hinaufzusteigen. Ebenso leicht würde es dann sein, von dort auf Lottes Rücken überzuwechseln; vorausgesetzt, er bekam sie in die Nähe des schiefen Baumstammes.

Es war wirklich nicht einfach gewesen, die junge Stute zu der krummen Weide zu locken. Horst versuchte es zuerst mit besonders saftigen Grasbüscheln, dann mit allerhand Kräutern, die er darunter mischte. Zwei- oder dreimal hatte er Lotte schon ganz nahe an den Baum gelockt, doch kurz vor dem Stamm drehte sie immer wieder ab.

Horst wurde immer aufgeregter, er fing an zu schwitzen. „Komm, Lottchen, komm!", lockte er die Stute. „Komm doch mal her zum krummen Bäumchen!"

Aber Lotte sah ihn nur ab und zu freundlich an und pustete ein paar Mal durch die Nüstern. Dann rupfte sie wieder am Gras und entfernte sich langsam.

Irgendwann hatte es schließlich doch geklappt. Die

93

junge Stute war kaum in die Nähe der Weide gekommen, da kletterte Horst ganz schnell den schiefen Stamm hinauf und bemerkte nicht einmal, dass die Rinde ihm die Knie aufschabte.

Und auf einmal saß Häuptling Fliegender Pfeil im Baum, der zweikampferprobte, stolze Mohikaner! Mit einem gewaltigen Kriegsschrei würde er im nächsten Augenblick, einem Panter gleich, auf den Rücken des wildesten Mustangs springen, der jemals über das Gras der Prärie galoppiert war.

Und alle Apachen und Sioux, besonders aber diese feigen Komantschen, würden sehen, wie Fliegender Pfeil einem Hurrikan gleich über die Prärie brauste; den Tomahawk in der erhobenen Faust!

Horst ließ sich locker vom Baum fallen. Der Abstand zu Lottes breitem Rücken war so gering, dass er die Stute nicht verfehlen konnte. Schnell griff er mit beiden Händen in ihre lange Mähne. Er blieb einen Augenblick lang ausgestreckt auf dem Rücken der Stute liegen – froh darüber, dass er diese schwierige Aufgabe zu Winnetous vollster Zufriedenheit gelöst hatte.

Doch schon ein paar Augenblicke später erwachte in ihm neuer Tatendrang. Häuptling Fliegender Pfeil richtete sich vorsichtig vom Pferderücken auf, die Hände jedoch fest in die Mähne gekrallt. „Hüh!", rief er. „Los, Lotte, hüh!"

Und dann versuchte er mit den Fersen seiner nackten Füße der jungen Stute die Sporen zu geben.

Doch Lotte rührte sich nicht. Sie stand unbeweglich da, wie aus Stein gemeißelt, den Kopf zu Boden gesenkt; aber sie hatte aufgehört zu grasen und es schien, als lauschte sie auf etwas.

„Los! Komm, Lotte!", schrie Horst nun noch lauter. „Los!"

Er trommelte mit der rechten Faust gegen den Pferdehals und mit den Fersen gegen den Bauch der Stute.

Auf einmal fühlte Horst die Augen aller Indianerkrieger auf sich gerichtet. Ja, die ganze Prärie schien nur noch aus Augen zu bestehen und ihn anzuschauen!

Beim großen Manitu, dachte er, *der tapfere Häuptling Fliegender Pfeil vom ruhmreichen Stamme der Mohikaner hockt wie ein zahnloses Weib auf dem Rücken eines feurigen Mustangs. So eine Schande darf ich nicht zulassen!*

Er hörte auf mit den Fäusten zu trommeln und mit den nackten Fersen die Sporen zu geben und dachte nach. Und wenn in diesen Augenblicken jemand die beiden aus der Ferne gesehen hätte, könnte er gemeint haben, da stünde ein Reiterdenkmal im Grün der Wiese.

„Zum Teufel noch mal!", rief Horst plötzlich laut. „Dem listigen Häuptling Fliegender Pfeil ist es gelungen, den hohen Rücken des feurigsten Mustangs aller Zeiten zu besteigen! Es wird ihm doch noch gelingen, dieses faule Pferd in Schwung zu kriegen! Hugh, ich habe gesprochen!"

Und schon bearbeitete er mit Händen und Füßen die

junge Stute, sodass es aussah, als mache er einen Indianertanz auf dem Rücken des Pferdes.

Da bäumte sich Lotte plötzlich auf. Mit wildem Wiehern riss sie den Kopf nach oben, stieg in die Höhe und warf sich herum. Und dann jagte der schnellste Mustang aller Zeiten im wildesten Galopp aller Zeiten über die Prärie.

Da aber schien Häuptling Fliegender Pfeil den Mustang verlassen zu wollen. Es hatte den Anschein, als wollte er im Galopp abspringen, um spurlos irgendwo im Gebüsch zu verschwinden. Um sich Mut zu machen, schrie Horst in den Galopp hinein: „Ein Indianer kennt keine Angst!"

Lottes Hufe flogen über die Wiese. Sie fetzten Grasbüschel heraus; zertraten Maulwurfshügel; brachten den Boden zum Dröhnen.

Als Lotte die Wiese zum zweiten Mal umrundet hatte, machte sie einen Satz und eine plötzliche Wendung nach links.

Horst spürte einen mächtigen Ruck in den Armen, dann hatte er für einen Augenblick das Gefühl des Fliegens.

Lotte setzte hart wieder auf, Horst flog beinah über ihren Hals. Schnaubend jagte die Stute weiter, dann sprang sie über das Gattertor. Nun federten ihre Hufe bereits über den Waldweg, sie jagten in wilden Sätzen die ausgefahrenen Wagenspuren entlang.

Horst hing lang gestreckt über der Mähne. Bei jedem

Absprung, bei jedem Aufprall schlug sein Körper gegen den Rücken des jungen Pferdes – und das tat weh!

„Ein Indianerherz kennt keinen Schmerz!", schrie der tapfere Häuptling der Mohikaner.

Aber Lotte steigerte noch ihren Galopp. So dicht jagte sie jetzt unter den Ästen der Bäume dahin, dass Horst die Zweige ins Gesicht peitschten.

Da kam die Angst. Und auf einmal war er ganz allein, verlassen von allen Apachen, ja, auch vom Letzten der Mohikaner. Er war allein mit sich und seiner Angst, auf dem harten Rücken eines wild galoppierenden Pferdes.

Wenn uns nur keiner entgegenkommt!, dachte Horst in seiner großen Angst. Doch Lotte jagte weiter. Sie ließ seinen Körper auf und nieder hüpfen wie einen Ball. Der Angstschweiß machte seine Handflächen feucht, Horst fürchtete, dass er ihre Mähne bald nicht mehr fest halten konnte. Er hatte Angst, die wilden Sprünge dieses rasenden Galopps nicht mehr länger auszuhalten.

Eingehüllt in eine Staubfahne preschte Lotte nun auf das Dorf zu. In gestrecktem Galopp bogen Ross und Reiter in die Dorfstraße ein.

„Pferd ist durchgegangen!", hörte Horst jemanden schreien.

Karschinskis Alfred rannte auf die Straße.

Schon waren sie an ihm vorbeigeprescht.

Leute liefen auf die Straße.

Schreien und Rufen.

Lotte raste dem Hof entgegen.

Ein Torflügel stand offen, Lotte jagte wild über den Hof.

Horst hörte Hühner kreischen, sah Federn fliegen.

Eine Frauenstimme schrie auf.

Die dunkle Öffnung der Stalltür schoss bedrohlich auf Horst zu.

„Nein!", schrie jemand.

Horst spürte einen dumpfen Schlag. Dann war es vorbei. *Bin ich tot?*, dachte er. Es war alles so seltsam um ihn herum, so feucht und so weich. Und dann dieser durchdringende Gestank, fürchterlich!

Erschrocken riss Horst die Augen auf, er sah kleine weiße Wolken und einen blassblauen Sommerhimmel. Dann hörte er Großmutter Luises Stimme. Sie kam von irgendwo über ihm. Sie fragte und er antwortete.

Jetzt erst erkannte er, was los war: Er war drei Schritte vor der Stalltür vom Pferd gestürzt. Zu seinem großen Glück, denn die Türöffnung war so niedrig, dass er unweigerlich gegen die Mauer geschleudert worden wäre.

Horst hörte Gelächter, es wurde lauter. Und da sah er, dass sich das halbe Dorf um ihn versammelt hatte; es war ja Sonntagnachmittag und man hatte Zeit. Nun begriff er auch, warum die Leute lachten: Er war auf den Misthaufen gefallen! Horst lag auf dem Rücken, mitten in einer stinkenden Brühe. Und um ihn standen Leute, die lachten und lachten!

98

Welch eine Schande, durchzuckte es ihn, *welch bodenlose Schande für den großen Häuptling der Mohikaner!*

Fliegender Pfeil ist nicht nur vom Mustang gefallen, son-
dern dazu noch auf einen riesigen stinkenden Misthau-
fen! Beim großen Manitu, was würde nur Winnetou dazu
sagen? Doch Gott sei Dank wusste ja keiner im Dorf,
dass auf dem Misthaufen eigentlich ein Indianerhäupt-
ling lag.

Nach diesem anrüchigen Ende seines Rittes über die
sonntägliche Prärie hatte ihn Oma Luise ins Waschfass
gesteckt. Da half ihm kein Sträuben. Energisch drückte
sie seinen Kopf so lange unter Wasser, bis Horst schließlich alles über sich ergehen ließ.

„Man sollte dich drei Tage wässern lassen wie einen
Salzhering", sagte sie, „du Stinktier!"

Und dann scheuerte sie mit der Wurzelbürste so fest
seinen Rücken, dass er schrie.

Zweieinhalb Jahre waren seit diesem Sommernachmittag
vergangen. Lotte war zu einem kräftigen Pferd herangewachsen, das gewohnt war, vor Pflug und Erntewagen gespannt zu werden. Nun war Lottes erstes Fohlen unterwegs. In zwei Monaten sollte sie Mutter werden.

Es war Anfang Januar des Jahres 1945. Ein auch für
masurische Verhältnisse eiskalter Januar hatte begonnen.
Die Schneeverwehungen auf der Dorfstraße reichten
Horst bis zum Hals.

Das Donnern der Geschütze kam jeden Tag näher. Die
Front, sagten die Erwachsenen, sei inzwischen diesseits

der ostpreußischen Grenze. Und eines Morgens bekamen sie den Befehl, das Dorf zu verlassen.

In klirrender Kälte nagelten Opa Jakob und Boleslaw schwere Bretter an den großen Leiterwagen und machten ihm ein Dach. Und dann, am Nachmittag, stand er, zu einem unförmigen Planwagen verwandelt, im Hof.

So schnell es nur ging, beluden sie den Wagen, mit Hausrat, Lebensmitteln, mit dem Futter für die Pferde.

Sie hatten so viel auf die Ladefläche des Wagens gepackt, dass die drei Pferde – Lene, Hans und die trächtige Lotte – ihn kaum zu bewegen vermochten. Denn alles schien lebenswichtig um die eisige Fahrt in eine ungewisse Zukunft zu überstehen.

Schwerfällig war der überladene Wagen die verschneite Dorfstraße entlanggerumpelt. Mit all ihrer Kraft hatten die drei Pferde das schwere Gefährt durch den knirschenden Schnee gezogen.

Nun warteten Menschen und Tiere an der Straße, die zur nächsten Stadt führte, um sich irgendwann in den Strom der Flüchtlinge einzureihen.

Schwer beladene Pferdewagen mit Bauernfamilien, Lastwagen mit Soldaten, dicht hintereinander, in endloser Kolonne, so bewegten sie sich langsam durch die Abenddämmerung des eisigen Wintertages.

Opa Jakob versuchte eine Lücke zwischen den Flüchtenden zu finden, in die er den schwer beladenen Planwagen lenken konnte. Mit Schreien und Peitschenschlägen trieb er die keuchenden Pferde an. Die stemmten sich in die Sielen, ihre Hufe rutschten auf dem vereisten Schnee und fanden keinen Halt. Die Räder des unförmigen Planwagens drehten sich auf der Stelle. Das Fell der Pferde war nass vom Schweiß.

Horsts Mutter kletterte vom Wagen. Sie redete beruhigend auf die Pferde ein. „Die Lotte kann nicht mehr!", sagte sie schließlich.

Jetzt stiegen alle ab und griffen in die Holzspeichen der Räder. Doch auch das nützte nichts.

„Ihr habt zu viel geladen", rief ein Soldat. „Schmeißt runter, was runtergeht!"

Sie warfen Dinge in den Straßengraben, die sie vor kurzer Zeit noch für unentbehrlich gehalten hatten.

Der Soldat half ihnen dabei. „Haut ab, so schnell es geht!", rief er ihnen zu. „Die Russen können schon morgen hier sein!"

Der Wagen war immer noch schwer beladen und die Pferde hatten Mühe, ihn über die vereiste Straße zu ziehen.

Nun rollten sie langsam und schwerfällig zwischen den anderen Flüchtenden mit. Sie fuhren die ganze Nacht hindurch. Immer ganz im Dunkeln; denn jeder Lichtschimmer war streng verboten, damit kein feindliches Flugzeug sie entdeckte.

Militärfahrzeuge drängten sie einige Male von der Straße. Dann, im Morgengrauen, entdeckten sie einen verlassenen Gutshof. Er lag etwas abseits der Straße. Ein paar andere Pferdewagen schlossen sich ihnen an.

Sie fuhren auf den großen Hof. Hier wollten sie den Tag über bleiben, weil sie hofften, in der Dunkelheit wieder schneller fahren zu können.

Die Pferde könnten sich auf diese Weise etwas ausruhen und die Straßen wären dann freier, sagte Opa Jakob; der größte Teil des Flüchtlingstrecks wäre schon weiter nach Westen gezogen.

Sie brachten die Pferde in die Ställe, tränkten und fütterten sie. Man machte Feuer in den großen Kachelöfen und kochte mit den mageren Vorräten Essen. Dann versuchten einige zu schlafen.

Am Nachmittag kamen die Tiefflieger. Ganz niedrig flogen sie über die Straße, die noch immer mit Flüchtlingen voll gestopft war, und schossen auf Menschen und Tiere.

Eines der Kampfflugzeuge drehte ab und raste auf den Gutshof zu. Horst hörte das Nahen der explodierenden Geschosse. Schreiend lief er auf das tief verschneite Feld hinaus. In panischer Angst stürzte er durch Gebüsch und Schneewehen. Er lief, bis er nicht mehr konnte. Weinend hockte er sich in den Schnee.

Die Mutter war seinen Spuren nachgegangen und brachte ihn zum Hof zurück. Es begann bereits zu dämmern.

„Wir müssen weg!", sagte Kalchowitz, der Nachbar aus ihrem alten Dorf. „Die Russen sollen nur noch zehn Kilometer entfernt sein!"

Opa Jakob und Boleslaw holten die Pferde aus dem

Stall. Sie spannten nur Lene und Hans vor den Wagen. Lotte wurde hinten angebunden, sie sollte sich schonen.

Bevor Horst auf den großen Wagen stieg, ging er noch einmal zu Lotte. Er streichelte ihren Hals. Sie wieherte leise und rieb ihre Nase an seiner Pelzmütze.

Als sie die Straße in Richtung Allenstein erreicht hatten, war es dunkel geworden. Überall waren Soldaten. In den Straßengräben lagen zerstörte Fuhrwerke und tote Pferde.

„Das waren die Tiefflieger", sagte Opa Jakob leise.

Oma Luise begann zu beten.

Erika, Horsts kleine Schwester, wachte auf und fing an zu weinen. Die Mutter wiegte sie in ihren Armen und versuchte sie zu beruhigen. Horst biss in den Lederriemen seiner Pelzmütze.

Ein Panzer kam ihnen entgegen. Sie mussten in den Straßengraben ausweichen. Nun saßen sie dort fest. Alle mussten vom Wagen klettern. Auch Lotte wurde wieder angespannt. Sie schoben den Wagen mit aller Kraft. Glatteis. Die Räder drehten sich auf der Stelle.

In der Nähe explodierte eine Granate. „Deckung!", brüllte eine Stimme.

Sie warfen sich in den Straßengraben.

Eine zweite Explosion. Noch eine, und noch eine. Aber jede klang weiter entfernt.

Schließlich stiegen sie aus dem Schnee des Straßengrabens und schoben den Wagen wieder an. Die Pferde zogen mit aller Kraft.

Sehr, sehr langsam, Schritt für Schritt, kamen sie voran. Endlich konnten sie weiterfahren.

Sie hörten noch einige Male das schrille Pfeifen vorüberfliegender Granaten, etwas später dann den Donner der Explosionen. Aber es klang immer weiter entfernt.

Später sahen sie auf der rechten Seite ein großes Feuer am Nachthimmel. Der flackernde Widerschein färbte den Schnee rot. Dann hörten sie vereinzeltes dumpfes Krachen und schnelle Folgen knatternder Schüsse.

Nach etwa einer Stunde kamen sie zu einem umgestürzten Planwagen. Er war verlassen und lag mit der hinteren Hälfte im Graben. Als Opa Jakob ihren Wagen um das große Hindernis herumlenkte, rutschten die hinteren Räder von der Straße.

Wieder mussten sie schieben. Die Pferde keuchten. Sie zogen mit letzter Kraft, ihre Flanken bebten.

Sie hatten den Wagen gerade wieder halbwegs auf der Straße stehen, da hielt ein Militärwagen neben ihnen. Ein junger Offizier sprang heraus und schrie: „Die Straße muss frei bleiben! Machen Sie sofort die Straße frei!" Und schon versuchte er die Pferde zur Seite zu drängen.

Hans bäumte sich auf. Schrill wiehernd stieg er und riss Lene mit. In panischer Angst begannen die Pferde mit den Hufen zu schlagen. Sie trafen sich gegenseitig, rissen an den Sielen und dem Zaumzeug.

104 Dann Mutters Schrei, so laut, dass er den Lärm übertönte: „Lotte!"

Die trächtige Stute wurde zu Boden gerissen. Hart

schlug ihr schwerer Leib auf das harte Eis. Dann lag sie, noch in den Sielen, regungslos auf der linken Seite.

Opa und Boleslaw griffen nach dem Zaumzeug, sie versuchten Lene und Hans zu beruhigen.

Die Mutter schrie den Offizier an. Sie lief ganz nahe an ihn heran und schrie ihm ins Gesicht: „Lassen Sie die Pferde in Ruhe! Sehen Sie nicht, was Sie angerichtet haben!"

Der junge Offizier lief ein paar Schritte zurück. Die Mutter lief ihm nach: „Fassen Sie an! Los, Mann, helfen Sie! Das Pferd stirbt! Mensch, die Stute stirbt doch!"

Dann befreiten Opa und Boleslaw die Stute aus dem Zuggeschirr. Die Mutter warf Decken auf das Eis der Straße, die schoben sie unter Lottes Beine. Dann versuchten sie, die Stute aufzurichten. Auch einige Soldaten fassten mit an.

Endlich kam die Stute hoch, zitternd stand sie da.

Ein Soldat ließ eine Taschenlampe aufblitzen.

Da sah Horst das Blut im Schnee. „Blut!", schrie er. „Lotte blutet!"

Beim Aufprall auf die vereiste Straße hatte sich die trächtige Stute die Zunge zerbissen. Schaum und Blut tropften ihr aus dem Maul, fielen in den Schnee.

Zitternd stand das Tier zwischen den Menschen. Plötzlich knickten ihre Hinterbeine ein. Lotte versuchte aufzustehen, kam aber nicht mehr allein hoch.

Die Männer fassten wieder zu, sie schoben Lotte mühsam hoch. Für einen Augenblick stand die junge Stute breitbeinig da, seltsam steif, dann sank sie wieder zu Boden.

Die Mutter kniete sich in den Schnee und streichelte sie. Leise redete sie zu Lotte.

„Sie schafft das nicht mehr", hörte Horst Opa Jakob sagen.

Die Mutter fing an zu weinen.

„Sie müssen weiter", sagte der junge Offizier. Er sprach jetzt leise, fast verlegen. „Die Front kommt immer näher. Denken Sie an die Kinder! Wir kümmern uns um das Pferd."

Horst wollte zu Lotte, aber Oma Luise fasste ihn am Arm. Er riss sich los, fiel in den Schnee. Blind von Tränen richtete er sich auf, fiel wieder hin. Dann hielt ihn die Mutter fest.

Boleslaw hob ihn auf den Wagen.

Hans und Lene begannen zu ziehen.

Schwerfällig rollte der Planwagen über die vereiste Straße.

Dann fiel der Schuss.

Omas Trakehner

„Vati, erzähl mir etwas von den Trakehnern!"

„Also, das sind Pferde, weißt du", der Vater blickte über den Rand seiner Zeitung, „die werden als Trakehner gezüchtet!"

Mark sah seinen Vater wieder hinter der Zeitung verschwinden.

„Ach, nee", sagte er da, „richtige Pferde also! Ich hatte schon befürchtet, das wäre eine Kaninchensorte oder Hunderasse!"

Vaters Gesicht tauchte wieder über der Zeitung auf. „Hunderasse?", fragte er verständnislos. „Seit wann interessierst du dich für Hunde?"

„Eigentlich interessiere ich mich nicht für Hunde", sagte Mark. „Besonders deshalb nicht, weil man auf Hunden so schlecht reiten kann."

Der Vater ließ die Zeitung sinken. „Wer will auf Hunden reiten?", fragte er seinen Sohn. „Das wäre doch glatte Tierquälerei!"

Mark nickte. „Das wäre es sicher! Aber ich wollte ja nichts von dir über Hundereiten wissen."

„Wer denn?", fragte der Vater und war schon wieder hinter der Zeitung verschwunden.

„Hörst du mir überhaupt zu?", fragte Mark. Langsam wurde er ungeduldig.

„Klar", behauptete der Vater und raschelte mit seiner Zeitung. „Was war mit den Hunden los?"

„Es hat heute keinen Zweck", stellte Mark nüchtern fest. „Wenn du dich einmal an deiner Zeitung festgebissen hast, dann ist nichts zu machen!"

„Ja", sagte der Vater und blätterte geräuschvoll die Zeitung um, „Hunde sind bissig, da ist wirklich nichts zu machen."

„Du sagst es." Mark stand auf. „Vielleicht weiß Mutti etwas über Trakehner."

„Das sind doch Pferde", hörte er seinen Vater noch sagen, dann hatte Mark schon das Wohnzimmer verlassen.

„Na", meinte seine Mutter, als er in die Küche kam, „was hat mein Sohn denn auf der Seele?"

Mark setzte sich zu ihr an den Tisch. „Mensch, bin ich froh", sagte er, „dass du keine Zeitung liest!"

„Aber natürlich lese ich Zeitung", bemerkte die Mutter. „Willst du wissen, was heute drinstand?"

Mark schüttelte energisch den Kopf. „Mama", seine
108 Stimme zitterte ein bisschen, „kannst du mir was über Trakehner erzählen?"

„Davon stand nichts in der Zeitung!"

Mark räusperte sich. „Weißt du, Mama", sagte er dann übertrieben ruhig, „ich hab doch wegen der Trakehner vorhin schon Vati gefragt. Ich hab ihm auch schon erzählt, dass ich weiß, dass das keine Hunderasse ist."

Die Mutter stutzte. „Hunderasse?", fragte sie verdutzt.

„Nun ja", Mark kratzte sich am linken Ohr, „wenn Vati seine Zeitung liest, hört er doch nicht zu."

„Ach so", meinte die Mutter. Sie schien erleichtert zu sein. „Ich dachte schon, du hättest das mit der Hunderasse ernst gemeint."

„Also, was ist, erzählst du mir etwas über Trakehner?"

„Ich?", fragte die Mutter gedehnt.

„Schick mich um Himmels willen nur nicht wieder zu Vati." Mark stand auf. „Bei dem war ich eben, und bei ihm hat es im Moment überhaupt keinen Zweck!"

Da wurde die Küchentür aufgemacht, und der Vater kam herein. Er hielt die Zeitung noch in der Hand.

„Du wolltest doch vorhin etwas über Trakehner wissen", sagte er zu Mark. „Oder hab ich mich da geirrt?"

Mark war zu überrascht, um zu nicken.

„Er wollte es", antwortete die Mutter an seiner Stelle. „Schön, dass du unserem Jungen jetzt etwas über sie erzählen willst."

„Wieso ich? Na, hör mal, ich dachte, dein Sohn hätte seine Pferdeliebe von deiner Familie geerbt?"

„Ihr wisst es also beide nicht", stellte Mark fest und wollte aus der Küche gehen.

„Moment", rief ihm die Mutter nach. „Vielleicht finden wir doch noch eine Lösung!"

„Warum willst du das überhaupt wissen?", fragte der Vater.

„Ich bin vom Geheimdienst und darf nichts verraten." Mark öffnete die Küchentür.

„Sei nicht albern!", sagte der Vater.

„Bis wann müsstest du es denn wissen?", erkundigte sich die Mutter vorsichtig.

„Möglichst bis gestern", meinte Mark.

„Und da fragst du erst heute?"

„Hättest du gestern mehr gewusst?"

„Das ist eine ziemlich blöde Frage", bemerkte der Vater.

„Weißt du denn eine Antwort?" Mark sah ihn an.

„46 52 19", sagte die Mutter.

Mark blieb in der offenen Küchentür stehen.

„Aber klar", rief er, „dass ich nicht selbst draufgekommen bin!"

Und schon lief er zum Telefon.

„Hallo, Oma, hier ist Mark!"

„Schön, dass du anrufst, wie geht es euch so?"

„Na ja, Mutti und Vati reden gerade über Pferde."

„Das ist gut! Und was macht dein Reiten?"

„Wir sollen nächste Woche einen jungen Trakehner bekommen, hat uns die Reitlehrerin gestern gesagt."

„Schade, dass mich mein Rheuma nicht mehr aufs Pferd lässt", die Oma lachte, „sonst würde ich euch jungem Gemüse schon zeigen, wie man mit einem Trakehner umgeht!"

„Oma, erzähl mir was über Trakehner!"

„Zuerst einmal, der richtige Name ist: Ostpreußisches Warmblutpferd Trakehner Abstammung."

„Klar, Oma, Ostpreußisches Warmblutpferd Trakehner Abstammung", wiederholte Mark, „aber einfach Trakehner reicht doch auch!"

Oma lachte wieder. „Keine Angst, mein Junge, wir bleiben bei den Trakehnern. Als ich noch in Ostpreußen lebte, heute gehört es ja zu Polen, war es das größte Pferdeland Deutschlands. Trakehner galten als die beste deutsche Pferdezucht. Damals gab es allein bei den Trakehnern über 50 000 Zuchtstuten."

„50 000", rief Mark überrascht. „Das sind ja riesig viele!"

„Weißt du", sagte die Oma, „Trakehnerpferde sind eine besondere Züchtung. Schon vor über siebenhundert Jahren hat man in Ostpreußen durch die Kreuzung von Pruzzenpferden mit den schweren Pferden der Ordensritter eine gezielte Zucht betrieben ..."

„... Ritterpferde mussten ja schwer und kräftig sein", unterbrach Mark seine Großmutter, „sie hatten schließlich schwere Eisenrüstungen zu schleppen!"

„Eigentlich wollte ich nicht von Ritterpferden, sondern von Trakehnern erzählen", sagte Oma etwas ungeduldig, „und das möchte ich so machen, wie ich es für richtig halte!"

„Ich hör dir auch genau zu", sagte Mark schnell und setzte sich in einen Sessel.

„Also: Im 16. und 17. Jahrhundert wurden auch türkische Pferde bei den Trakehnern eingekreuzt. Als Deckhengste nahm man hauptsächlich Araber und englische Vollbluthengste. In der damaligen Zeit waren Pferde das wichtigste Transport- und Fortbewegungsmittel zu Lande; man benutzte sie als Zugtiere und als Reitpferde. Sie waren auch im Krieg unentbehrlich.

Friedrich Wilhelm der Erste, der im Jahre 1713 zum König von Preußen gekrönt wurde, baute eine mächtige Armee von über 80 000 Soldaten auf. Der König galt als sehr streng, er wurde auch der Soldatenkönig genannt. Er wusste genau, wie wichtig gute Pferde für seine Soldaten waren, daher baute er die Kavallerie, die berittenen Soldaten, besonders sorgfältig auf. Friedrich Wilhelm liebte Pferde; auf seinen Befehl wurde im Jahre 1732 das Hauptgestüt Trakehnen gegründet und die Zucht dieser großartigen Pferde wurde staatlich gefördert und unterstützt ..."

Mark wechselte den Telefonhörer vom rechten ans linke Ohr und klappte das Telefonbuch auf. Er nahm mit der rechten Hand einen Bleistift vom Tisch und zog tief in Gedanken den ersten Strich auf das Papier.

„Vor dem Zweiten Weltkrieg", hörte er die Oma weiter sagen, „da waren die Aufzucht und der Fohlenverkauf der Remonten ein gutes Geschäft. Es wurde behauptet, dass es nirgends auf der Welt so eine harte

Zuchtauswahl gegeben habe wie in Trakehnen. Als Zeichen ihrer reinen Rasse trugen die Pferde aus dem Gestüt Trakehnen das Brandzeichen mit der berühmten Elchschaufel auf der Hinterhand.

Waren die Pferde drei Jahre alt, kamen sie ein Jahr lang ins Training. Als Vierjährige mussten sie dann bei Fuchsjagden und harten Querfeldeinrennen, die über Zäune, Hecken, Erdwälle und offene Wassergräben führten, ihre Leistungsfähigkeit und Ausdauer beweisen.

Nach dieser Zeit wurden sie weiter ausgemustert und nur die besten Tiere blieben im Hauptgestüt. Die zweitbesten wurden an Staatsgestüte überstellt und erst die so genannte dritte Wahl wurde an Privatleute verkauft. Und auch diese Pferde hatten noch hervorragende Eigenschaften. Diese strenge Auslese brachte den Trakehnern den Ruf ein, eine ganz besonders edle Rasse zu sein."

Mark zog gedankenverloren die Spitze des Bleistifts über das Papier.

„Bist du noch da, Mark?", fragte Oma. „Du bist so still geworden. Allerdings hab ich ja auch die ganze Zeit geredet!" Sie lachte.

Mark schreckte auf und legte hastig den Bleistift aus der Hand. „Ja, klar bin ich da", sagte er schnell und ärgerte sich, dass er den Bleistift weggelegt hatte, obwohl ihn die Oma gar nicht sehen konnte. Er nahm den Stift wieder in die Hand und sagte ins Telefon: „Du hast Trakehner geritten, Oma?"

„Das ist schon sehr lange her", antwortete seine

Großmutter, „aber ich kann mich noch gut daran erinnern. Trakehner sind sehr zuverlässige Pferde von großer Zähigkeit und Ausdauer, aber manchmal auch nervös und von eigenwilligem Charakter. Sie haben schmale und charaktervolle Köpfe, große Augen, eine feine Mähne und einen schön gebogenen Hals. Seit dem Ende des Zweiten Weltkrieges werden Trakehner im Westen weiter gezüchtet, besonders in Niedersachsen, Schleswig-Holstein und Nordrhein-Westfalen. Doch damals, nach der harten, mühseligen Flucht aus Ostpreußen, schien das Ende der berühmten Trakehner-Zucht gekommen. Nur etwa 800 Zuchtstuten und 45 Hengste konnten gerettet und in den Westen gebracht werden!"

Mark hörte plötzlich auf zu zeichnen. „Und was ist aus den anderen geworden?", fragte er aufgeregt. „Es gab doch in Ostpreußen über 50 000 Stuten, hast du vorhin gesagt!"

Am anderen Ende der Leitung war es still geworden, eine ganze Zeit lang. Als Omas Stimme dann wieder zu hören war, klang sie sehr leise.

„Weißt du, mein Junge, es war eine schreckliche Zeit, damals im Krieg, im Januar 1945. Die Menschen flohen aus Ostpreußen durch Eis und Schnee, mussten ihr ganzes Hab und Gut zurücklassen. Viele versuchten im Pferdewagen über das zugefrorene Frische Haff zu entkommen. Russische Kriegsflugzeuge warfen Bomben auf die Fliehenden, die Explosionen rissen Löcher ins Eis, Menschen und Pferde ertranken. Über unseren Köpfen jagten Tiefflieger dahin und schossen auf Menschen und Tiere. Die Straßengräben waren voll von zerstörten Pferdewagen und vielen Toten …"

Die Großmutter hatte zu sprechen aufgehört, und Mark saß da, ganz still. Er hatte den Hörer an sein linkes Ohr gepresst und hörte die Großmutter weinen.

Da nahm er den Hörer langsam vom Ohr und legte ihn vorsichtig auf. Dann sah er auf seine Zeichnung. Es war ein Pferdekopf mit einem langen, eleganten Hals, mit edlem Gesicht und großen Augen.

„Na, ist alles geklärt?", fragte die Mutter, als sie ins Wohnzimmer kam. „Ist alles klar mit den Trakehnern?"

Mark legte ganz schnell seine linke Hand über den Pferdekopf, er drehte sich zu ihr um und nickte. Als er dann aber das Telefonverzeichnis möglichst unauffällig weglegen wollte, sah es die Mutter. Widerstrebend reichte ihr Mark seine Zeichnung.

„Toll!", sagte seine Mutter und sah überrascht auf den Pferdekopf. „Wirklich, Mark, das ist ein schönes Bild!"

„Omas Trakehner", sagte der Junge etwas verlegen. „Weißt du, ich hab's gar nicht gemerkt, dass ich auf das Telefonbuch gezeichnet habe!"

Die Mutter lachte. „Wir werden ja wieder ein neues Telefonbuch bekommen. Auf jeden Fall hast du für Oma jetzt eine Überraschung. Das ist ein schönes Geschenk für sie!"

Geschichten von heute und morgen

Zwischen den
weißen Hügeln

Vor ihr liegt eine unermessliche Weite.

In weißen Wellen breiten sich Hügel über die Landschaft bis zum fernen Horizont. Weiß, weit und still.

Sie sieht keinen Anfang, und auch ein Ende sieht sie nicht. Sie steht nur da und blickt nach vorn, sieht in das weiße Schimmern am Horizont. Und überall, wo ihre Blicke auch hinfallen, sieht sie dieses Weiß, ein reines, schimmerndes, ununterbrochenes Weiß, wie sie es bisher noch nie gesehen hat. Sie steht auf einer Anhöhe. Direkt unter ihr ist das Tal.

In immer flacher werdenden Bogen senkt sich die Höhe zum Talgrund hinab, um dann zu einem neuen Hügel anzusteigen; zu einem neuen Gipfel, der ihr flacher als der erste erscheint. Sie sieht lange hinaus, und je länger sie hinsieht, desto mehr ist ihr, als sei alles nur ein Traum. Langsam wendet sie sich um.

Hinter ihr am Hügel, vielleicht zehn Meter von ihr entfernt, steht das Pony. Sie gleitet auf ihren Skiern durch

den Schnee auf das Pony zu. Als sie bei ihm ist, schnaubt
es kleine Atemwolken aus seinen Nüstern. Sie streichelt
seinen Hals. Dann bückt sie sich, nestelt an den Bindun-
gen ihrer Ski und nimmt die Leinen fest in ihre Hände.

Noch einmal schweifen ihre Blicke über die sanften
Linien des Hügels und folgen ihnen in die Tiefe, weit
hinab bis zum Grunde des Tals.

Sie hatten Elke das Pony einfach mitgegeben, heute
am frühen Morgen.

„Lena weiß ja Bescheid", Inger hatte gelächelt und auf
das Pony gedeutet, „die findet immer den Weg zurück in
den Stall."

Die Stute Lena hatte sie leicht vom Hof gezogen und
war mit ihr in die weiße Weite hinausgetrabt. Und die
hellen Atemwölkchen vor ihren Nüstern erinnerten Elke
an ein kleines Lokomotivchen, eine Spielzeugeisenbahn,
die sie irgendwo einmal gesehen hatte. Lächelnd hatte
Elke die langen Leinen in beiden Händen gehalten, die
sie mit dem Pony verbanden. So war sie über die makel-
lose Schneefläche geglitten, die sich weiß und glitzernd
vor ihren Blicken ausbreitete.

Elke lächelt in der Erinnerung daran und senkt den
Blick auf die Schneefläche vor ihren Füßen. Sie neigt den
Oberkörper etwas vor und beugt ein wenig die Knie.

Sie wartet noch einen tiefen Atemzug lang, ehe sie das
Pony mit leisem Schnalzen antreibt. Lena macht die ersten Schritte ins Weiß. Zögernd beginnen die Bretter zu
gleiten.

Elke sieht das helle Schneeglitzern, spürt das sanfte Gleiten unter ihren Füßen und fühlt, wie sie schneller in die Tiefe fährt.

Sie kann das Gleiten hören. Der Schnee knirscht leise unter den Skiern. Sie hört auch ein Knistern, das Wehen des Fahrtwindes und das Rauschen ihres Pulsschlags in den Ohren. Sie spürt alle Geräusche auch in ihrem Inneren. Es ist wie ein freudiges Erzittern, das sich mit dem Schlag ihres Herzens mischt. In gleitendem Schwung fährt sie der Tiefe entgegen, gezogen von Lena folgt sie der Linie des Hügels hinab ins Tal. Sie spürt die Geschwindigkeit, fühlt sie durch ihren Körper wehen, hört sie als Rauschen und nimmt sie als wirbelnden Wind wahr. Sie spürt eine seltsame Erregung und folgt, von diesen Gefühlen getragen, dem Zug des Ponys über den weißen Hang nach unten.

Sie hat sich vorgebeugt, tiefer nach unten, zu einem federnden Bogen aus Sehnen, Muskeln und Haut. Und hinter ihnen weht eine schimmernde Staubspur, ein luftiger Schleier aus feinstem, weißem, glitzerndem Schneekristall.

Dann beginnt Elke zu schwingen, gleitet in immer weicheren Bögen hinab, schwingt immer tiefer nach unten. So nähern sie sich gleitend dem Talgrund, das Mädchen und die Ponystute, getragen von der Zugkraft des kleinen Pferdes und dem Schwung der Höhe; eingehüllt in eine weiße Wolke aus glitzerndem Schneestaub.

Das Pony wird langsamer, ihr Gleiten wird sanfter –

und auch der Rausch der Geschwindigkeit vergeht. Das Pony zieht sie sanft das letzte Stück des Hügels hinab.

Sie haben den Grund des Tals erreicht, Lena und Elke. Das Pony wiehert hell, doch ohne stehen zu bleiben beginnt es, sie wieder bergauf zu ziehen.

Sie sieht seinen Atem im Gegenlicht, sieht die kleinen Hufe im Schnee verschwinden. Sie spürt in den langsamer werdenden Schritten die Mühe des Weges bergauf.

Nun beginnt auch sie die Schwere zu spüren. Sie hängt mit den Händen und der Muskelkraft ihrer Arme an den Leinen. Das Pony hält den Kopf gesenkt, die Blicke im nahen Weiß, und zieht sie langsam nach oben.

Als sie dann auf der Höhe sind, lässt Elke das Pony ausruhen.

Sie gleitet zu ihm hinüber und klopft seinen warmen Hals. Lena schnaubt ein paar Mal. Sie hat sich angestrengt, scheint aber nicht erschöpft zu sein. Elke gibt ihr ein paar Zuckerstücke, die Lena eifrig nimmt.

Elke ist durch eine Brieffreundschaft nach Norwegen gekommen. Die Osterferien waren ideal für einen Besuch. Als ihre Brieffreundin Inger im letzten Sommer in Deutschland war, hatte sie Elke eingeladen.

Für Inger war Elkes Stadt ein einziges Abenteuer gewesen. Elke hatte Mühe gehabt, ihre norwegische Freundin daran zu gewöhnen, dass der Autoverkehr mit jungen Radfahrern nicht besonders nachsichtig ist und dass es meistens zu wenig Radwege gibt, auf denen man ungefährdet fahren kann.

Trotzdem, es hatte den beiden viel Spaß gemacht, zusammen zu sein. Und Elke hatte sich sehr gefreut, Ostern nach Norwegen zu kommen.

Sie hatten sie mit einem Schlitten von der Bahnstation abgeholt, und sie war zum ersten Mal im Leben in so einem großen Schlitten gefahren.

Der Bauernhof von Ingers Eltern lag ziemlich weit von der Bahnstation entfernt. Sie waren fast eine Stunde lang mit dem Schlitten zum Hof gefahren.

Zwei stämmige kleine Islandpferde hatten den Schlitten gezogen. Und als sie mit bimmelnden Glöckchen über den glitzernden Schnee geglitten waren, da hatte Elke gewusst, dass die Tage hier in Norwegen schön werden würden!

Es war die erste Reise, die Elke allein machte. Ihre Mutter hatte ein wenig gezögert, ehe sie die Einwilligung dazu gegeben hatte. Doch schließlich hatte sie das Argument überzeugt, dass ja auch Inger allein nach Deutschland gekommen war.

„Und die ist noch jünger als ich!", hatte Elke gesagt.

„Ja", die Mutter hatte gelächelt. „Ganz gewaltig jünger, nämlich genau siebzehn Tage!"

„Jünger bleibt jünger", hatte Elke gelacht.

Nun war sie schon die zweite Woche hier und hatte noch immer kein Heimweh.

122 Elkes Blick fliegt bis zum Horizont, senkt sich dann wieder zu Tal. Und während sie erneut die Leinen fasst, läuft das Pony schon den Hang hinunter.

Und wieder sieht Elke den weißen Glanz vor ihren Augen und spürt das gleichmäßige Gleiten unter den Füßen. Eingehüllt in diese Wolke aus frischem Pulverschnee wird sie von Lena wieder den Hügel hinuntergezogen. Elke hält sich mit beiden Händen an den langen Leinen fest und möchte vor Freude schreien.

Vom Talgrund zieht das Pony sie den nächsten Hang wieder hinauf. Als Lena oben zur Ruhe kommt, steht ihr Atem eine Zeit lang dampfend vor ihren Nüstern, ehe er sanfter und ruhiger wird.

Während Elke noch neben dem Pony steht, fällt Schnee vom Himmel. Elke zieht den rechten Handschuh aus, öffnet die Hand und fängt eine Flocke auf. Da liegt sie auf ihrer warmen Haut: ein zerbrechliches Filigran aus weißem Schneekristall, kalt und ganz leicht. Ein glitzerndes Gebilde liegt in ihrer Hand, hauchfein und zart, vielleicht fünf Herzschläge lang; dann beginnt die Schneeflocke zu schmelzen.

Immer dichter fallen die Flocken über das Land.

Noch einmal sieht Elke über die geschwungenen Hügelwellen aus Weiß, die sich in immer engeren Bogen einander zu nähern scheinen, bis sie am Horizont verschmelzen.

Und während sich ein dichter Flockenvorhang über die Landschaft schiebt, sieht Elke weit unten im Tal den Bauernhof liegen.

Da wird das Pony unruhig. Erwartungsvoll wirft es den Kopf auf.

123

Elke begreift: Es will in den Stall zurück. Schnell fasst sie die Leinen und fährt hinter Lena den letzten Hügel hinab.

Sandras Traumpferde

„Wir müssen mindestens vierzig Kilometer Vorsprung haben, ehe die anderen kommen", hatte Papa gesagt.

„Mindestens vierzig", hatte Opa hinzugefügt, „noch besser wären fünfzig!"

Das war gestern Abend gewesen, nachdem Papa Oma Christa und Opa Erwin abgeholt hatte. Sie wollten diese Nacht bei ihnen bleiben, damit sie am Morgen ganz früh losfahren konnten.

Es war das erste Mal, dass sie mit Oma und Opa Ferien machten. Mama und Oma hatten Opa überredet, in diesem Jahr nicht mit dem eigenen Auto in Urlaub zu fahren. Denn obwohl Opa sich selbst immer noch zu den besten Autofahrern der Welt, na, wenigstens Europas, zählte, er sonst auch noch ziemlich rüstig war, hatten die anderen doch das Gefühl, dass er als Beifahrer einfach besser war als hinter dem Lenkrad. Man durfte es ihm nur nicht sagen, wenigstens nicht so direkt.

Schließlich war es Oma gemeinsam mit Mama dann doch gelungen, ihn zu überreden, sein Auto in diesem Jahr nicht zu benutzen und stattdessen mit ihnen im VW-Bus mitzufahren. Und Sandra hatte nichts dagegen, denn eigentlich kam sie mit den Großeltern gut aus, manchmal sogar besser als mit Mama, besonders wenn es ums Aufräumen und solche Sachen ging.

Natürlich hatten sie schon gepackt, bevor Oma und Opa kamen. Eigentlich hatte das hauptsächlich Mama gemacht. Sandra hatte nur die für sie allerwichtigsten Sachen, zum Beispiel die Reithosen, in ihre Reisetasche gestopft.

„Ich bin fertig!", hatte sie dann gerufen und wollte ganz schnell aus dem Zimmer huschen.

Zuerst hatte die Mutter überhaupt nichts gesagt. Sie nahm nur Sandras Reisetasche und schüttete den Inhalt einfach auf den Tisch.

Verdutzt war Sandra im Türrahmen stehen geblieben, etwas ratlos, wie es schien.

„Damit willst du vier Wochen auskommen?", hatte die Mutter gefragt und auf das Häuflein gedeutet. „Ist das dein Ernst?" Und sie hatte ihre Tochter dabei mit einem Blick angesehen, auf den diese ihr keine rechte Antwort geben konnte. Als Sandra dann das Durcheinander auf dem Tisch zu ordnen begann, half Mama ihr ein bisschen. Und als Papa mit Oma und Opa ankam, war das Urlaubsgepäck bereits fertig gepackt gewesen.

Sie waren sehr zeitig zu Bett gegangen, damit sie am

nächsten Morgen die Reise gut ausgeruht beginnen konnten.

Zuerst hatte sich Sandra noch unruhig herumgewälzt. Immer wieder musste sie an ihr Reiseziel denken. In ihrer Vorstellung sah sie den alten Bauernhof neben dem kleinen See. Sie sah die schwarzen Balken des Fachwerkhauses, die das weiße Mauerwerk umrahmten, sah die gelben Blüten der Sonnenblumen im Garten neben dem Haus und das leuchtende Rot der Geranien.

Sie sah die Wiese am Waldrand und den kleinen Bach, der sich das Tal hinabschlängelte. Und auf der Wiese sah sie die Pferde weiden. Schon hatte sie Winnetou entdeckt, den jungen Rappen, der ihr Lieblingspferd war.

Und während sie sich immer wieder ausmalte, wie Winnetou sich freuen würde, wenn sie ihm zur Begrüßung all die Zuckerstückchen gab, die sie schon seit Wochen in ihrer Anoraktasche versteckte, hatte sie auf einmal das Gefühl, wieder auf seinem Rücken zu sitzen, wie damals. Sie hatte doch ein wenig Angst gehabt, als sie zum allerersten Mal im Leben vor einem richtigen Pferd gestanden hatte.

Der Rappe hatte sie aufmerksam angesehen. Dann schob er seinen Kopf so nah an ihr Gesicht, dass sie seinen warmen Atem spürte, und sog mit geblähten Nüstern ihren Geruch ein. Und auf einmal spürte sie seine weiche Nase an ihrer rechten Wange. Als sie erschrocken zurückweichen wollte, hörte sie den Bauern sagen: „Du, er kann dich gut leiden."

Ehe sie noch überlegen konnte, hatte er sie schon mit einem Schwung auf Winnetous Rücken gesetzt.

Unbeweglich hatte das große Tier dagestanden; es war, als würde es ihre Angst spüren und alles vermeiden wollen, was sie noch mehr beunruhigen konnte.

Sandra versank immer weiter in ihren alten Erinnerungen; sie mischten sich mit ihren Wünschen ... und irgendwann schlief sie ein.

Als Mama sie um halb fünf weckte, war Sandra mitten in einem Traum gewesen, in dem es um Pferde ging. An Einzelheiten konnte sie sich nicht mehr erinnern, nur so viel war sicher: Es war ein schöner Traum gewesen. Deshalb war sie auch ein bisschen sauer, denn eigentlich hätte sie ja an ihrem ersten Ferientag gern länger geschlafen, statt schon um halb fünf mitten aus den schönsten Träumen gerissen zu werden.

Obwohl sich Sandra gleich nach dem Wecken wieder in die Kissen gekuschelt hatte, nützte es nichts, denn nach dem dritten Weckversuch hatte Mama ihr kurzerhand die Bettdecke weggezogen. Da half kein Protest, schließlich wollten sie so früh wie möglich auf der Autobahn sein, um vor den anderen Ferienreisenden jene vierzig bis fünfzig Kilometer Vorsprung zu haben, die Papa und Opa für nötig hielten.

Doch anscheinend hatten das auch eine ganze Menge anderer Leute gedacht. Denn als sie jetzt die Abkürzung zur Autobahn fuhren, die Papa zuvor als seinen „geheimen Schleichweg" bezeichnet hatte, da war es dort trotz der frühen Morgenstunde schon ziemlich voll. Lauter schwer beladene Autos fuhren vor ihnen her, und viele hatten sogar noch Sachen aufs Dach gepackt.

„Das ist wirklich ein echter Schleichweg, mein Junge", sagte Oma. „Wirklich, und so ganz und gar total geheim!"

Papa, der gerade ziemlich schräg *Das Wandern ist des Müllers Lust* gepfiffen hatte, hörte mitten in der Melodie auf. Er räusperte sich. Dann sagte er mit besonderer Betonung: „Besser schlecht gefahren als gut gelaufen, oder?"

„Da könntest du durchaus Recht haben", meinte Opa und versuchte auch *Das Wandern ist des Müllers Lust* zu pfeifen. Es klang nicht besonders. Erst als Oma und Mama mitflöteten, allerdings nicht so falsch wie Papa und Opa, hörten die beiden Männer auf.

Ihren ersten Stau hatten sie am Ende des „geheimen Schleichweges", dort wo er in die große Vorfahrtstraße mündete, die direkt zur Autobahn führte. Dort mussten nämlich alle Autos vor dem Stoppschild anhalten, ehe sie auf die Vorfahrtstraße einbiegen konnten. Das dauerte ziemlich lange.

„Ach, das ist ja nur ein Stauchen", hatte Papa fröhlich gesagt, „das schaffen wir doch mit links!"

„Klar", sagte Opa, „mit so was muss man immer rechnen. Das ist ja heutzutage nicht mehr wie früher, als man mit dem Pferdewagen unterwegs war!"

129

„Pferdewagen fände ich gemütlicher", meinte Oma

lächelnd, „zumindest habe ich damals nie einen Pferde-
wagenstau erlebt!"

Es dauerte tatsächlich nur eine Viertelstunde, dann
waren sie auf der großen Straße – und bald auch schon
auf der Autobahn. Dort ging es dann ziemlich flott weiter. Na ja, so flott eben, wie Papas alter VW-Bus, beladen
mit fünf Personen und dem ganzen Urlaubsgepäck, vo-
rankommen konnte.

Es war ein schöner sonniger Vormittag und sie waren
inzwischen ihrem Reiseziel schon ein Stück näher gekommen – wenn auch längst nicht so weit, wie Papa das
ursprünglich vorgehabt hatte. Ein paar ziemlich lang-
same Viertelstunden hatte es gegeben und zwei- oder
dreimal mussten sie auch fast stehen bleiben. Aber so
einen ganz dicken Stau wie im letzten Jahr, in den waren
sie diesmal noch nicht geraten.

Opa Erwin, der neben Oma Christa in der zweiten
Reihe saß, war eigentlich ganz fröhlich und gut gelaunt.
Er hatte Papa zwar einige Male ein paar Ratschläge gegeben, wie er nach seiner Ansicht besser und schneller
fahren könnte, aber nachdem ihm Oma einmal den Ellbogen ziemlich kräftig in die Rippen gestoßen hatte, ließ
er Papa allein fahren.

Sandra saß auf der letzten Bank im Bus, sie hatte sich
in ein Buch mit Pferdegeschichten vertieft. So verging ihr
die Zeit am schnellsten.

Es musste so gegen Mittag sein, als sie an einer Auto-
bahnbrücke das große Schild *Vorsicht Stau!* bemerkten.

„Deine fünfzig Kilometer Vorsprung sind jetzt wohl endgültig futsch", sagte Oma zu Opa.

„Na, bis jetzt sind wir aber doch ganz gut durchgekommen", bemerkte Opa, als der Vater bremste.

Ganz langsam rollten sie in drei endlos langen Reihen dicht an dicht über die Autobahn. Sie fuhren immer langsamer. Dann saßen sie fest. Doch schon nach ein paar Minuten ging es wieder weiter, allerdings stockend und so langsam, dass man zu Fuß hätte mitgehen können. Aber nach einem knappen Kilometer war auch das zu Ende. Jetzt standen sie endgültig, Stoßstange an Stoßstange, und ihr VW-Bus mittendrin.

Heiß brannte die Sommersonne vom wolkenlosen Himmel.

Im Auto wurde es immer wärmer. Mama hatte die Fenster heruntergekurbelt und verteilte lauwarmen Sprudel.

Inzwischen war die Sonne bis zur Mittagshöhe gestiegen und trotz der geöffneten Fenster wurde es im Wagen nun unerträglich heiß.

Sandra hörte auf zu lesen. „So eine Affenhitze!", sagte sie.

„Wo hast du denn diese Weisheit her?", fragte Vater erstaunt. „Etwa aus der Schule?"

„Guck in den Spiegel", antwortete seine Tochter und lachte ihn an.

Oma kicherte, Opa drehte sich zu Sandra um. „Ich dachte, du wärst eingeschlafen", sagte er.

Mama warf Sandra einen verstohlenen Blick zu und lächelte. Papa wischte sich den Schweiß von der Stirn, sagte aber nichts.

Sandra starrte wieder angestrengt in ihr Buch.

Nun begannen einige Leute aus ihren Autos auszusteigen und sahen nach vorn. Aber die Wagenkolonne rührte sich nicht von der Stelle.

Sandra versuchte wieder zu lesen, doch die Hitze machte ihr zu schaffen, und immer noch standen sie auf der gleichen Stelle. „Wenn ich doch bloß ein Pferd hätte", seufzte sie plötzlich und klappte ihr Buch zu. „Dann bräuchte ich hier nicht rumzuhocken und meine Schweißperlen zu zählen! Dann wäre ich nämlich gar nicht weggefahren, sondern bei meinem Pferd geblieben!"

Oma lachte. „Das Glück dieser Erde liegt für deine Tochter auf dem Rücken der Pferde!", sagte sie zu Sandras Mutter.

„Glück im Lotto wäre mir lieber", bemerkte Opa Erwin. „Auf dem Rücken der Pferde ist es mir zu gefährlich!"

Vater drehte sich nach hinten um und lächelte etwas gequält. „Was ist schon ein Pferd gegen diese achtzig PS hier", sagte er und klopfte dabei gegen das Lenkrad des Busses. „Achtzig Pferdestärken unter der Motorhaube sind achtzigmal so viel wie ein einzelnes Pferd. Ihr werdet ja sehen, wie wir gleich losbrausen, wenn der Stau zu Ende ist."

„Ja, wenn." Mama kurbelte nervös an ihrer Fensterscheibe, obwohl die doch schon ganz weit unten war.

Wozu brauche ich achtzig PS, dachte Sandra, *mir würde ein einziges Pferd genügen!* Laut sagte sie: „Na ja, ewig kann das hier auch nicht dauern!" Sie wusste aus Erfahrung, dass man Papa nicht aufregen durfte, wenn man so lange wie jetzt im Stau stand.

Der Vater sagte nichts. Er blickte ziemlich angestrengt durch die Windschutzscheibe, obwohl es dort vorn nichts Neues zu sehen gab. Denn vor ihnen stand noch immer der große Wohnwagen, der hinten auch noch zwei Motorräder auf einem Gestell angehängt hatte.

Rechts neben sie hatte sich ein riesiger Lastwagen geschoben. Er stand so dicht neben ihrem Bus und war so hoch und lang, dass Sandra nur die graue Wand des großen Anhängers sehen konnte. Hinter ihnen war ein zweiter Lastwagen herangefahren. Er war so nahe gekommen, dass es aussah, als wollte er seinen riesigen Kühler durch ihre Heckscheibe schieben.

Links von ihrem Bus stand ein großer Wagen, der auf dem Dach zwei Paddelboote hatte. Sie waren ziemlich lang und ragten vorn und hinten noch ein Stück über den Wagen hinaus.

So standen sie seit einer halben Stunde eingekeilt im dichten Stau, und die Sonne schien und schien, und die Luft wurde immer heißer. Die Hitze flimmerte über der Autobahn.

Nun war das nicht Sandras erster Ferienstau. Spätestens seit ihren allerersten Schulferien hatte sie auf jeder Autoreise regelmäßig ihre Stauerlebnisse gehabt. Zwar wurden die Staus jedes Jahr länger, was Sandra bescheuert fand, aber sie wusste auch, dass es ihren Bus keinen Zentimeter weiterbrachte, wenn man sich aufregte. Sie machte es sich auf dem Rücksitz so bequem wie möglich, schob das Gepäck, so gut es ging, zusammen, kuschelte sich in eine Ecke und versuchte wieder in ihren Pferdegeschichten zu lesen.

Die Hitze wurde aber immer unerträglicher. Das Lesen wurde mühsamer. Manchmal verschwammen Sandra die Buchstaben vor den Augen. Es wurde noch wärmer im Auto, immer wärmer …

Als das erste Wiehern zu hören war, drehte sich der Vater zu Sandra um. „Lass das!", rief er nach hinten.

Ehe sie antworten konnte, wieherte es zum zweiten Mal.

Jetzt geriet Mutter in Verdacht.

Doch da wieherte es zum dritten Mal.

Vater sah ratlos von Mutter zu Oma und Opa und dann wieder zur Mutter zurück. Er machte den Mund auf und wollte gerade etwas sagen, da wieherte es wieder. Jetzt aber viel lauter.

Mit einem Ruck drehte sich Vater um und starrte nach hinten.

Genau in diesem Augenblick sprang die Motorhaube auf. Sie schoss so plötzlich in die Höhe, dass sie alle fünf wie angewurzelt dasaßen.

Und dann hob sich langsam ein Pferdekopf aus dem Motorraum nach oben. Schon schaute das Pferd mit großen Augen durch die breite Rückscheibe in den Wagen.

„Was ist das?", fragte Mama, sie schien echt erschrocken zu sein.

Gerade wollte Sandra halb im Scherz sagen: „Das nennt man wohl ein Pferd!" – da begann der Rotfuchs schon aus dem Motorraum zu klettern.

Sandra hielt den Atem an, denn kaum war der Fuchs draußen, da kam schon das nächste Pferd nach oben.

Nach dem siebten Pferd schrie Vater plötzlich: „Um Gottes willen, mein VW-Bus hat achtzig PS!"

Ohne zu drängeln kletterten die Pferde zügig aus dem Motorraum. Kaum war eins draußen, tauchte auch schon der nächste Kopf auf. Als dann das neunundsiebzigste Tier draußen war – die letzten fünf waren übrigens Ponys – hörte Sandra ein vertrautes Wiehern.

Das kann doch nicht wahr sein!, dachte sie. Doch da streckte Winnetou schon seinen schönen Kopf aus dem Motorraum. Er zeigte die Zähne und wieherte, als würde er lachen.

„He, Winnetou!", rief Sandra und schob die Tür des Busses auf. Mit einem Satz war sie draußen. Schon stand sie neben dem Rappen, der seine Nüstern sanft an ihrer Schulter rieb.

„Komm sofort in den Bus zurück!", rief Vater.

Und Opa meinte: „Also, das ist doch die Höhe!"

Aber da saß Sandra schon auf Winnetous Rücken.

Die Autobahn wimmelte jetzt von Pferden, wohin man auch blickte. Überall waren weiße, schwarze, braune und gefleckte Pferde und Ponys zu sehen; viele Rassen in jeder Größe waren da. Sie tänzelten elegant zwischen den unbeweglich dastehenden Autos im Stau hin und her.

Für Sandra war das der schönste Anblick, den sie sich vorstellen konnte!

Inzwischen begannen immer mehr Kinder auf die Rücken der Pferde zu steigen. Und plötzlich sah es so aus, als wären nur Kinder im Stau.

„Mir nach!", rief Sandra plötzlich.

Winnetou sprang mit einem hellen Wiehern über das nächste Auto.

Sandra spürte Wind in den Haaren. Weit dehnte sich das Land vor ihren Blicken aus und ihr war, als berührten die Hufe des Pferdes den Boden nicht mehr. In gestrecktem Galopp jagten sie dahin, eine weite Ebene entlang, die sich in wechselnden Farben bis zum Horizont breitete.

Sandra lag über den Hals des Pferdes gebeugt. Sie hörte das Pfeifen des Windes in seiner Mähne. Auf einmal spürte sie, wie sich der Schlag ihres Herzens mit dem des Tieres verband. Und mit jedem Sprung, bei jedem Schritt fühlte sie, wie sie freier wurde. So flog sie über das weite Land, sicher getragen auf dem breiten Rücken des Pferdes. Irgendwann sah sie dann in der Ferne das Meer. Auf fliehenden Hufen flogen sie ihm entgegen.

Sandra hatte keine Angst, als sie den Strand erreichten

und in die Brandung tauchten. Sie ritt mit Winnetou durch die aufspritzenden Wellen, sicher und leicht. Und Sandra wunderte sich nicht einen einzigen Augenblick, dass das Wasser sie nicht berührte. Das Rauschen des Meeres verwandelte sich plötzlich in ein Flügelschlagen. Schon flogen sie empor.

Sandra sah, dass sich an den Flanken des Rappen Flügel bewegten; seidig schimmerndes Weiß des Gefieders, glänzend im Licht der Sonne.

Als sie nach unten blickte, sah sie die anderen Kinder. Sie flogen, so wie sie, auf ihren Pferden dem hellblauen Sommerhimmel entgegen. Mit leichten Flügelschlägen trieben sie durch das Himmelsblau. Sie sahen aus wie ein Schwarm großer, fremdartiger Vögel, deren Schwingen im Licht der Sonne wie weiße Muschelschalen blinkten.

Weit unter sich in der Tiefe sah Sandra die Autobahn. Eine endlos lange Autoreihe kroch sehr langsam über die Erde. Die Wagen fuhren so dicht, dass es schien, als wären sie miteinander verbunden. Es war, als bewege sich ein riesenlanger, endloser Blechwurm über die Oberfläche der Erde. *Autoschlange*, dachte Sandra und bemerkte auf einmal, dass alle Autos rückwärts fuhren.

Und während sie sich noch darüber wunderte, flogen sie höher hinauf. Sie stiegen immer weiter nach oben. So hoch flogen sie hinauf, dass sich schließlich das Blau des Himmels in tiefe Schwärze verwandelte, aus der unzählige Sterne leuchteten. Aber sie flogen noch weiter, immer weiter hinauf. Sie flogen so hoch, dass Sandra die

Erde als Kugel sehen konnte. Und sie sah diese riesige Kugel immer kleiner werden, bis es schien, als sei sie nur noch ein zartblauer Luftballon. Von feinem Blau umhüllt, so drehte sich die Erde jetzt tief unter den Kindern; und sie sah so klein und zerbrechlich aus, dass Sandra Angst um sie bekam …

Der Vater ließ den Motor anspringen, der Stau begann sich aufzulösen.

Sandra erwachte. „Wo ist denn Winnetou?", fragte sie schlaftrunken.

„Wer?", fragte die Mutter.

„Auf der Autobahn gibt's keine Indianer", bemerkte der Vater und schaltete in den zweiten Gang.

Sandra murmelte etwas Unverständliches zur Antwort. Dann fragte sie: „Und wo sind die anderen Pferde?"

„Welche Pferde?", wollte Opa wissen.

Der Vater hatte inzwischen in den dritten Gang geschaltet und versuchte gerade einen Lastwagen zu überholen.

„Deine Enkelin sieht Indianer und Pferde auf der Autobahn", sagte Opa Erwin zu Oma Christa. „Mitten am hellen Tag und im dichtesten Ferienverkehr. Vielleicht kümmerst du dich um das Kind!"

Oma hatte sich zu Sandra umgedreht. Doch ehe sie etwas sagen konnte, hatte sich das Mädchen schon wieder auf der Rückbank zusammengerollt. Sie hatte den Kopf auf ihre große Reisetasche gelegt und hielt die Augen geschlossen.

„Möchtest du was trinken?", fragte jetzt die Mutter. Sandra hielt die Augen geschlossen. „Die ganze Autobahn ist voller Pferde", sagte sie leise, „tausend und abertausend Pferde."

Der Vater schien es gehört zu haben. „Aber klar", meinte er und gab noch etwas mehr Gas. „Und auch ich lasse jetzt meine achtzig PS über die Fahrbahn galoppieren!"

„Winnetou kann fliegen", murmelte Sandra kaum noch verständlich, „und die Erde ... die Erde ist ... eine kleine blaue Kugel ..."

„Wir sollten das Kind schlafen lassen", sagte Oma jetzt leise nach vorn.

Der Vater schaute in den Innenspiegel. Dann schaltete er in den dritten Gang zurück und steuerte den VW-Bus vorsichtig in eine Lücke zwischen zwei schwer beladenen Autos, die ziemlich langsam auf der äußersten rechten Spur fuhren. „Wir müssen ja nicht unbedingt mit fünfzig Kilometern Vorsprung ankommen", flüsterte er.

„Auch nicht mit vierzig", flüsterte Opa Erwin.

„Müssen wir wirklich nicht", sagte nun auch die Mutter ganz leise. „Hauptsache ist, wir kommen gut an!"

Der letzte Ritt

Unter den Hufen der Strand, zitterndes Weiß im Licht des Mondes, aber fest genug für den Tritt.

Sie schienen zu fliegen, im weit ausgreifenden Schwung der Beine, als würden die Hufe den feinen Sand überhaupt nicht berühren; als würden sie eine Handbreit über dem Boden auf eine unsichtbare federnde Schicht treffen, die sie jedes Mal wieder nach oben warf. Doch ihre Spuren im feuchten Sand bewiesen, dass sie die Erde trafen. Sicher und fest.

Der Mond stand voll und silbern über dem Meer. Weiß schäumend warfen sich die Wellen der beginnenden Flut gegen den weiten Strand. Schaumspitzen fielen über den Sand, breiteten sich aus, ehe sie unter dem schäumenden Weiß der neuen Wellen verschwanden, sich mit ihnen vermischten und dann erloschen.

Er lag weit über den Hals des Pferdes gebeugt, fühlte jede Regung des federnden Körpers, passte sich ihr an. Er spürte das sanfte Peitschen der langen Mähne in sei-

nem Gesicht, hörte das Pfeifen des Windes im flattern-
den Haar und fühlte sich frei.

Zu seiner Rechten das Meer. Ausgebreitet bis zum
funkelnden Zitterhorizont; ein weites, schimmerndes,
lebendiges Netz aus Wellen und Mondlicht, Reflexen
und bewegtem Wasser.

Und links die Kuppen der Dünen – Urzeittiere aus
Sand, die im Mondlicht schliefen.

Sie jagten über den Strand, galoppierten zwischen der
rauschenden, blinkenden Flut und den Hügeln unbeweg-
licher Dünen. Sie spürten die enge Verbundenheit dieser
Gemeinsamkeit, fühlten das Aufeinander-Angewiesen-
sein in dieser Nacht. Und vor ihnen flog der gemeinsame
Schatten ihres Rittes über den silbernen Sand und machte
sie frei und stark.

Als die Flut den Strand immer weiter zusammen-
schob, zwang sie die Enge zur Langsamkeit. Dann, als
die Wellen nur noch einen schmalen Streifen Sand übrig
gelassen hatten, kehrten sie um.

Als sie im flachen Wasser zurücktrabten, spritzten
kleine Wellenkämme um die Beine des Pferdes – und der
Mondlichtschatten ihrer Reitergestalt lief jetzt hinter
ihnen her über die bewegte Flut.

Später, als sie die Dünen erklommen hatten, ein Rei-
terstandbild zwischen Mond und Meer, sah er noch einmal zum Horizont hinüber. Er sah das silberne Netz aus
Wellenkämmen, ausgebreitet zwischen Horizont und
Land, blickte auf die sanften Hügel der bläulich weißen

Dünen, wo in der Ferne das regelmäßige Streifenlicht des Leuchtturms blitzte.

Dann senkte er seine Blicke auf das Silberfell des Pferdes, auf dem das Mondlicht den Schweiß zu winzigen Perlen geformt hatte. Er neigte seinen Kopf so tief gegen den Hals des Pferdes, bis seine Wange das Fell berührte. Er spürte die Wärme der feuchten Haut und das Pulsieren des Blutes in der Halsschlagader. Dann griff er mit beiden Händen um den Hals des Apfelschimmels und hatte für einen Augenblick das Gefühl, die Zeit sei stehen geblieben.

Opa hatte Jens mitten in der Nacht geweckt. Verschlafen war ihm der Junge in den Stall gefolgt. Nun standen sie vor dem alten Pferd. Es lag so still da, als ob es schliefe.

„Der Tierarzt wird bald kommen", sagte Opa leise.

Jens schaute auf den alten Apfelschimmel. „Ist es schlimm?", fragte er dann.

Opa antwortete nicht, er schwieg eine ganze Weile. Schließlich sagte er: „Leo ist sehr alt, mein Junge. Er ist fast dreimal so alt wie du."

Er machte eine Pause und schien zu überlegen:

„Wenn er ein Mensch wäre, dann wäre er jetzt uralt."

„Älter als du?", fragte Jens.

142   Ein winziges Lächeln huschte über das Gesicht des alten Mannes und machte es für Augenblicke jung.

„Älter als ich", sagte Opa, „noch älter!"

„Und du hast den Leo schon gekannt, als er noch jung war?"

„Ich war sogar bei seiner Geburt dabei", antwortete Opa, „und ich war auch der Erste, der ihn ritt." Er lächelte wieder ein wenig. „Du kannst dir das sicher nicht vorstellen, dein alter Opa auf einem pfeilschnellen Apfelschimmel?"

„Doch, doch", sagte Jens ein Spur zu schnell, „doch, kann ich!"

Sie waren losgestürmt, als hätte ein Pfeil die Bogensehne verlassen. So dicht lag er über dem Rücken des Pferdes, dass sie zu einem Wesen verschmolzen schienen, hätte man sie aus der Ferne gesehen.

Sie jagten den flachen Hügel hinab zu Tal. Vor ihnen, in der Weite der grünen Gräser, nur unterbrochen von kleinen Büschen, breitete sich die Ebene aus.

Die Mittagssonne warf einen sehr kurzen Schatten ins Grün. Er ritt rechts neben ihnen über das Gras, huschte über die Büsche und glitt mit ihnen zu Tal.

Der Körper des Pferdes streckte sich, zog sich wieder zusammen, streckte sich wieder; unglaublich schnell, im galoppierenden Rhythmus, so federten seine Hufe über das Gras, preschten zwischen den Büschen dahin, ließen den Körper des Reiters an den wilden Bewegungen teilnehmen; gaben ihm das Gefühl, für winzige Augenblicke im Flug zu sein.

Dann kam der Wald. Dunkel reckten sich seine hohen Stämme dem klaren Blau entgegen. Sie trugen den dichten Baldachin aus Blättern, der das Sonnenlicht filterte und nur gedämpft einließ. Schon waren sie in das grünliche Halbdunkel eingetaucht. Ein toter Baumstamm lag quer in ihrer Bahn. Ohne zu zögern flog der Apfelschimmel hinüber, setzte mit den Vorderhufen auf, die Hinterhand folgte. Dann fand das Pferd den Weg, es begann zu traben.

Jens kauerte sich neben den alten Apfelschimmel nieder. Er hörte ihn leise keuchen und sah, wie sich seine Flanken langsam hoben und senkten. Vorsichtig legte er seine Hand auf das feuchte graue Fell und spürte den Schweiß zwischen seinen Fingern und auf seiner Handfläche. Er streichelte Leos Hals, strich ihm langsam über die eisgraue Mähne. Dann sah er fragend zum Großvater empor.

Opa räusperte sich. Als er dann zu sprechen begann, war seine Stimme sehr leise. „Der Leo…", sagte er und stockte, er suchte nach Worten. Er räusperte sich wieder. „Ich dachte", sagte er dann, „du solltest es wissen, schließlich kennst du den Leo so lange, wie du lebst!"

Jens senkte den Kopf.

144 „Er war das erste Pferd, auf dem du gesessen hast", sagte der alte Mann, und seine Stimme war nur noch ein heiseres Flüstern.

Sie waren zum Fluss geritten, der alte Mann und das Kind. Langsam war der Apfelschimmel über den Uferweg gegangen. Ab und zu blieb er stehen um zu grasen.

„Hüh, Leo, hüh!", hatte der Junge dann gerufen.

Der alte Mann, der hinter ihm saß, hielt ihn fest umschlungen. „Er hat Hunger", hatte er dem Kind erklärt, „er muss uns ja beide tragen."

Dann war das Pferd ins Wasser gewatet. In langen und durstigen Zügen hatte der Apfelschimmel das kühle Wasser getrunken, bis zu den Knien im strömenden Fluss.

Der Reiter hielt mit der linken Hand die Zügel, mit der rechten das Kind. Schließlich reichte er dem Jungen die Zügel. „Fest halten!", sagte er dabei. „Mit beiden Händen!"

Dann beugte er sich hinab, tauchte die linke Hand in den Fluss und kühlte sich damit das Gesicht. Dann klopfte er mit der freien Hand sanft den Hals des Pferdes.

Der Apfelschimmel hob den Kopf vom Wasser empor und sah ihn an. Er schnaubte, dann wieherte er leise.

Der Tierarzt war gekommen. „Soll der Junge hier bleiben?", fragte er den Großvater.

Jens, der an der Tür gestanden hatte, trat zwei Schritte näher.

Großvater sah den Jungen an.

„Ich bleibe", sagte Jens leise.

„Na gut", sagte der Arzt, „geh aber lieber ein Stückchen zurück, man kann nie wissen!"

Jens wich bis zur Wand zurück, lehnte sich dagegen. Er hatte seine Hände zu Fäusten geschlossen und presste sie krampfhaft gegen die rauen Ziegel der Wand. Als sich seine Fingernägel in die Haut seiner Hände gruben, spürte er keinen Schmerz.

„Sie brauchen sich keine Sorgen zu machen", sagte der Tierarzt zu Großvater, als er die Spritze aufzog. „Es wird ihm nicht wehtun."

Der alte Mann antwortete nicht. Er ging zu dem liegenden Pferd und kniete vor ihm nieder. Er streichelte seinen Hals. Langsam versuchte der alte Apfelschimmel den Kopf ein wenig zu drehen. Er mühte sich sehr. Dann sah er den hageren Mann an. Der Alte neigte sich noch tiefer hinab. Es fiel ihm sichtlich schwer. Nun war er so tief gebeugt, dass sein Gesicht den Kopf des Pferdes berührte. Er schlang seine Arme um den schweißfeuchten Hals des Apfelschimmels und hielt ihn ganz fest. Als die Injektionsnadel des Tierarztes die Haut des Tieres durchstach und er das Zucken des todkranken Pferdes spürte, da begann er laut zu weinen.

Rotes Land

Weit in der Ferne sah sie den Tafelberg. Er stieg aus dem Rot der Wüste wie ein gigantischer Amboss empor, blaugrau im zitternden Dunst der Hitze.

Die Mittagssonne stand hoch im Zenit. Mary zog das Kinnband ihres Hutes fester. Dann drückte sie dem Hengst die Stiefel in die Weichen. Schnaubend stieg der Schimmel ein wenig empor, ehe er in die Ebene lief.

Endlich hielt Mary ihn leicht zurück und parierte ihn aus dem Trab zum Schritt. Es war heiß, er sollte jetzt nicht mehr laufen.

Um sie das rote Land, nur unterbrochen von grünen Inseln, die fast in der Röte verschwanden. Kärgliche Reste von Vegetation im Rot des Outbacks.

Sie ritt wohl zwei Stunden der Sonne entgegen, ehe das Grün sich verstärkte. Und aus den kleinen Inseln aus Gras waren nun kleine Büsche geworden.

Ein unbewegliches Gebilde im Dunstlicht der Ferne, jetzt aber zu gelblichem Blau umgeschmolzen, so stand noch immer am Horizont der riesige Amboss des Tafelberges.

Mary schien ihm kaum näher gekommen zu sein, bei ihrem langen Ritt über den staubigen roten Boden. Und durch den unruhigen Dunst der heiß zitternden Mittagsluft sah sie die große monolithische Gestalt hoch über die Wüste ragen.

Als die ersten Büsche die Größe von kleineren Kindern erreichten, sah sie ein Känguru springen. Es war durch die Büsche zu sehen, hatte graubraunes Fell und sprang mit kräftigen Sätzen zu ihrer rechten Seite davon.

Als Mary vorübergeritten war, blieb das Känguru stehen. Es stand noch eine Weile da und sah ihr nach. Aus seinem Fellbeutel heraus blickte neugierig ein Kängurukind.

Mary war am Morgen von der Farm ins Outback geritten. Sie tat es nicht zum ersten Mal. Seit zwei Jahren schon, immer wenn sie ihren ältesten Bruder besuchte, wagte sie sich ins rote Land.

Sie lebte in Sydney und ging dort zur Schule. Sydney war eine große Stadt; eine besondere Großstadt allerdings mit ihren verwinkelten Buchten am Pazifischen Ozean und modernen Gebäuden im Zentrum. Obwohl eine Millionenstadt, war Sydneys Atmosphäre doch freundlich geblieben.

148   Mary lebte gern in dieser Stadt, doch wenn sie zu ihrem Bruder kam, hatte sie Sydney beinahe vergessen.

Der Schimmel trug sie dem Tafelberg zu. Umgeben

vom Rostglanz der Wüste, so ritt sie dem riesigen Felsen entgegen, behielt ihn als Zielpunkt vor Augen. Hoch über dem Horizont ragte er in das strahlende Blau des Himmels. Sein oberer Teil bildete eine Fläche, die sich weit nach allen Seiten dehnte. Es sah aus, als hätte vor Urzeiten ein Riese mit einem gigantischen Messer den Gipfel vom Berg geschnitten, sodass nur der Rumpf blieb.

Sie gab dem Schimmel die Zügel frei, er ließ entspannt den Kopf sinken.

Und während sie zwischen den grünen Inseln der Büsche dahinritt, an Gesträuch vorüber, dem mächtigen Felsen entgegen, dachte sie plötzlich an Sydney. Sie sah für Augenblicke die gewaltigen weißen Muscheln des Opernhauses im Nachmittagslicht, sah blaue Wellen im Hafen blitzen. Doch schon hatte die Wüste diese Bilder verschluckt und brachte das Mädchen ins Outback zurück. Das rote Land hatte ihre Gedanken wieder gefangen.

Vor ihr der steinerne Amboss, jetzt aber in mehr gelblichem Blau, der sich über der Wüste erhob. Mary sah hinüber, sie dachte daran, dass sich der Fels später, im Abendlicht, zu Violett wandeln würde.

Ihr Bruder John lebte schon längere Zeit auf der Farm, die dem Schwiegervater gehörte. Damals, als John seine Frau kennen lernte, hatten sie eine Zeit lang gezögert, ob sie die Farm dem Leben in der großen Stadt vorziehen sollten. Nun hatte sich John an das Leben dort so gewöhnt, dass ihm seine Geburtsstadt Sydney fast fremd geworden war.

Marys Bruder war zwanzig Jahre älter als sie, das machte ihn ihr fast zum Vater. Und manchmal, wenn sie mit ihm und seiner Frau ins Outback ritt, nannte sie das in fröhlicher Übertreibung einen Ausflug mit ihren Pflegeeltern.

Mary ritt durch die Wüste, deren Farben im Nachmittagslicht deutlicher wurden: Leuchtendes Gelb, verschiedene Töne von Braun und zartes Violett begannen sich ins Rotgrün des Outbacks zu mischen.

Als sie zur Wasserstelle kamen, die klein war und seicht, schnaubte der Schimmel. Mary stieg vom Pferd und nahm ihm das Sattelzeug ab. Es war ein anstrengender Ritt gewesen. Sie strich über die Mähne des Schimmels, er senkte den Kopf und trank in durstigen Zügen.

Einmal hatte Mary diesen Ort in der Regenzeit gesehen. Der winzige Tümpel war damals ein reißender Fluss gewesen. Und das rote Land ringsumher war grün gewesen und von Wildblumen übersät, schöner als jeder Garten.

Sie hatte in der Schule gelernt, dass die australische Wüste vor langer Zeit sehr fruchtbar gewesen war. Ein üppig grüner Pflanzenteppich hatte den roten Boden bedeckt.

150 Sie hatte die Reste dieser großen Fruchtbarkeit bei einem Ausflug nach Palm Valley gesehen, einer geschützten Wüstenoase im Süden von Alice Springs. Diese Oase

ist heute noch mit uralten Palmen bestanden, die aus jener Zeit stammen, da das Outback nicht von leuchtendem Rot, sondern üppigem Grün bedeckt war.

Jetzt war der wilde Fluss der Regenzeit nur noch eine kleine Wasserstelle für Tiere. Doch jeder Wassertropfen in der Wüste war wertvoll und den Eingeborenen heilig.

Sie wusste es aus der Schule, dass die Aborigines seit 50 000 Jahren auf diesem Kontinent zu Hause waren. Sie hatten im Einklang mit der Natur gelebt, auch in den großen Wüsten, ja, besonders dort. 50 000 Jahre, eine unvorstellbar lange Zeit. Mary sah über die Weite des Landes, hinüber zum Tafelberg. In der Nähe hatte sie eine Felsmalerei gesehen. Es gab viele Felsenbilder im Land. Sie waren über den ganzen Kontinent verstreut und oftmals in Höhlen versteckt.

Manche der Bilder, mit weißer Farbe auf Felswände aufgetragen, waren mehr als zehntausend Jahre alt. Es waren die Kultstätten der Eingeborenen und sie erzählten von einer uralten Vergangenheit, die sie Traumzeit nannten.

Marys Bruder, der mit Aborigines befreundet war, hatte ihr viel davon erzählt; auch von den langen Wanderungen der Eingeborenen auf ihren geheimen Wegen, die sie Traumpfade nennen.

„Manche Aborigines waren früher sehr lange unterwegs, oft quer durch den ganzen Kontinent. Sie mussten die riesigen Entfernungen zu Fuß zurücklegen, denn es gab für sie kein anderes Transportmittel als ihre Beine."

Mary hatte an ihren Wochenendflug von Sydney nach Alice Springs gedacht, dem roten Zentrum des Kontinents. Von dort hatte ihr Bruder sie mit seinem kleinen Flugzeug zur Farm geflogen. In wenigen Stunden hatte sie mehr als zweitausend Kilometer zurückgelegt. Auch wenn sie mit dem Zug gefahren wäre, hätte sie Alice Springs frühestens in zwei Tagen erreicht. Doch wie lange sie zu Fuß hätte gehen müssen, das wusste sie nicht. „Das kann ich mir überhaupt nicht vorstellen", hatte sie zu ihrem Bruder gesagt, „zu Fuß von Sydney durchs Outback bis zu euch!"

Seine Frau und er hatten darüber gelacht.

„Das kann ich mir auch nicht vorstellen", hatte John gesagt. „Wenigstens ein gutes Pferd wäre auf so einem langen Weg dein zuverlässiger Begleiter gewesen."

„Die Aborigines kannten keine Pferde", hatte seine Frau hinzugefügt, „sie waren selbst bei den längsten Traumpfaden auf ihre Füße angewiesen."

„Sie hatten ja auch mehr Zeit als ich", hatte Mary geantwortet. „50 000 lange Jahre!"

Traumzeit, dachte Mary. Sie sah den ersten Ghost Gum leuchten; so nannten sie den weißrindigen Eukalyptusbaum. Hell stand seine glatte schneeweiße Rinde vor dem tiefen Blau des Wüstenhimmels, umgeben vom roten Ton der Erde, die sich immer mehr in grünes Grasland verwandelte. *Traumzeit*, dachte das Mädchen und sah zum Tafelberg hinüber. Sie waren ihm so nahe gekommen, dass sie jetzt seine steinernen Formationen bemerkte. In waagerechter Anordnung zogen sich farbige Streifen quer durch den Berg, die sich in Schichten überlagerten. Sie waren von leicht ockerfarbenem Braun und einem hellen Graublau, immer wieder unterbrochen von grünlichen Streifen.

Als habe der Schimmel die Nähe der Farm gewittert, federte er über das Land. Mary ließ ihn gewähren. Und während des schnellen Ritts dachte sie an die Traumzeit der Aborigines, an die seltsamen Wesen und die bizarren Tiere, die sie auf den Höhlenbildern gesehen hatte. *Die Aborigines kannten keine Pferde*, dachte Mary, *50 000 Jahre lang!* Das war ihr ebenso unvorstellbar wie der Gedanke, dass sie nie mehr auf dem Rücken eines Pferdes sitzen würde.

Das Sternenpferd

Es war in der großen Pause gewesen. Irina ging so dicht an Konny vorüber, dass sie ihn streifte. Unauffällig blickte er ihr aus den Augenwinkeln nach und sah, dass sie die linke Hand um die rechte Faust legte und beide Daumen nach oben hielt. Das war ihr verabredetes Geheimzeichen, wenn einer den anderen ganz allein sprechen wollte.

Irina ging weiter, bis zu den Fahrradständern. Und Konny, der mit Heiko und Stefan zusammengestanden hatte, trennte sich kurz darauf von den beiden und ging, lässig vor sich hin pfeifend, in die gleiche Richtung.

Irina fummelte schon an ihrem Gepäckträger herum, als Konny kam. Sofort machte er sich an seinem Lenker zu schaffen.

„Die Stella soll verwurstet werden!", flüsterte Irina.

Konny hielt mitten in der Bewegung inne. Er stand für einen Augenblick wie erstarrt da. „Sie soll *was* werden?", fragte er nach einer Pause.

„Mensch, hast du aber 'ne lange Leitung!", flüsterte Irina aufgeregt. „Und schrei um Gottes willen nicht so rum!"

Konny schaute sich unauffällig um. „Was ist mit Stella?", flüsterte er schließlich.

„Sie wollen sie verwursten", wiederholte Irina rasch. „Im Schlachthof!"

„So ein Quatsch, das glaube ich nicht." Konny wischte mit dem Jackenärmel über seine Fahrradklingel. „Der alte Prottka würde das nie machen!"

Irina nickte. „Der Prottka bestimmt nicht, aber sein Sohn!"

„Ich wusste gar nicht, dass Prottka einen Sohn hat", sagte Konny.

„Und was für einen!" Irinas Stimme war nun so laut geworden, dass Konny jetzt „Pst!" machte.

„So ein Mist!", flüsterte Irina und schaute sich um.

Konny sah sich ebenfalls um, denn so was ist ansteckend. „Was ist nun mit Stella?", fragte er dann hastig. „Los, erzähl!"

„Sie soll verwurstet werden", behauptete Irina nun schon zum dritten Mal. „Ehrlich!"

„Quatsch mit Soße!", meinte Konny.

„Doch, ich hab's selber gehört!"

„Das kannst du einem erzählen, der sich die Hose mit der Kneifzange anzieht", meinte Konny. „Das ist doch glatt 'ne Räuberstory, glaub ich einfach nicht!"

„Das ist keine Räuberstory." Irina schien beleidigt zu

sein. „Seit wann erzähl ich dir Räuberstorys? Und dann noch in der großen Pause!"

„Reg dich nicht auf!" Konny ging in die Hocke und sah so interessiert auf die Speichen seines Vorderrades, als wären sie eines der sieben Weltwunder, von denen ihr Geschichtslehrer ihnen erzählt hatte. „So war das doch nicht gemeint!"

Irina ließ den Dynamo an den vorderen Reifen schnappen, zog ihn wieder zurück, sagte aber nichts.

„Ich meine nur", Konny tat, als schraube er an seinem Ventil herum, „dass der alte Prottka ganz sicher was dagegen machen würde, wenn sein Sohn auch nur versuchen sollte, der Stella ans Fell zu gehen."

„Würde er", flüsterte Irina zurück, „wenn er könnte."

„Was heißt denn das schon wieder?"

„Der Prottka ist doch nicht mehr auf dem Schrottplatz!"

„Echt nicht? Und warum nicht?"

„Er soll im Krankenhaus sein, aber frag mich nur nicht, in welchem."

Konny sprang aus der Hocke auf und sah wie ein lebendiges Fragezeichen aus. „Au Mann!", sagte er jetzt ziemlich laut. „Was Schlimmes?"

„Nichts Schlimmes, ich glaub, er hatte nur einen Schwächeanfall; das sagte sein Sohn zumindest gestern."

156 „Dann kommt er bald wieder zurück", sagte Konny. „Kein Grund zur Aufregung."

„Du sitzt wohl den ganzen Tag auf deinen Stehohren

rum, was?" Auch Irina wurde jetzt lauter. „Wie oft soll ich's noch sagen: Sie wollen die Stella abholen. Zum Schlachthof!"

Konny war wegen der Stehohren überhaupt nicht beleidigt. Erstens wusste er, dass er welche hatte, zweitens konnte Irina ungestraft so etwas zu ihm sagen und drittens begann er zu begreifen, dass an Irinas Behauptung etwas dran sein musste.

In diesem Augenblick schellte es, Ende der Pause.

„Um fünf an der Pommesbude", sagte Irina schnell und schon war sie weg. Und ehe Konny schalten konnte, war sie im Haupteingang der Schule verschwunden.

Als Konny wie vereinbart kurz nach fünf zur Pommesbude kam, hatte sich Irina schon eine Portion bestellt.

„Wie immer?", fragte Frau Schilcher.

„Nee", sagte Irina, „heute mit Majo."

„Oh, ist was passiert?", fragte Frau Schilcher.

„Noch nicht", antwortete Irina.

Konny balancierte sein Fahrrad zur Bude.

„Noch mal das Gleiche?", fragte Frau Schilcher.

„Um Gottes willen!" Konny stellte sein Fahrrad an den Papierkorb. „Von Pommes mit Majo bekommt man Stehohren!"

Frau Schilcher lachte und drückte ihm eine große Portion Ketschup auf seine Pommes.

„Angeber", sagte Irina.

Konny nahm den Pappteller in die linke Hand und begann hastig zu essen.

„Sollst sehen", sagte er mit vollem Mund, „spätestens nach der dreihundertdreiunddreißigsten Portion hast du Ohren wie eine indische Elefantenkuh."

Irina tauchte genüsslich ein paar Pommes in die Majonäse und schob sie sich in den Mund. „Du hast wohl schon lange nicht mehr in den Spiegel gesehen", sagte sie so nebenbei.

Heute war der erste Tag nach den Herbstferien. Bis gestern war Irina mit ihren Eltern bei Tante Susanne in Stuttgart gewesen. Kaum dass sie wieder zu Hause waren, hatte sie sich eine Möhre aus dem Gemüsefach des Kühlschranks geangelt. Und ehe ihre Mutter etwas fragen konnte, war sie schon nach draußen gelaufen. Sie hatte die Mohrrübe in ihre Anoraktasche geschoben und war zum Schrottplatz gegangen. Zuerst wollte sie beim alten Prottka vorbeigehen um ihm nach der Ferienzeit mal wieder Guten Tag zu sagen. Aber im Wohnwagen war er nicht.

Wahrscheinlich ist er bei Stella, hatte Irina gedacht und war zu der alten Baubude gegangen, die jetzt als Pferdestall diente. Sie nahm die Möhre aus ihrer Anoraktasche und rieb sie an ihrem Ärmel blank.

Wenn Mutti wüsste, was ich mit all diesen Möhren mache, dachte sie zufrieden, *dann würde sie nicht mehr so viele kaufen!*

158   Die Mutter hatte gestaunt, als Irina von einem Tag zum anderen zur Möhrenesserin geworden war.

„Jeden Tag ein Möhrchen ist gut für die Öhrchen!",

hatte Irina gesagt und dann behauptet, von heute an würde sie jeden Tag eine Möhre essen, wegen der Vitamine und so.

Vati hatte zwar gemeint, auf diese Weise könnte sie spielend leicht zum Kaninchen werden, aber Mutti hatte gesagt: „Wenn das Kind was für seine Gesundheit tun will, dann sollte man es unterstützen, anstatt dumme Sprüche zu kloppen!"

Vati hatte nur lächelnd in sein Kotelett gebissen und „Hm!" gemacht. Und Irina hatte an ihrer Möhre herumgeknabbert, obwohl sie eigentlich keinen besonderen Appetit darauf gehabt hatte.

Seit diesem Tag war im Gemüsefach immer jener Vorrat an Möhren, von dem Irina regelmäßig ihr Geschenk für Stella holte.

Sie kannten den alten Prottka und sein Pferd nun schon seit mehr als einem halben Jahr. Es war an einem Sonntag im Frühling gewesen. Irina war mit Konny in der Gegend herumgestrolcht, dabei hatten sie den alten Schrottplatz entdeckt.

Ganz toll vergammelte Sachen lagen da herum. Manche wirkten richtig abenteuerlich: Maschinenteile und Dinge, die aussahen, als wären sie von einem anderen Stern, mindestens aber, wie Konny meinte, als hätten da ein paar Außerirdische beim Sammeln mitgeholfen. Er hatte auch gleich ein total verdrehtes Gestell gefunden, das er auf Anhieb als Superantrieb eines Raumschiffs erkannte.

„Das muss von einem Raumschiff sein", sagte er zu Irina, „oder kannst du dir vorstellen, wofür das sonst noch gut sein soll?"

„Für mein Fahrrad kann man das nicht gebrauchen", sagte Irina nach einem kurzen Blick, „dann muss es ja wohl von einem Raumschiff sein."

„Klar", sagte Konny, „ich glaub, ich hab so was Ähnliches schon auf der *Enterprise* gesehen."

„Kann durchaus sein", meinte Irina, die lieber Tierfilme sah. „Im Weltraum kennst du dich eben besser aus als ich."

Gerade als Konny ein weiteres Stück des Raumschiffs Enterprise gefunden hatte, tauchte der alte Mann auf. Er war so unerwartet aus den verbogenen Schrottbergen herausgekommen, dass Konny für einen Augenblick wirklich glaubte, einem leibhaftigen Außerirdischen gegenüberzustehen. Schon wollte er durchstarten, denn bei unvermutet auftauchenden Außerirdischen konnte man ja nie wissen!

Irina wollte sich ihm gerade anschließen, und zwar aus ähnlichen Gründen – sie hatte nämlich schlicht Angst –, als der bärtige Alte fragte: „Ihr habt doch nicht etwa Schiss?"

Konny blieb sofort stehen, denn ihm war klar, dass ein Außerirdischer keine so dummen Fragen stellt. „Wir wollten hier gar nicht abhauen", sagte er deshalb so lässig wie möglich. „Das war bloß 'ne optische Täuschung von Ihnen!"

Da hatte der alte Mann so gelacht, dass ihm die Tränen kamen. Und dann hatte er ihnen den alten Wohnwagen gezeigt, in dem er zu Hause war, ganz hinten am Rande des Platzes.

Aber die größte Überraschung war doch der alte Bauwagen gewesen, der wiehern konnte. So wenigstens hatte es Irina in ihrer ersten Überraschung gesagt; und da hatte der Alte zum zweiten Mal gelacht. Als das Mädchen dann die Stella gesehen hatte, eine schneeweiße zierliche Stute, da war es Liebe auf den ersten Blick gewesen.

„Stella heißt lateinisch Stern", hatte ihnen der alte Prottka später dann erzählt, als sie auf seinem alten Pferdewagen saßen und mit ihm unterwegs waren. Er war der einzige Schrottsammler der ganzen Stadt, der das noch mit einem Pferdewagen machte. Früher war er Kohlenhändler gewesen, hatte er den beiden Kindern erzählt. „Dann aber ging's bergab, von Mal zu Mal schneller. Erstens brauchten die Leute für ihre Ölheizung keine Kohlen mehr, und zweitens sind Lastwagen schneller als Stella. Aber da mir die Stella viel, viel lieber als ein Lastwagen ist, musste ich Schrotthändler werden."

„Versteh ich", sagte Irina leise und streichelte der Stute über die Mähne.

„Die Stella hab ich bekommen, als sie noch ein Fohlen war", erzählte Prottka den Kindern. „Damals war sie noch nicht ganz weiß. Sie ist erst mit etwa zehn Jahren so schön wie ein Schneestern geworden!"

Als habe die Stute verstanden, dass man über sie

sprach, wieherte sie hell. Und der alte Prottka meinte, die Stella könnte Gedanken lesen, wenn sie nur wollte. Dabei lächelte er verschmitzt.

„Vielleicht ist sie wirklich eine Außerirdische", hatte Konny wieder sein Lieblingsthema aufgenommen. „Die können auch Gedanken lesen."

„Vielleicht", hatte der alte Prottka geantwortet. „Bei Stella ist so was durchaus möglich."

Ob irdisch oder außerirdisch, das ist mir piepegal, hatte Irina damals gedacht, *die Hauptsache ist, dass ich Stella immer wieder besuchen kann.*

So oft es ging, war sie den Sommer über mit Konny zum Schrottplatz gekommen. Und jedes Mal hatte sie der Schimmelstute eine Mohrrübe mitgebracht.

Als Irina gestern Nachmittag vom Wohnwagen zum Pferdestall gehen wollte, hatte sie auf einmal zwei fremde Stimmen gehört. *Wer ist das?*, dachte sie, *und was wollen die hier?*

Sie blieb hinter einem Schrotthaufen stehen und hörte zu.

„Was ist der ganze Schrott hier wert?", fragte ein Mann.

„Ich glaube, dafür bekommen Sie nicht mehr allzu viel", sagte der andere. „Und so auf den ersten Blick kann man das auch nicht sagen. Da müsste man sich die einzelnen Teile schon genauer ansehen."

162

„Ich möchte das alles so schnell wie möglich weghaben", sagte die erste Stimme wieder. „Jetzt, da mein

Vater nicht hier ist, muss der ganze Plunder rasch verschwinden!"

„Das mit Ihrem Vater kam sehr plötzlich", sagte der andere Mann.

„So plötzlich nun auch wieder nicht", erklärte Prottkas Sohn. „Er ist eben nicht mehr der Jüngste. Und auf die Dauer ist das doch wirklich kein Zustand, so ganz allein im Wohnwagen hier auf dem Schrottplatz zu hausen."

„Hoffentlich macht er Ihnen keine Schwierigkeiten, wenn es ihm wieder besser geht."

„Lieber Herr Moosgruber, wenn es danach ginge, wäre er auch nicht freiwillig ins Krankenhaus gegangen. Bei meinem Vater muss man eben etwas nachhelfen!"

Sie lachten beide.

Es war ein hässliches Lachen, fand Irina.

„Ein gutes Stück Bauland wäre das hier", bemerkte Moosgruber. „Wirklich ein wunderschönes Stück!"

„Wem sagen Sie das." Prottkas Sohn lachte wieder. „Und deshalb muss alles hier verschwunden sein, bevor mein Vater aus dem Krankenhaus kommt."

„Das lässt sich machen", sagte der Mann, der Moosgruber hieß. „Wenn Sie nichts dagegen haben, fangen wir gleich morgen mit dem Abtransport an."

„Ich verlasse mich ganz auf Sie", sagte der junge Prottka. „Je schneller das Gerümpel hier verschwunden ist, desto eher können wir die Baugrube baggern!"

„Hoffentlich redet uns Ihr Vater nicht ins Geschäft!"

„Der erfährt doch von allem erst, wenn schon die Fundamente stehen!"

Moosgruber lachte wieder.

„Von jetzt an wird er nicht einen Augenblick mehr ohne Aufsicht gelassen", sagte Prottkas Sohn. „Wir wollen ihn gleich vom Krankenhaus ins Altersheim bringen!"

„Nur gut, dass Sie so schnell einen Heimplatz gefunden haben!"

„Ich habe seit einiger Zeit vorgeplant", sagte der Sohn von Prottka. „Schließlich kenne ich meinen Vater lange genug!"

„Das hier war wirklich kein Aufenthaltsort für Ihren alten Herrn", meinte Moosgruber. „So viel schönes Bauland lässt man doch nicht ungenutzt herumliegen!"

Und wieder lachten die Männer.

Da ertönte Stellas Wiehern und unterbrach ihr Gerede.

„Was ist denn das?", fragte der Mann, der Moosgruber hieß.

„Ach, das ist der Gaul", sagte der Sohn von Prottka. „An den hab ich gar nicht mehr gedacht."

„Gehört das Pferd Ihrem Vater?"

„Von wegen Pferd", antwortete Prottkas Sohn. „Das ist eine alte Mähre, gerade gut genug zum Verwursten!"

„Pferdewurst soll eine Delikatesse sein." Moosgruber lachte meckernd.

164

Der junge Prottka stimmte ein: „Damit könnten wir ja noch ein Zusatzgeschäft machen!"

„Das scheint hier wirklich eine Goldgrube zu sein", bemerkte Moosgruber fröhlich.

Die beiden Männer gingen auf den Pferdestall zu.

„Wir lassen den Gaul noch so zwei oder drei Tage hier stehen, bis ich was Passendes für ihn gefunden habe", hörte Irina noch den Sohn vom alten Prottka sagen. Dann rannte sie, so schnell sie konnte, vom Schrottplatz hinunter.

Und nun schoben Konny und Irina ihre Fahrräder in Richtung Stadion.

„Das mit der Pferdewurst glaube ich nicht", sagte Konny jetzt. „Aber etwas kann an der Sache dran sein. Wir sollten wirklich überlegen, was wir tun können!"

„Stimmt." Irina nickte. „Nur überleg nicht zu lange. Ewig lassen sie Stella nicht mehr in der Baubude stehen!"

„Da könntest du ausnahmsweise mal Recht haben", sagte Konny und kratzte sich an der Baseball-Mütze. „Hast du 'ne Idee?"

„Wenn ich eine hätte, wär doch längst was passiert", antwortete sie mürrisch.

Konny kaute nachdenklich an seiner Unterlippe. „Ein Pferd kann man nicht in einen Schuhkarton packen und einfach wegtragen."

„Nee", meinte Irina, „das hat aber auch keiner verlangt!"

„Sei mal still", meinte Konny, „ich glaub, ich hab da 'ne Idee!"

Irina sagte nichts, und auch Konny schwieg. Stumm gingen sie eine Weile nebeneinander her.

„Verdammt noch mal", sagte der Junge schließlich, „ich dachte, ich hätte eine Idee gehabt, und dann hab ich sie wieder vergessen!"

„Und deswegen machst du so einen Aufstand? Stell dir vor, wenn jeder, der was vergessen hat, deswegen so einen Aufstand machen würde!"

„Du hast wohl noch nie etwas vergessen?"

„Auf jeden Fall nicht, dass wir Stella retten müssen!"

Inzwischen waren sie am Stadion angekommen.

„Ich glaub, wir kehren jetzt lieber um", meinte Konny. „Sonst läuft uns womöglich hier am Stadion noch jemand aus meiner Klasse über den Weg, und dann ist es aus mit unserem Geheimnis."

Sie schoben ihre Fahrräder in die andere Richtung. Etwa zwanzig Schritte waren sie zurückgegangen, als Irina rief: „Das ist es! Klar!"

„Was meinst du?", fragte Konny verdutzt.

„Dass ich nicht eher draufgekommen bin!", sagte Irina und klatschte mit der rechten Hand auf ihren Fahrradsattel. „Das ist die Lösung!"

„Welche Lösung?"

Als Irina nicht gleich antwortete, hielt Konny ihren Gepäckträger fest. „Mach's nicht so spannend", sagte er.

166   Für Irina schien alles klar zu sein. „Entführung", sagte sie einfach und ganz selbstverständlich. „Wir machen einfach 'ne bildschöne Entführung!"

„Was machen wir?" Konny ließ ihren Gepäckträger so schnell los, als hätte er sich die Finger verbrannt. „Sag mal, spinnst du?"

Irina hörte ihm gar nicht zu.

„Das wird eine ganz tolle Sache werden!", sagte sie. „Eine total heiße Super-Schau! Schließlich müssen wir etwas tun. Das hast du selbst gesagt!"

Konny kam wieder näher. „Das war doch nur ein Scherz?", fragte er. „Sag, dass es nur ein Scherz war!"

Irina sah ihn an, als erwache sie aus einem Traum. „Was soll ein Scherz gewesen sein?"

„Na, das mit der Entführung!"

Irina schüttelte langsam den Kopf. „Ich mein's ernst!"

„Sag mal, bist du bescheuert?" Konny starrte Irina fassungslos an.

Fast fröhlich erklärte sie: „Uns bleibt doch nichts anderes übrig!"

„Du, da mache ich nicht mit!" Konny stieg auf sein Fahrrad. „Dabei kannst du nicht mit mir rechnen!"

„Ich dachte, du bist mein Freund!"

„Bei Entführung hört jede Freundschaft auf!", sagte er entschlossen. „Auch jede Verwandtschaft!"

„Aber wo Stella doch jetzt keinen Herrn mehr hat!"

„Sollen da etwa auch noch Pferde mitmachen?" Er begriff es immer noch nicht.

Nun sah Irina ihn verdutzt an.

In diesem Augenblick begann Konny zu begreifen. „Du meinst ... die Stella?", fragte er gedehnt.

Irina nickte. „Klar. Wen denn sonst?"

Konny sprang vom Fahrrad. „Ja, aber", rief er, „was machen wir mit einem entführten Pferd ohne Pferdestall?"

„Das weiß ich auch noch nicht", antwortete Irina. „Aber wir müssen etwas tun, jetzt, wo die Stella ein Waisenkind geworden ist."

„Waisenmädchen", sagte Konny.

„Ist doch egal", meinte Irina. „Auf jeden Fall hat sie außer uns beiden jetzt keinen Menschen mehr, der ihr helfen könnte, wo doch der alte Prottka im Krankenhaus ist! Du hast ja gehört, was die beiden Kerle gesagt haben!"

„Stimmt", sagte Konny, „da hast du Recht. Und außerdem können wir die einzige Außerirdische in unserer Stadt nicht im Stich lassen."

„Komm, lass uns mal zur Pommesbude fahren", schlug Irina vor. „Bei Pommes mit Majo fällt mir garantiert was ein."

Es war etwa eine halbe Stunde später, als sie von der Pommesbude zum Schrottplatz fuhren. Moosgrubers Leute hatten inzwischen schon ziemlich viel Schrott abgefahren. Nun hatten sie Feierabend gemacht und der Platz lag wieder verlassen da. Prottkas Wohnwagen und Stellas Bauwagen standen noch an den gewohnten Plätzen.

168

Die weiße Stute wieherte leise, als sie zu ihr gingen. Konny strich über die weiße Mähne und Irina gab Stella nacheinander drei Möhren zu fressen. Endlich sagte das Mädchen leise: „Bis heute Abend, mein Schimmelschatz!"

Dann kurvten sie wieder vom Schrottplatz hinunter.

Als sie auf der Straße waren, sagte Konny: „Jetzt hast du unserem Sternenpferd aber ein echtes Versprechen gegeben."

„Klar." Irina nickte. „Und ich werde es auch halten, so wahr ich Irina Müller heiße!"

„Wir haben aber noch gar keinen neuen Pferdestall für Stella", sagte Konny.

„Stimmt", meinte Irina.

„Und wenn wir einen finden, wie kriegen wir Stella dorthin?", überlegte Konny.

„Hmm", machte Irina.

„Das Einfachste wäre, wenn wir den Bauwagen dort mit einem Trecker wegholen könnten", sagte Konny nachdenklich.

„Am besten mit einer fliegenden Untertasse!", sagte Irina spöttisch.

„Jetzt spinnst du aber", meinte Konny, „ganz kräftig sogar!"

„Das mit dem Trecker war auch nicht viel besser. Da könnten wir ja gleich das Überfallkommando und die Feuerwehr anrufen!"

Die Ampel sprang auf Gelb, Irina bremste. Sie hielten an und warteten.

„Wenn Oma Mallorca jetzt zu Hause wäre", sagte

169

Konny plötzlich. „Die würde uns schon sagen, wo's langgeht!"

Oma Mallorca hieß eigentlich Oma Elfriede, aber weil sie jeden Herbst nach Mallorca flog, um dort ein paar Wochen zu bleiben, nannte Konny sie nur „Oma Mallorca".

Oma Mallorca war schwer in Ordnung. Und wenn Konny ein echtes Problem hatte, auf Oma Mallorca konnte er sich verlassen.

„Sie ist also wieder ausgeflogen?", wollte Irina wissen.

Konny nickte. „Sie hat mir schon eine Karte geschrieben, als wir noch in den Herbstferien in der Lüneburger Heide waren!"

Die Ampel schaltete auf Grün, sie fuhren los.

„Mallorca", rief Irina ganz plötzlich, „natürlich, Mallorca!"

Und sie bremste so plötzlich, dass Konny ihr beinahe gegen das Hinterrad fuhr.

„Pass doch auf!", schimpfte er, aber Irina fuhr schon weiter. Als er sie wieder eingeholt hatte, rief sie ihm zu: „Damit wäre der Fall klar: Mallorca!"

Konny radelte ganz dicht an sie heran. Er war noch etwas außer Puste: „Ich versteh nur Mallorca!"

„Dann ist auch bei dir alles klar", sagte Irina und trat wieder in die Pedale.

Konny strampelte hinterher. „Was ist klar?", fragte er, als er sie wieder erreichte.

„Alles." Irina radelte jetzt ganz gemütlich dahin. „Ab jetzt haben wir alles im Griff."

Ehe Konny weiter fragen konnte, redete sie schon weiter: „Die Bude von Oma Mallorca ist doch frei! Und so hat die Stella einen neuen Stall!"

Konny schwenkte so überrascht seinen Lenker zur Seite, dass er Irina streifte. Sie musste bremsen.

„Aber Omas Wohnung ist doch im dritten Stock", rief er ratlos. „Wie stellst du dir das vor, heimlich und mitten in der Nacht mit einem alten Pferd die Treppen rauf bis in den dritten Stock?"

Irina lachte so, dass sie beinahe vom Rad fiel.

„Auf diese Idee wäre ich einfach nicht gekommen!", sagte sie schließlich und wischte sich die Lachtränen aus den Augen. „Mann, bist du blöd!"

Konny sah wirklich nicht besonders geistreich aus.

„Ich meine doch die andere Bude", erklärte Irina jetzt, „die im Schrebergarten!"

„He, sag das doch gleich!" Konny schien erleichtert. „An Oma Mallorcas Gartenlaube hab ich gar nicht gedacht!"

„Ich merke schon, man kann sich nicht alles beim Fahren erzählen." Irina stieg vom Rad.

Als sie ihre Fahrräder schoben, erzählte sie Konny ausführlich ihren Plan.

„Geheime Kommandosache Mallorca", rief Konny fröhlich zum Abschied. „Das Raumschiff Stella ist schon gesattelt!"

Sie trafen sich bei Anbruch der Dunkelheit auf dem Schrottplatz wieder.

„Im Wilden Westen hat man Pferdediebe aufgehängt", flüsterte Irina.

„Lass den Quatsch", flüsterte Konny nervös.

Irina sagte nichts mehr, sie gab Stella ihre gewohnte Möhre und zog das weiße Pferd dann am Halfter nach draußen.

„Was machen wir bloß, wenn Stella unterwegs wiehert?"

„Die wiehert doch nur, wenn sie Angst hat", antwortete Irina.

„Bist du sicher?"

„Ziemlich", meinte das Mädchen und hielt der Stute den Rest der Möhre hin. „Und wenn sie was zu kauen hat, dann ist sie voll beschäftigt, dann wiehert sie nicht. Was meinst du, warum ich heute Nachmittag drei Kilo Möhren im Supermarkt gekauft habe?"

Sie klopfte auf ihre Anoraktaschen: „Das müsste bis zum Schrebergarten reichen. Außerdem frisst Stella langsam!"

Sie führten die Stute vom Schrottplatz.

„Die Indianer früher", flüsterte Konny, „die haben ihren Pferden bei Gefahr Felle um die Hufe gebunden, dann waren keine Spuren zu entdecken!"

„Als wenn man auf Asphaltstraßen Hufspuren sehen könnte", flüsterte Irina verächtlich.

„Sicher ist sicher", meinte Konny.

„Wir könnten der Stella ja deinen Anorak und dein Hemd um die Hufe binden", bemerkte Irina.

„War ja bloß 'ne Idee!" Konny nahm Stellas Halfter auf der anderen Seite von Irina. Dann gingen sie mit dem Pferd auf Schleichwegen zum Schrebergarten, so leise wie möglich.

Sie kannten sich in dieser Gegend am Stadtrand gut aus. Nur ein einziges Mal mussten sie mit der Stute im Gebüsch verschwinden, als ihnen eine Gruppe von Leuten entgegenkam.

Als sie das Pferd schließlich in Oma Mallorcas Gartenhaus hatten, waren sie beide sehr froh.

„Mensch, hatte ich Schiss", sagte Irina, „die ganze Zeit über!"

„Warum denn Schiss? Ich war doch bei dir!"

„Du alter Angeber! Hätte ich dir nicht ab und zu eine Möhre zwischen die Zähne geschoben, dann wäre die ganze Stadt von deinem Zähneklappern wach geworden!"

„Du hattest also doch Angst, dass Stella wiehern könnte", stellte Konny fest.

Irina lachte. „Hast du schon mal ein Raumschiff wiehern gehört?" Dann knipste sie die Taschenlampe an und leuchtete auf die Tür. „Stell dir vor, ich hatte nur Schiss den ganzen Weg über, dass Stella nicht durch diese Tür hier passen würde! Was hätten wir dann gemacht?"

„Au Mann", rief Konny verblüfft. „Daran hatte ich überhaupt nicht gedacht!"

„Macht nichts", sagte Irina, „Hauptsache, sie ist jetzt drin!" Sie streichelte Stellas Hals.

Irina nahm den leeren Wassereimer und gab ihn Konny. „Mach ihn mal eben draußen am Wasserhahn voll. Ich bin ein Mädchen und hab Angst im Dunkeln. Und du bist doch der Stärkere!" Sie lachte.

Konny knurrte etwas und ging hinaus. Als er den vollen Eimer wieder hereinschleppte, sagte er schnaufend: „Ich tue das alles nur für unsere außerirdische Stute!"

Sie stellten Stella den Eimer hin und legten ihr das Heu vor, das sie von der Baubude mitgenommen hatten. Schließlich konnte Stella nicht nur die paar Möhren fressen. Dann verschlossen sie die Tür gut.

Als sie nach Hause kamen, hatten sie wieder Glück, weil niemand ihr spätes Kommen bemerkte. Und wenn ihnen das Aufstehen am Morgen auch ziemlich schwer fiel, so waren sie beide doch mächtig stolz darauf, ein richtiges Pferd gerettet und sicher versteckt zu haben.

Sie hatten sich einen Plan gemacht, wie sie Stella versorgen würden. Das gehörte zur „Geheimen Kommandosache Mallorca".

Damit alles nicht allzu sehr auffiel, teilten sie sich die Arbeit. Einer sollte sich vor Beginn der Schule um das Pferd kümmern, der andere hinterher. Am Abend wollten sie dann immer zusammen hingehen.

174   Am Abend des dritten Tages waren sie zum Schrottplatz gegangen, ganz unauffällig, versteht sich. Der Schrott war zum großen Teil abtransportiert worden.

Stellas ehemaliger Stall stand weit offen, und vor Prottkas Wohnwagen hatten sie einen Trecker gespannt.

„Das mit dem Trecker war ja wohl meine Idee", bemerkte Konny grinsend.

„Du kannst das ja dem Sohn vom alten Prottka sagen." Irina lachte. „Vielleicht bekommst du dafür noch 'ne satte Belohnung."

„Du bist nur neidisch, weil das meine Idee gewesen ist", stellte Konny fest.

„Klar, bin ich", meinte Irina, „denn du hast wirklich tolle Ideen! Wenn ich noch dran denke, dass du die Stella über die Treppen in Oma Mallorcas Wohnung im dritten Stock bringen wolltest!"

„Das war ein Missverständnis", gab Konny schnell zu. „Aber nur, weil ich nicht genau wusste, was du vorhattest."

Sie gingen wieder zurück.

„Ob der junge Prottka wohl die Polizei angerufen hat?" Konny sah sich um.

„Der ist doch froh, dass er sich nicht mehr um Stella zu kümmern braucht", sagte Irina. „Jetzt kann er seinem Vater sagen, dass das Pferd geklaut wurde, und da braucht er noch nicht mal zu lügen!"

Konny sah sich immer wieder um.

„Hör endlich auf, dich dauernd umzusehen!" Irina stieß ihm den Ellbogen in die Seite. „Sonst glauben die Leute noch, wir hätten sie gestohlen!"

Konny grinste. Sie bogen in einen Seitenweg ein.

„Wenn wir nicht rechtzeitig gekommen wären", Irina war jetzt sehr nachdenklich, „dann wäre die Stella jetzt vielleicht schon im Pferdehimmel!"

In Oma Mallorcas Laube schien sich die Schimmelstute ganz wohl zu fühlen. Nur rauslassen durften sie sie nicht, das wäre zu gefährlich gewesen. Bis jetzt hatte ja auch alles so gut geklappt, dass die beiden Freunde von Tag zu Tag sicherer wurden.

Sie waren gerade auf dem Weg zur Pommesbude.

„Ich glaube, wir sind übern Berg", sagte Irina.

„Stella ist doch ein Sternenpferd", meinte Konny. „Und einer außerirdischen Stute kann eben nichts passieren."

Sie kurvten zur Bude.

„Wie immer?", fragte Frau Schilcher.

Sie nickten. Gerade hatten sie ihre Portionen entgegengenommen, als ein Lastwagen hielt. Zwei Arbeiter kamen zu der Bude.

„Der Alte hat getobt", hörten sie einen der Männer sagen. „‚Die Arbeiten unverzüglich einstellen!', hat er geschrien!"

„Wer war das eigentlich?", fragte der andere Mann. „Den hab ich dort noch nie gesehen!"

„Dem soll der ganze Schrott gehört haben", meinte der Erste wieder. „Und dem gehört auch das Land."

„Au Backe", sagte der Zweite, „dann werden wir jetzt mit dem Ausbaggern wohl noch Jahre warten müssen!"

Sie holten sich ihre Würstchen und fuhren wieder davon. Konny und Irina hatten gespannt zugehört. Kaum waren die beiden verschwunden, da fuhren sie los.

„Das ging ja schneller, als ich dachte", rief Irina Konny zu. „Jetzt weiß der alte Prottka wenigstens Bescheid und macht Dampf bei seinem Sohn!"

Bald standen sie in einiger Entfernung vor Prottkas ehemaligem Schrottplatz. Er war fast leer, sogar Stellas alter Stall und der Wohnwagen waren verschwunden.

„Kein Wunder, dass Prottka getobt hat", sagte Irina leise. „Sein weißes Pferd!"

„Würdest du doch auch machen", bemerkte Konny, „wenn du nach Hause kommst, und alles ist verschwunden!"

„Und das Sternenpferd dazu", sagte Irina.

„Der alte Prottka wird echt froh sein, dass wir seine Stella gerettet haben", meinte Konny. „Es hätte ja viel schlimmer kommen können! Denk nur an den Schlachthof!"

„Zum Glück ist Stella ein Sternenpferd", sagte Irina leise.

„Sie ist eine echte Außerirdische, das kannst du ruhig glauben!"

„Glaub ich doch, Konny. Und ehe deine Oma wieder nach Hause kommt, ist alles bestens geregelt."

Am nächsten Tag suchten sie die Rufnummern der Altersheime der Stadt aus dem Telefonbuch heraus und fingen an. Sie gaben sich als Enkel von Prottka aus, die ihren Großvater sprechen wollten.

In drei Heimen hatten sie schon angerufen, und von einem Anruf zum anderen wurden sie mutiger.

„Hier Seniorenheim Abendgold", sagte eine Frauenstimme. „Was kann ich für Sie tun?"

„Sie können mir mal meinen Großvater rüberreichen", sagte Irina. „Ich möchte bitte mit ihm reden!"

Die Frau vom Seniorenheim lachte.

„Wir haben zurzeit zweiundsiebzig Großväter im Haus", sagte sie. „Welchen von ihnen soll ich dir denn rüberreichen?"

„Wir möchten Herrn Prottka sprechen", sagte jetzt Konny ins Telefon.

„Da ist ja noch jemand", sagte die Frau. „Da wird sich euer Opa aber freuen, dass ihr an ihn denkt!"

„Wir freuen uns auch", meinte Konny.

„Moment mal", sagte die Frau vom Seniorenheim. „Ich muss mal in der Kartei nachschauen, denn die Namen von zweiundsiebzig Großvätern kann man ja schließlich nicht alle auswendig kennen!"

Sie hörten Papier rascheln.

„Da habe ich ihn", sagte die Frau dann. „Joseph Prottka, Zimmer achtundzwanzig. Wie heißt ihr beiden denn?"

„Grüßen Sie Opa bitte von Irina und mir", rief Konny in den Hörer.

Die Frau fragte: „Hast du auch einen Namen?"

„Zwei sogar", antwortete Konny, „alle sagen Konny zu mir, aber in Wirklichkeit heiße ich Konrad!"

„Mann, Konrad", rief Irina überrascht, „das hab ich ja gar nicht gewusst!"

„War noch was?", fragte die Frau am Telefon, sie hatte Irinas Bemerkung nicht verstanden.

„Nein", sagte Irina, „bei uns ist alles klar!"

„Gut", meinte die Frau vom Seniorenheim, „dann wartet mal auf euren Opa."

Nun war eine Zeit lang Stille.

„Wer will mich sprechen?", hörten sie auf einmal Prottkas Stimme. „Ich habe keinen Enkel, der Konrad heißt!"

„Einen schönen Gruß von Stella", rief Irina schnell.

Da entstand eine lange Pause.

„Was hast du gesagt?" Prottkas Stimme war jetzt ganz aufgeregt.

„Einen schönen Gruß von Stella", sagte nun auch Konny.

„Moment mal, wo seid ihr?", rief Joseph Prottka ins Telefon. „Und wo ist Stella?"

„In Sicherheit", sagte Irina einfach. „Und um Stella brauchen Sie sich keine Sorgen zu machen. Der geht's gut! Stimmt's, Konrad?"

Konny nickte, aber das konnte der alte Prottka am Telefon ja nicht sehen.

Nachdem die beiden mit Joseph Prottka vereinbart hatten, ihn am nächsten Tag zu Stella zu bringen, gingen sie noch einmal zu Oma Mallorcas Gartenlaube. Sie redeten mit Stella und versorgten die weiße Stute, so gut sie konnten. Endlich gingen sie zufrieden nach Hause.

Es war so gegen fünf Uhr morgens, als bei Konnys Eltern das Telefon läutete.

„Was ist los?", fragte der Vater schlaftrunken. „Nein, wir haben kein Polizeipferd. Wie bitte?"

Konnys Mutter sah ihren Mann verständnislos an. „Was haben wir nicht?", fragte sie ihn.

Er antwortete nicht auf ihre Frage. „Sie sind von der Polizei und Sie brauchen kein Pferd? Ja, Mann, das kann jeder sagen! Deswegen müssen Sie mich doch nicht mitten in der Nacht aus dem Bett klingeln!"

„Was ist los?", wollte die Mutter wissen.

„Natürlich haben wir einen Schrebergarten und eine Laube, vielmehr, sie gehört meiner Mutter. Aber ein Pferd haben wir nicht. Wie kommen Sie überhaupt darauf? Hier im dritten Stock?" Konnys Vater lachte. Dann redete er weiter: „Das ist nicht zum Lachen? Das ist ruhestörender Lärm? Und Wiehern? Na, erlauben Sie mal, ich wiehere nicht, ich lache!"

Die Mutter schüttelte fassungslos den Kopf.

„Welches Pferd denn?", rief ihr Mann nun ins Telefon. „Wir haben kein Pferd in der Gartenlaube! Wie bitte? Es hat die ganze Nacht gewiehert?" Konnys Vater sah seine Frau an. „Hältst du vielleicht heimlich ein Pferd?"

Ratlos sah sie ihn an.

„Ich komme sofort!", rief ihr Mann da in den Hörer. Und bald darauf waren sie beide auf dem Weg zu Oma Mallorcas Laube.

„So, so", sagte der Polizist am nächsten Tag zu den beiden Kindern. „Ihr habt das Pferd also nur versteckt, um es vor dem Schlachthof zu retten?"

Konny nickte.

„Das hatten wir doch der Stella versprochen", sagte Irina leise. „Und Versprechen muss man halten!"

„Das ist ja eine tolle Geschichte", sagte ein zweiter Polizist. „Und das sollen wir euch glauben?"

„Es war aber so", erklärte Irina. „Ehrlich!"

„Und das habt ihr euch alles so ganz allein überlegt?", fragte der erste Polizist wieder.

„Haben wir", erklärte Konny. „Das war unsere geheime Kommandosache Mallorca."

„Eure geheime Kommandosache?" Der zweite Polizist sah seinen Kollegen an. „Und warum ausgerechnet Mallorca?"

„Nur so", sagte Irina schnell. „Weil alle geheimen Kommandosachen ja einen Namen haben müssen!"

„Das leuchtet mir ein", sagte der Beamte. „Ich merke schon, du kennst dich aus!"

„Ich glaube, wir haben da eine ganz gefährliche Bande von Pferdedieben erwischt!", sagte nun ein dritter Polizist und deutete auf die beiden. „Das mit dem Verwursten glaubt doch kein Mensch!"

Konny wurde blass.

„Moment mal, Herr Oberkommissar", rief Irina jetzt. „Darf ich mal telefonieren?"

„Sie möchte ihren Rechtsbeistand sprechen", sagte der dritte Beamte und reichte Irina den Hörer. „Bitte schön!"

Die Polizisten grinsten.

Irina sagte nichts, sie wählte nur die Nummer des Altenheims Abendgold. „Ich möchte ganz dringend Herrn Prottka sprechen", rief sie ins Telefon.

Schon konnte sie Prottka hören.

„Sag mal", rief er, „wollt ihr mich verarschen, oder was? Ich warte! Ich dachte, wir wollten zu Stella!"

„Wollten wir auch", sagte Irina, „aber da kam uns die Polizei dazwischen."

„Seid ihr im Knast?", fragte Prottka, und es klang, als sei er erschrocken.

„Nein, auf der Polizeiwache, Herr Prottka", sagte Irina schnell. „Aber vielleicht sagen Sie selbst der Polizei, was wir mit Stella vorhatten! Und warum!"

Sie reichte dem Polizisten den Hörer, und der hörte Prottka zu. Dann stellte er noch ein paar Fragen. Als er schließlich den Hörer auflegte, nickte er Konny und Irina zu. „Da haben wir ja alle noch einmal Glück gehabt", sagte er lächelnd. „Und wie es aussieht, ist der Fall jetzt gelöst." Er sah Konnys Eltern an. Dann wandte er sich wieder an die Kinder: „Wie mir Herr Prottka gerade sagte, habt ihr sein verlassenes, entlaufenes Pferd gefunden und anständig versorgt, als er im Krankenhaus lag. Stimmt's?"

Die beiden nickten heftig.

„Ich glaube, dafür könnt ihr einen anständigen Finderlohn erwarten", erklärte der zweite Polizist, „obwohl ja Kinder so spät am Abend nicht mehr auf der Straße sein sollten!"

„Sind wir jetzt frei?", fragte Konny ungeduldig. Sie mussten doch zu Prottka. Und vor allem zu Stella.

Die Polizisten lachten.

„Da haben wir noch einmal Glück gehabt", sagte Irina, als sie die Fahrräder bestiegen.

„Das hab ich dir doch schon immer gesagt", erklärte Konny. „Stella ist eine Außerirdische, sie bringt einem Glück!"

Irina nickte. Sie wusste es ja.

„Lass uns noch mal zur Pommesbude fahren", schlug Konny vor. „Nach all der Aufregung brauch ich 'ne anständige Portion Pommes mit Majo."

„Mit Majo?" Irina staunte. „Aber Pommes mit Majo machen Stehohren!"

„Als wenn das für mich ein Problem wäre", Konny grinste. „Stehohren sind übrigens bei Außerirdischen ziemlich beliebt! Du solltest dir unbedingt mal die Ohren von Mister Spock in der Enterprise ansehen!"

„Wenn ich unbedingt schöne Stehohren sehen will",

183

Irina lachte nun auch, „dann gehe ich zu Stella. So eine Wunderstute wie sie, die kann es im Fernsehen gar nicht geben! Komm mit!"

Drosselgesang

Das muss eine Singdrossel sein!", sagte Wolfgang sehr bestimmt.

Ira zügelte ihr Pferd und lauschte. Nun hörte auch sie das leise „Judit-Judit-Judit".

Es klang weit entfernt, und sie hätte den leisen Gesang sicher nicht bemerkt, wenn Wolfgang es ihr nicht gesagt hätte.

„Lass uns näher reiten!" Wolfgang lenkte seine Fuchsstute schon in die Richtung, aus der der Gesang kam.

Schnell folgte ihm Ira. Sie überholte ihn und ritt nun wieder vor ihm.

Sie ritten einen Feldweg entlang, der zwischen Kornfeldern hindurchführte. Er endete vor dem Koppeltor einer Wiese.

„Der Weg geht hier nicht mehr weiter", sagte Ira, „Ende der Vorstellung."

Das Flöten des Vogels war jetzt ganz deutlich zu hören.

„Wir sind schon ganz nahe", sagte Wolfgang.

Ira sah sich um. Seitlich des Weges entdeckte sie eine Wagenspur, die an der Grenze von Kornfeld und Wiese verlief. Sie lenkte ihr Pferd in die Spur und Wolfgang folgte ihr.

So ritten sie bis zum Waldrand. Kurz vor den ersten Bäumen hielten sie an.

Der Gesang der Drossel war jetzt sehr nahe, schien noch weicher geworden. Der Vogel hatte seine Melodie variiert und veränderte sein Flöten zu verschiedenen Motiven.

Wolfgang ließ die Zügel der Stute locker. Auch das Pferd hatte den Kopf zur Seite gewandt und lauschte.

„Sie müsste jetzt eigentlich zu sehen sein", sagte Wolfgang leise zu Ira.

Das Mädchen schaute sich um. Das Grün der Blätter über ihr war sehr dicht. Angestrengt suchten ihre Augen.

„Sie scheint direkt über uns zu sein", flüsterte Wolfgang, „ein wenig rechts von mir, nur etwa fünf Meter entfernt." Er sagte es sehr leise, aber ganz sicher.

Ira sah in das Gewirr der Blätter und Äste. Sorgfältig tasteten sich ihre Blicke durch das flirrende Grün. Sie suchte nach einer Lücke im dichten Laub des Baumes.

Und auf einmal sah sie den braunen Fleck im Grün. Die Singdrossel saß im Geäst der Buche, direkt über ihren Köpfen. Sie schien ins Land hinauszusehen und sang ihre Melodie. Wie versunken in ihren eigenen Gesang saß sie auf einem Ast und flötete wunderschön.

Die Pferde hatten die Köpfe gesenkt und zupften am Gras.

„Wie sieht sie aus?", flüsterte Wolfgang nach einer Weile.

„Ein helles Bauchgefieder mit braunen Tupfen", flüsterte Ira zurück, „der Kopf ist leicht gesprenkelt, die Flügel hellbraun."

„Sie ist sehr einfallsreich", sagte Wolfgang nach einer Weile leise. „Sie erfindet immer neue Motive und Tonfolgen!"

Ira hörte zu. Sie hatte die Augen geschlossen und lauschte dem melodischen Gesang der Drossel über ihr. Dann, plötzlich, schnaubte Iras Pferd, und der Gesang verstummte.

Sie hörten nur noch ein leichtes Rascheln der Blätter, als der Vogel aufflatterte und mit kräftigem Flügelschlag den Baum verließ. Und ehe Ira die Augen öffnete, war die Singdrossel schon irgendwo in der blauen Weite verschwunden.

Sie ritten die Wagenspur zurück, bis sie zum Feldweg kamen.

Wolfgang hob den Kopf zur Sonne, nun schien sie ihm voll ins Gesicht. „Mittag?", fragte er Ira.

Sie sah auf ihre Armbanduhr. „Viertel nach zwölf", antwortete sie.

„Schön", meinte Wolfgang, „du musst mich doch erst um eins abliefern."

Ira lächelte dem Jungen zu. Doch schon fiel ihr ein,

dass er ihr Lächeln nicht sehen konnte. „Ich habe deiner Mutter versprochen, dich rechtzeitig zum Essen zurückzubringen", sagte sie.

„Wenn ich so besorgt um mich selbst wäre wie meine Mutter", Wolfgang lachte, „dann hätte ich nie im Leben ein Pferd bestiegen!"

„Deine Mutter ist schon in Ordnung", sagte Ira. „Wirklich!"

„Mag sein", sagte Wolfgang, „ja, aber manchmal geht sie mir mit ihrem Besorgtsein auf den Geist!"

Ira lachte.

Wolfgang klopfte der Fuchsstute mit der rechten Hand den Hals. „Wäre es nach Mutter gegangen, so hätte ich mich doch niemals auch nur in Olgas Nähe trauen dürfen!"

Sie waren jetzt auf dem Feldweg angekommen. Als sie zwischen den Kornfeldern ritten, hob Wolfgang schnuppernd den Kopf.

„Der Weizen riecht gut", sagte er zu Ira und ritt die Fuchsstute nahe ans Feld.

Als die ersten Ähren seine Stiefel berührten, bückte er sich zur Seite hinunter und pflückte eine Ähre vom Halm. Er nahm sie in die linke Hand, die die Zügel hielt, und ließ die Fingerspitzen der rechten über die Kornähre gleiten. Er tat es langsam und sehr sorgsam. Dann löste er zwei Körner heraus und steckte sie in den Mund.

188

„Sie schmecken süß", sagte er und holte die restlichen Körner aus der Ähre. Er sammelte sie in seiner rechten

Hand. Dann beugte er sich weit über den rotgoldenen Hals seiner Stute und reichte ihr das Korn.

Als er die samtweichen Lippen des Pferdes an seiner Handfläche spürte, lächelte er versonnen.

Sagen- und Märchenpferde

Ein Pferd aus purem Gold

Es war einmal ein Mann, der hatte drei Söhne; zwei kluge und einen, den sie den Dummen nannten.

Da nun der Vater alt und krank im Sterben lag, sprach er zu seinen Söhnen: „Wenn ich begraben bin, sollt ihr an meinem Grabe Wache halten. Jeder Einzelne von euch eine ganze Nacht."

Und die drei Söhne versprachen es zu tun.

Als nun der Vater tot und beerdigt war und die erste Nachtwache nahte, befiel den Ältesten große Angst.

Da sagte der Jüngste zu ihm: „Lass mich doch für dich zum Friedhof gehen, um an Vaters Grab zu wachen."

Und er ging auf den Friedhof. Es war eine finstere Nacht, kein Stern blinkte vom Himmel. Der Wind heulte, ein Käuzchen schrie, und dem Jüngsten war nicht geheuer zu Mute. Doch trotz seiner Angst blieb er am Grab seines Vaters um zu wachen.

Es war um die Stunde der Mitternacht, da öffnete sich das Grab und der Vater kam hervor. Er sagte kein einziges Wort, doch reichte er seinem jüngsten Sohn drei Birkenzweige, die dieser nach Hause trug, sie jedoch vor seinen Brüdern versteckte.

Als nun die zweite Nacht anbrach und der zweitälteste Bruder am Grabe wachen sollte, hatte auch der so große Angst, dass wieder der Jüngste statt seiner zum Friedhof ging.

Und wieder um die Stunde der Mitternacht öffnete sich das Grab. Wieder sagte der Vater kein einziges Wort. Dieses Mal reichte er dem Jüngsten ein Knäuel mit Garn, das der Junge ebenfalls nach Hause trug und vor seinen Brüdern versteckte.

Die dritte Nacht war noch finsterer als die beiden anderen zusammen. Und in dieser Nacht war der Jüngste so müde, dass er beinahe im Stehen eingeschlafen wäre. Aber trotz seiner großen Müdigkeit schleppte er sich zum dritten Mal auf den dunklen Friedhof hinaus, um dort das Versprechen zu erfüllen, das er dem Vater gegeben hatte.

Und es war wieder um die Stunde der Mitternacht, als sich das Grab öffnete und der Vater zu ihm kam. Doch in dieser Nacht blieb der Vater nicht stumm, sondern sprach zu seinem jüngsten Sohn.

„Es ist gut zu wissen", sagte der Vater, „dass wenigstens einer meiner Söhne jenes Versprechen hält, das mir alle drei auf dem Sterbebett gegeben haben! Nimm du jene Birkenzweige, die ich dir vorgestern gab und gehe damit zu der uralten Eiche in unserem Garten. Wenn du mit den drei Zweigen dreimal gegen ihren Stamm schlägst, wirst du erfahren, was du weiter zu tun hast!"

Und nach diesen Worten stieg der Vater wieder ins Grab und der Jüngste ging nach Hause und legte sich todmüde schlafen.

Nun lebte in derselben Stadt auch der König des Landes. Und dieser König hatte eine Tochter, die hoch oben im vierten Stockwerk seines Schlosses wohnte. Eines Tages nun ließ er bekannt geben, dass seine Tochter denjenigen heiraten würde, dem es gelänge, auf seinem Pferd zweimal bis in das vierte Stockwerk des Schlosses hinaufzureiten.

Es kamen viele Prinzen und Edelleute auf prächtigen Pferden geritten. Es kamen auch andere reiche Männer um ihr Glück zu versuchen. Sie kamen aus dem eigenen Land, aber auch aus ganz fremden Ländern; manche von ihnen sogar von sehr weit her.

Doch was sie und wie sie es auch versuchten, keinem gelang es, auf seinem Pferd in das vierte Stockwerk zur Königstochter hinaufzureiten.

Es war am Morgen nach jener dritten Nacht, da der Jüngste am Grabe seines Vaters Wache gehalten, als die beiden älteren Brüder beschlossen, sich um die Hand der Königstochter zu bewerben. Sie kauften von dem ererbten Geld ihres Vaters zwei schöne Rappen und prächtige Kleider und sagten zu ihrem Bruder: „Wir wollen zur Tochter des Königs ins vierte Stockwerk reiten. Du aber bleibst zu Hause und hütest die Schweine!"

Dann ritten die zwei gemeinsam zum Schloss der Prinzessin.

Sie waren kaum davongeritten, als der Jüngste in den Garten lief um das zu tun, was ihm sein Vater in der letzten Nacht geraten hatte. Kaum hatten die drei Birkenzweige zum dritten Mal die Rinde des uralten Baumes berührt, da öffnete sich der mächtige Eichenstamm weit wie ein Tor. Und wiehernd kam ein Pferd hervorgetänzelt, das glänzte wie pures Gold.

Da nun der Junge sah, dass auf dem goldenen Rücken die prächtigsten Kleider lagen, zögerte er nicht lange und zog die vornehme Kleidung an. Und als er sie angezogen hatte und das goldene Pferd bestieg, da sah er aus wie der allerschönste Prinz.

Wie er nun auf seinem golden schimmernden Pferd zum Schloss geritten kam, traten alle, die dort versammelt waren, ehrfurchtsvoll zur Seite. Der Jüngste aber ritt im Galopp auf die Mauer des Schlosses zu und ohne auch nur einen winzigen Augenblick zu zögern bis in das vierte Stockwerk hinauf.

Als er dort oben dann angekommen war, sagte er zu der Tochter des Königs: „Hochverehrte Prinzessin, als Zeichen meiner glücklichen Ankunft hier im vierten Stockwerk, da wünsche ich mir jenes goldbestickte Taschentuch, dass Ihr in Euren schönen Händen haltet."

Und die Königstochter erfüllte sofort seinen Wunsch. Dann ritt er wieder die Wand hinab und durch die Gasse der Wartenden auf und davon.

Als seine Brüder nun nach Hause geritten kamen, sie hatten, wie alle anderen auch, vergeblich versucht, ins vierte Stockwerk hinaufzureiten, da waren die prächtigen Kleider, das goldene Pferd und auch das goldbestickte Taschentuch längst wieder im mächtigen Stamm der Eiche verschwunden.

Die beiden älteren Brüder verspotteten ihren jüngsten, der wieder bei den Schweinen saß und seine schmutzigen Kleider trug. Und sie erzählten ihm, dass sie im Schloss einen so prächtigen Prinzen gesehen hätten, wie noch keinen zuvor. Der wäre auf einem Pferd geritten, das ausgesehen hätte, als sei es aus purem Gold!

Da sagte ihr jüngster Bruder, den sie den Dummen nannten: „Die Klugen sehen es nur, doch die Dummen besitzen es!"

Da lachten die beiden Brüder noch lauter über ihn und riefen: „Du denkst wohl, der Prinz auf dem goldenen Pferd war so dumm wie du? Das kann gar nicht sein, denn deine Dummheit ist riesengroß, wirklich, sie schreit ja zum Himmel!"

Am nächsten Tage ritten die beiden Brüder wieder zum Schloss. Und wieder ging der Jüngste zum uralten Eichenbaum. Als er die drei Birkenzweige wieder dreimal gegen den Stamm geschlagen hatte, kam wieder das goldene Pferd hervor, das er erneut bestieg, um in prächtigen Kleidern zum Schloss zu reiten.

Dort ritt er zum größten Erstaunen aller Versammelten wieder die Mauern des Schlosses empor. Er ritt ohne

Mühe ganz hoch hinauf, bis er das vierte Stockwerk erreichte. Sein Ritt schien so mühelos zu sein, als sei das große goldene Pferd, das ihn trug, federleicht wie ein Vogel im Flug.

Die Prinzessin hatte schon voller Ungeduld auf ihn gewartet.

„Nimm diesen Ring aus rotem Gold", sagte sie zu ihm, „damit du ein weiteres Andenken an unsere zwei Begegnungen hast!"

Der Jüngste nahm dankend den Ring aus der Hand der Prinzessin und ritt dann auf seinem goldenen Pferd wieder die Mauern des Schlosses hinab.

Kaum war er hinuntergeritten und wollte zum Schlosstor hinaus, da schoss voller Neid ein Wartender dem Prinzen einen Pfeil hinterher. Der Pfeil sirrte durch die Sommerluft und traf die rechte Ferse des Reiters!

Trotz seines Schmerzes gelang es dem Jüngsten noch, in höchster Eile nach Hause zu reiten und sein goldenes Pferd, die prächtigen Kleider und auch den Ring der Prinzessin im uralten Eichenstamm zu verstecken.

Als seine Brüder heimkehrten, fragten sie ihn, warum er lahmen würde.

Da sagte er mit trauriger Stimme: „Ich bin über unser dickstes Schwein gestolpert und dann in den Schweinetrog gefallen. Bei diesem Sturz habe ich mir meinen rechten Fußknöchel verstaucht. Und der tut jetzt weh! Ihr glaubt nicht, wie weh das tut!"

Da lachten seine beiden Brüder so, dass ihr Lachen

kein Ende finden konnte und riefen immerzu: „Die Klugen sehen es nur, doch die Dummen besitzen es! Ach, die Klugen sehen es nur, doch die Dummen besitzen es!"

Die Königstochter hatte drei Tage und Nächte vergeblich darauf gewartet, dass der vermeintliche Prinz auf seinem goldenen Pferd wieder zu ihr geritten käme. Doch er kam und kam nicht zurück!

Da ließ der König den fremden Reiter im ganzen Lande suchen. Und als er dann von seiner Verwundung erfuhr, mussten seine Diener jeden lahmen Mann, den sie fanden, ins Schloss bringen. Doch es war keiner dabei, der als untrügliches Zeichen den goldenen Ring und das goldbestickte Taschentuch der Königstochter vorweisen konnte.

Auf ihrer Suche nach dem unbekannten Reiter kamen die Diener auch in das Haus der drei Brüder. Und auf die Frage, ob es in ihrem Hause jemanden geben würde, der auf seinem rechten Fuß humpelte, sagte der Älteste lachend: „Aber ja, wir haben einen lahmen Bruder! Doch der ist so dumm und so ungeschickt, dass er sogar über unsere eigenen Schweine stolpert!"

Und der Zweitälteste fügte noch hinzu: „Sie sollten sich wirklich die Mühe ersparen, ihn anzusehen. Er ist so dumm und so schmutzig, dass es schon eine Schande ist, einen solchen Bruder zu haben!"

Aber die Diener des Königs ließen keine Ruhe, bis sie den Jüngsten gesehen hatten. Und weil er auf dem rechten Fuß wirklich lahmte, musste er, so schmutzig und so zerlumpt wie er war, mit ihnen ins Schloss kommen, denn das hatte der König befohlen.

Als die Königstochter ihn in seinen Lumpen so vor sich stehen sah, da rief sie voller Entsetzen: „Dieser elende, schmutzige, lahme Schweinehirt kann doch um alles in der Welt niemals der Rechte sein!"

Doch nachdem der Leibarzt des Königs die Schusswunde gründlich betrachtet hatte, musste der Schweinehirt jener fremde Reiter sein. Und weil der König versprochen hatte, dass er seine Tochter demjenigen zur Frau geben würde, der auf seinem Pferd bis ins vierte Stockwerk geritten käme, musste er sein gegebenes Versprechen auch halten.

Da begann die schöne Tochter des Königs bitterlich zu weinen. Und sie war verzweifelt darüber, dass ein so schmutziger, humpelnder und, wie es schien, auch noch dummer Schweinehirt nun ihr Mann werden sollte!

Da humpelte der jüngste Bruder, den seine beiden ältesten immer den Dummen nannten, wieder nach Hause zum uralten Eichenbaum zurück. Dort angekommen, schlug er die drei Birkenzweige wieder dreimal gegen die alte, rissige Rinde. Und schon öffnete sich der riesige Baum und mit hellem Wiehern trabte das goldene Pferd hervor.

So schnell er nur konnte, zog der Junge die prächtigen Kleider an und jagte dann in gestrecktem Galopp zum Schloss zurück. Doch er kam nicht allein, denn ihm folgten in einer langen Reihe sechs goldene Hengste und zwölf silberne Stuten, neben denen zwölf silberne Fohlen munter und fröhlich sprangen.

Als ihn die Königstochter so reiten sah und auch ihr goldbesticktes Taschentuch und den Ring aus rotem Gold erblickte, da war sie glücklich wie niemals zuvor im Leben!

Als die Hochzeitskutsche dann, gezogen von goldenen Hengsten, begleitet von silbernen Stuten und silbernen Fohlen, durch die Straßen der Stadt gefahren kam, da war das ein so prächtiger Anblick, dass man davon noch lange und bis in ferne Lande erzählte.

Die beiden älteren Brüder jedoch, die sich so klug vorgekommen waren, die mussten seit dieser Zeit selbst ihre Schweine hüten.

Prinz Ludwig und die Prinzessin mit der schönen schwarzen Haut

Es war einmal ein König, der war von einem Tag auf den anderen blind geworden. Und obwohl seine Ärzte alles versuchten, es gelang ihnen nicht, ihm sein Augenlicht wiederzugeben.

Je mehr sich die Ärzte vergeblich bemühten, desto trauriger wurde der König. Und je mehr er trauerte, desto verzweifelter wurde er auch. Doch seine Verzweiflung und alle Kunst seiner Ärzte halfen nicht, die Sehkraft seiner Augen wiederzuerlangen.

Da kam eines Tages ein weiser Mann an den Hof des blinden Königs und erzählte, dass es in einem fernen Land einen Vogel gäbe, der sänge so wunderschön, dass von seinem Gesang alle blinden Menschen sehend würden. Wenn es dem König gelänge, diesen Vogel, der auf den Namen „Cäsarius" höre, an seinen Hof zu bekommen, würde ihm auf der Stelle das Augenlicht wieder geschenkt!

Da ließ der blinde König seinen ältesten Sohn zu sich

kommen und bat ihn, sich auf die Reise zu begeben, um in diesem fernen Land irgendwo auf der Welt den wundersamen Vogel zu finden.

Der älteste Königssohn rüstete sich zu seiner großen Reise. Und der Vater schenkte ihm ein prächtiges Pferd. Der Sohn bestieg den mächtigen Hengst und ritt in die Welt hinaus, um seinem Vater den Wundervogel zu bringen.

Er war einen ganzen langen Tag geritten, als er am späten Abend an eine Herberge kam, die mitten im tiefen Walde lag.

Er band sein Pferd an den Zaun vor der Herberge an und ging hinein. Als er den Raum betrat, fand er dort eine muntere Gesellschaft von Kartenspielern versammelt, die ihn sogleich zum Mitspielen aufforderten. Und da er für sein Leben gerne spielte, sagte er nicht Nein. Er spielte und spielte, bei Tag und bei Nacht. Und er verlor dabei all sein Geld. Doch er spielte immer noch weiter. Da verlor er schließlich auch seine schönen Kleider und endlich sogar sein prächtiges Pferd!

Als er nichts mehr hatte, was ihm gehörte, warfen ihn seine Spielgesellen in ein Verlies, wo er ohne Kleider, nur bei Wasser und trockenem Brot, elendig schmachten musste.

Als nun eine längere Zeit vergangen war und der Älteste nicht wiederkehrte, da bat der Vater den zweiten Sohn, den Wundervogel zu suchen.

Auch der zweite Sohn bestieg einen prächtigen Hengst

und ritt in die Welt hinaus, um seinem blinden Vater aus einem fernen Land den Wundervogel Cäsarius zu bringen.

Doch dem zweiten Sohn erging es ebenso, wie es seinem älteren Bruder ergangen war. Und seit dieser Zeit mussten beide Brüder bei Wasser und Brot und nackten Leibes im dunklen Verlies jenes einsamen Hauses in der Tiefe des Waldes schmachten.

Da nun auch der zweite Sohn verschollen war, beschloss der Jüngste, Ludwig mit Namen, den sie heimlich aber den dummen Prinzen nannten, sich auf die Reise ins Unbekannte zu begeben, um jenen Vogel zu finden, der seinen Vater von seiner Blindheit erlösen konnte.

Aber der blinde König wollte ihn nicht ziehen lassen aus Angst, nun auch noch den letzten der Söhne zu verlieren. Insgeheim fürchtete er auch, dass Ludwig dieser schweren Aufgabe nicht gewachsen sei. Doch der Prinz bat seinen Vater so lange, bis der ihm die Reise gestattete. Und zum Abschied schenkte er ihm dann eine sehr sanfte Stute, dachte er doch, dieses sanfte Tier würde so gemächlich traben, dass seinem jüngsten Sohn, den sie heimlich den dummen Prinzen nannten, beim Reiten auf holprigen Straßen kein Schaden entstünde.

Prinz Ludwig nun ritt den gleichen Weg entlang, den vor ihm seine Brüder geritten waren. Doch als er an der einsamen Herberge im Walde vorüberkam und man ihn dort zum Kartenspiel einlud, sagte er zu den Spielern, er müsse in wichtigen Geschäften weiterreiten. Bei seiner

Rückkehr dann sei er zum Spiel durchaus bereit; sprach es und ließ seine Stute sanft weitertraben.

So ritt er weiter bei Tag und bei Nacht und erreichte endlich einen noch größeren Wald, als es der erste gewesen war. Dort saß vor einer winzigen Hütte eine alte Frau.

„Prinz Ludwig", rief ihm die alte Frau entgegen, „komm, setze dich zu mir! Komm, iss und trink und ruhe dich aus, denn morgen hast du einen weiten Weg vor dir!"

Prinz Ludwig tat, was die Alte ihm sagte. Er versorgte seine Stute und setzte sich dann zu der alten Frau, um mit ihr zu essen und mit ihr zu reden.

Als er am nächsten Morgen sein Pferd besteigen wollte, da sprach die Alte zu ihm: „Höre mir ganz genau zu, denn ich will dir einen guten Rat geben! Lass deine sanfte Stute bei mir und nimm meinen Rappen dafür. Mein Rappe ist viel schneller als dein Pferd. Sitz auf und lass den Rappen gewähren, er kennt seinen Weg ganz genau!"

Der schöne Rappe war schnell wie der Wind und er trug den Prinzen zu einer anderen Frau, die war noch älter als die erste. Die lebte einhundert Meilen entfernt in einem anderen, noch größeren Wald. Diese sprach zu ihm die gleichen Worte wie die erste alte Frau und es war deren ältere Schwester. Auch sie schenkte ihm ein schönes Pferd.

Am nächsten Morgen bestieg Prinz Ludwig sein neues

Pferd, eine wunderschöne Fuchsstute. Die galoppierte noch schneller, als es der schnelle Rappe getan hatte. Und als er auf ihr mehr als hundert Meilen geritten war, traf er die dritte der Schwestern. Die war so alt, wie er es bisher nicht für möglich gehalten hatte.

Auch bei ihr ruhte er sich aus. Und am nächsten Morgen sprach sie zu ihm: „Wenn du meinen pfeilschnellen Schimmel besteigst, wird er dich zu jenem Ort tragen, an dem du den Vogel Cäsarius findest. Steige sofort ab, wenn der Schimmel stehen bleibt, und gehe geraden Weges zum Eingang des Schlosses, das dann vor deinen Augen entsteht. Dort angekommen musst du drei Zimmer durchschreiten. Im dritten wird, unter vielen anderen Vögeln, auch Cäsarius sein. Ergreife ihn und eile, so schnell du kannst, zum Schimmel zurück. Schwing dich sofort auf den Rücken des Pferdes und reite dann um dein Leben!"

Prinz Ludwig dankte der uralten Frau und bestieg den herrlichen Schimmel, der schneller war als der Wind. Als Ludwig nach einem Ritt über viele hundert Meilen am Ziel angekommen war, tat er alles genau so, wie es die Uralte gesagt hatte.

Das erste Zimmer, das er betrat, war vornehm und prächtig eingerichtet. Es zwitscherten dort so viele Singvögel, wie er sie noch nie zuvor auf einmal gehört hatte. Doch auch der allerschönste Vogelgesang konnte den Prinzen nicht zum Bleiben verführen und eilig ging er weiter.

Im zweiten Zimmer, noch prächtiger ausgestattet, flatterten noch mehr Singvögel als in dem ersten. Sie zwitscherten und jubelten, dass es eine Freude war, ihrem Gesang zu lauschen. Doch der Prinz durcheilte auch diesen Raum und war schon im dritten Zimmer. So kostbar war dieser Raum ausgestattet, dass die beiden ersten, so prächtig sie auch gewesen waren, vor seiner Pracht verblassten! Und er war angefüllt mit Vögeln des seltsamsten Gesanges, den Gott jemals geschaffen hatte.

Aber das Allerschönste in diesem Raum war eine schlafende Frau. Die lag auf einem goldenen Diwan und hatte eine glänzend schimmernde schwarze Haut. So wunderschön war diese Frau, dass Prinz Ludwigs Jugend nicht widerstehen konnte – und er küsste sie mitten auf den Mund!

Sein Kuss war jedoch so zärtlich, dass die Schöne nicht einmal erwachte. Dann ergriff er den Vogel Cäsarius und eilte mit ihm davon. Doch bevor er das Zimmer verließ, schrieb er auf ein Stückchen Papier seinen Namen und versteckte es hinter jenem Bild, das den Wundervogel zeigte.

Kaum hatte der Prinz das dritte Zimmer verlassen, als im Schloss ein fürchterliches Lärmen begann: Wilde Hunde bellten, Wölfe heulten, Löwen und Tiger brüllten so laut, dass sich dem Prinzen die Nackenhaare sträubten. Und da sprang er schon auf und davon und rannte um sein Leben! Hetzten doch die allerwildesten Raubtiere hinter ihm her!

Kaum hatte der Prinz seinen Fuß in den Steigbügel gehoben, da galoppierte der Schimmel schon mit ihm davon, noch schneller als der Wind! Und ehe es Abend wurde, waren Reiter und Ross und der Vogel Cäsarius unversehrt bei der uralten, weisen Frau.

„Nimm dieses Brot hier", sagte die uralte Weise, „es kann dir einmal behilflich sein; denn sobald du ein Stück davon abgebrochen oder auch gegessen hast, schließt sich die Lücke und das Brot hat wieder seine vollständige Gestalt."

Prinz Ludwig nahm dankend das Brot von der uralten Frau und ritt auf der Fuchsstute zur zweiten Schwester zurück.

Die schenkte ihm ein Stückchen Seife.

„Nimm diese Seife und trage sie stets bei dir", sagte sie dabei, „denn sollte der Tag jemals kommen, an dem du ganz plötzlich völlige Sauberkeit benötigst, so macht dich dieses Stück im Augenblick so rein, dass deine Haut glatt und schön wie die eines kleinen Kindes wird!"

Als Ludwig die dritte der Schwestern erreichte, da schenkte sie ihm ihren windschnellen Rappen. Und sie gab ihm auch den Rat, nicht in die Herberge im Walde einzukehren.

„Zwar werden dort deine Brüder gefangen gehalten", sagte sie zu ihm, „doch wäre es besser, dich jetzt nicht um die beiden zu kümmern!"

Aber das mitleidige Herz des Prinzen, den sie den Dummen nannten, ließ ein Vorbeireiten nicht zu. Und er kehrte in die Herberge ein, bezahlte alle Spielschulden seiner Brüder und löste sie aus dem Schuldgefängnis aus. Dann ritten die drei gemeinsam nach Hause.

Doch während sie so dahinritten, sagte der älteste Bruder heimlich zum zweiten: „Es kann doch nicht sein, dass unser dummer jüngster Bruder so ruhmreich nach Hause kommt!"

„Das darf nicht sein", antwortete ebenso heimlich der zweite, „denn dann sind wir beiden die wirklichen Dummen!"

Und da beschlossen sie ihren jüngsten Bruder zu töten. Doch es fehlte den beiden an Mut, diese ruchlose Tat mit eigenen Händen zu tun. Und als sie zum Strand eines Meeres kamen, gaben sie Fischern heimlich viel Geld und den Auftrag, ihren jüngsten Bruder in der Tiefe des Wassers zu ertränken.

Die Fischer nahmen Prinz Ludwig gefangen und segelten mit ihm auf das weite Meer hinaus, um ihn fern der Küste in der Tiefe des Wassers zu ertränken.

Die beiden Brüder aber nahmen den Vogel Cäsarius und ritten, so schnell sie nur reiten konnten, zum Schloss ihres blinden Vaters.

Als sie ins Schloss des blinden Königs geritten kamen, herrschte bei ihrer Ankunft große Freude. Doch bald schon kehrte die Trauer zurück, denn der wundersame Vogel mit Namen Cäsarius, dessen Gesang Blinde sehend machen konnte, ließ keinen einzigen Ton aus seiner Vogelkehle!

Da wurde der alte König noch trauriger, als er es vor der Reise seiner drei Söhne gewesen war! Denn zu seiner Blindheit gesellte sich noch der Verlust seines jüngsten Sohnes, der, wie seine beiden Brüder dem Vater heuchelnd berichteten, mit unbekanntem Ziel fortgeritten sei.

Prinz Ludwig jedoch war es durch Sanftmut und Überredungskunst gelungen, die Fischer dazu zu bringen, dass sie sein Leben verschonten. Und sie setzten ihn auf einer einsamen Insel aus, die von Menschen unbewohnt fernab jeder Küste in der großen Weite des Meeres lag.

Sieben Jahre lang blieb der Prinz dort als Mensch ganz allein. Er lebte wie ein Tier unter Tieren. Er lebte gemeinsam mit dem Wild des Waldes, mit den Bewohnern des Meeres und allem, was da kriecht, hüpft und fliegt am Strand und unter den Bäumen. Und da er allen von seinem unerschöpflichen Brot zu essen gab, wurden die Tiere bald so zutraulich, als sei der Prinz einer der ihren.

Doch in dem fernen Land, im verwunschenen Schloss, in dem einst der Vogel Cäsarius lebte, da hatte die wunderschöne Prinzessin mit der schwarzen Haut, als sie aus ihrem Schlaf erwachte, geglaubt, sie habe einen wunderbaren Traum gehabt. Ein Prinz aus einem fernen Land sei gekommen und habe sie geküsst – was bisher kein anderer gewagt hatte, da alle von ihrer Schönheit geblendet waren.

Immer wieder musste die Prinzessin an diesen Traum

denken. Und jedes Mal hoffte sie inständig, er würde in Erfüllung gehen und eines Tages würde ein Prinz kommen, der sie aus ihrer Einsamkeit erlösen möge.

Doch es sollte noch sieben Jahre dauern, bis sie eines schönen Tages wieder einmal verträumt auf jenem goldenen Diwan lag, auf dem Prinz Ludwig sie damals angetroffen hatte, und ihr Blick am Bild des Vogels Cäsarius hängen blieb. Sie stand auf, um das Bild, das sie magisch anzuziehen schien, aus der Nähe zu betrachten. Voller Neugier drehte sie es sogar um und fand hinter dem Bild jenes Papier, auf das Prinz Ludwig einstmals seinen Namen geschrieben hatte; damals, als er den Wundervogel entführte.

Ihr Herz tat einen Sprung – so war ihr Traum also wirklich wahr geworden! Auf der Stelle wollte sie sich auf die Suche nach jenem Prinzen machen und ihn notfalls sogar mit Gewalt für sich gewinnen. Sie versammelte ein großes Heer und zog mit vielen Reitern gegen jenes ferne Königreich, aus dem Prinz Ludwig damals gekommen war.

Da nun das gewaltige Reiterheer die Grenzen des Königreiches erreicht hatte, schickte die schwarze Prinzessin einen Herold aus, der vom blinden König verlangte, dass jener Mann, der den Vogel Cäsarius geraubt hatte, auf der Stelle zu ihr kommen müsste! Sollte der Mann sich jedoch weigern zu kommen, so ließ sie den Herold verkünden, würde das gewaltige Heer das Land und den Königspalast bis zur Unkenntlichkeit verwüsten!

Der blinde König, mutlos und voller Furcht, ließ seinen ältesten Sohn zu sich kommen.

„Mein Sohn", sagte der blinde König, „bist du es gewesen, der den Vogel Cäsarius fing?"

„Ja, Vater, ich war es!", rief der älteste Prinz voller Stolz.

Da schickte ihn der König in das feindliche Lager, damit er dort um Gnade für sein Vaterland bitten möge.

Der älteste Prinz schmückte sich mit seinen allerschönsten Kleidern. Er sattelte sein prächtigstes Pferd und ritt auf ihm dem feindlichen Heerlager entgegen. Als er die Stadt verlassen hatte, sah er die Heerstraße der fremden Prinzessin vor sich liegen; schimmernd, als sei sie gepflastert mit purem Gold. Da wagte er nicht, die Hufe seines Pferdes darüber traben zu lassen. Und so ritt er neben der glänzenden goldenen Straße auf das feindliche Lager zu.

Am Ende der goldenen Straße aber stand wartend die schwarze Prinzessin. Als sie nun den fremden Mann so auf das Lager zukommen sah, sprach sie zu sich: „Das kann er nicht sein! Der da geritten kommt, hat nicht den Mut meines Traumprinzen!"

Und sie behandelte den ältesten Prinzen, als sei er ein ganz gewöhnlicher Knecht. Dann schickte sie ihn mit der Nachricht zurück, sie wolle denjenigen haben, der wirklich den Wundervogel geraubt hatte!

Der blinde König rief nun den zweiten Sohn und befahl ihm, sich ohne zu zögern ins feindliche Heerlager zu begeben. Doch auch dem zweiten Prinzen erging es, wie es dem ältesten Bruder ergangen war; denn auch er traute sich nicht, sein Pferd auf die goldene Straße zu lenken. Und wie sein ältester Bruder kehrte er auch mit der gleichen Nachricht zurück.

Da wurde der blinde König sehr zornig. Und er befahl seinen beiden Söhnen, sein Schloss sofort zu verlassen. Nicht eher dürften sie zurückkommen, bis sie ihren jüngsten Bruder gefunden hätten!

Da nun die beiden Prinzen zum Strand des Meeres geritten kamen, trafen sie dort jene Fischer wieder, denen sie den Auftrag gegeben hatten, ihren jüngsten Bruder zu töten. Als sie nun erfuhren, dass ihr Bruder lebte und auf einer einsamen Insel sei, nahmen sie sich ein Schiff und segelten so lange, bis sie zu jener Insel kamen, auf der seit sieben Jahren ihr jüngster Bruder als einziger Mensch unter Tieren lebte.

Sie mussten lange suchen, ehe sie ihn fanden, denn er sah selbst aus wie ein wildes Tier. Mit allen Tieren der Insel befreundet, weigerte er sich, die Insel zu verlassen, um seinen Brüdern ins Schloss des Vaters zu folgen.

Aber den dringenden Bitten seiner beiden Brüder gelang es endlich, den jungen Prinzen zu überzeugen, dass ihn sein Vater unbedingt brauchte, um von seiner Blindheit erlöst zu werden.

212   Als Prinz Ludwig mit seinen Brüdern das Schiff bestieg, da sah er so wild aus, als sei er ein Tier des tiefsten Urwaldes. Und die Fischer fürchteten sich vor ihm.

Da zog der Prinz die Wunderseife hervor. Kaum hatte die Seife seine Haut berührt, da wurde Ludwig reiner und schöner noch, als er jemals im Leben gewesen!

So schnell es die Winde erlaubten, segelte das Schiff über das Meer. Dann galoppierten die drei Brüder zum Schloss ihres Vaters zurück.

Sie waren kaum dort angekommen, als der Vogel Cäsarius zu singen begann. Er sang so lieblich und so schön, dass alle, die seinen Gesang hörten, vor Freude weinen mussten. Und dem alten König gingen die blinden Augen auf und er sah von Stund an die Welt in der ganzen Pracht ihrer schönsten Farben und herrlichsten Formen!

Als nun Prinz Ludwig auf seinem prächtigen Rappen die golden glänzende Heerstraße entlang zum fremden Heerlager ritt, da stand wieder an ihrem Ende die fremde Prinzessin.

„Das muss er sein", sagte die Frau mit der schönen schwarzen Haut, „denn niemand sonst auf der Welt hätte den Mut, über eine Heerstraße, gepflastert mit purem Gold, so unbefangen zu reiten!"

Die Hochzeit Ludwigs mit der schönen Prinzessin wurde zu einem großen Fest. Und es feierten auch die Soldaten des Königs gemeinsam mit den Reitern des fremden Heeres. Der alte König, sehenden Auges nun, wollte seinem jüngsten Sohn sein ganzes Königreich zur Mitgift geben.

Doch die Prinzessin mit der schwarzen Haut sagte zu ihm: „Behalte dein Land, oh König, behalte es nur als dein Eigentum! Wir besitzen ein so großes Reich, dass es für deinen Sohn und auch für mich zur gemeinsamen Heimat werden wird. Wir haben in unserem Reich so viel Raum, wie man braucht, um ein Menschenleben lang miteinander glücklich zu sein!"

Dann zog die fremde Prinzessin mit ihrem Mann, jenem Ludwig, der früher heimlich der dumme Prinz genannt worden war, und ihrem gewaltigen Reiterheer wieder in das große fremde Land zurück; in jenes ferne Land, aus dem sie und auch jener Vogel Cäsarius, der mit seinem Gesang Blinden das Augenlicht wiedergeben konnte, einstmals gekommen waren.

Die beiden Prinzen aber, die so boshaft und falsch zu ihrem jüngsten Bruder gewesen waren, die wurden von ihrem königlichen Vater mit tiefer Verachtung gestraft. Erst als sie ihre Reue dauerhaft zeigten und ehrlich lebten, nahm er sie wieder in den Schoß der Familie auf.

Das sprechende Pferd
des Teufels

Es war einmal eine Wirtin, in deren Schänke die Bauern gerne eintraten, wenn sie an Markttagen ihre Pferde, ihr Vieh oder die Früchte des Feldes verkauft hatten. Sie hatten es sich zur Gewohnheit gemacht, hier noch ein wenig zu verweilen, um nach vollbrachtem Handel den Durst zu stillen und miteinander über dies und jenes zu plaudern.

Manche der Bauern blieben bis in den Abend hinein in der Schänke. Und wenn sie dann nicht mehr ganz so klar denken konnten wie bei ihrem Eintritt, schrieb ihnen die Wirtin die doppelte Anzahl von Getränken auf; statt eines Kruges oder eines Glases eben deren zwei, manchmal sogar drei.

Lange Zeit wurde das nicht bemerkt, war doch die Wirtin sehr geschickt darin, die Bauern durch allerlei fröhliches Reden abzulenken um sie auf diese Weise zu täuschen. Das gelang ihr auch vortrefflich, bis zu jenem Abend, da sie an einen besonders aufgeweckten Bauern geriet, der ihre unschönen Taten entdeckte und sich darüber empörte!

Die Wirtin jedoch tat sehr entrüstet und sagte laut, eine bekanntermaßen ehrbare Frau wie sie würde so etwas nie und nimmer tun!

Nun wurden auch andere Bauern aufmerksam und überprüften schweren Augenlides ihre Rechnungen.

Und der Älteste sagte: „Frau Wirtin, wenn Ihr zu Gott in den Himmel wollt, dann müsst Ihr ganz und gar ehrlich sein!"

Aber die Wirtin tat weiterhin sehr empört und sagte es auch ziemlich laut.

Da sprachen die Bauern zueinander: „Diese Frau will Gottes Worte nicht hören, sie hört wohl lieber auf den Teufel!"

Doch die Wirtin behauptete weiter, sie hätte nichts Unrechtes getan und sprach endlich diese Worte: „Falls ich Unrecht getan haben sollte, möge mich auf der Stelle der Teufel holen! Mit Leib und Seele und hier vor aller Augen!"

Ihre Worte waren kaum gesprochen, da wehte ein gewaltiger Sturmwind durch die Schänke, ein schreckliches Sausen und Brausen erfüllte die Luft und ein solcher Schwefelgestank, dass allen Anwesenden der Atem stockte.

Dann folgte ein Blitz und ein Donner von solcher Gewalt, dass sich die Bauern vor Angst auf den Boden warfen und um ihr Leben fürchteten.

Schon stand der gehörnte Leibhaftige im Raum und blickte aus glühend feurigen Augen in die Runde!

„Du hast mich gerufen", rief er mit schrecklicher Stimme, „und nun bin ich hier, um das zu tun, was du gewünscht hast!"

Bei diesen Worten verwandelte sich vor aller Augen die unehrliche Wirtin in ein tiefschwarzes Pferd. Schon sprang der Teufel auf seinen Rücken und galoppierte mit ihm aus der Schänke hinaus und in gestrecktem Galopp weiter durch die finstere Nacht. Er galoppierte, bis er zu einer Schmiede kam, die einsam am Rande eines Dorfes lag.

Dort zügelte er sein schwarzes Pferd und schlug mit der Faust ganz gewaltig gegen die Tür der Schmiede. Er schlug so lange, bis der Schmied erwachte.

Schlaftrunkenen Auges öffnete der Schmied seine Tür und der Teufel verlangte von ihm, er möge sofort die Hufe seines Pferdes beschlagen, denn er hätte noch einen weiten Weg vor sich und müsste in dieser Nacht noch zum Schloss des Fürsten reiten, um ihm einen überaus wichtigen Brief zu bringen!

Der müde Schmied versuchte die anstrengende Arbeit auf den nächsten Morgen zu verschieben. Und er erzählte dem Teufel, dass es sehr schwierig sei, jetzt mitten in der Nacht ein Schmiedefeuer zu entzünden, um dort das Eisen zur nötigen Weißglut zu bringen.

Doch der Teufel lachte nur höhnisch und meinte, vom Feuer machen, da verstünde er reichlich viel, das könne

217

er ihm ruhig glauben. Er sollte nur so rasch wie möglich ans Werk gehen, denn die Zeit würde drängen!

Aber der Schmied, der die harte Arbeit des langen Tages noch in den müden Armen spürte, versuchte wieder ins warme Bett zu kommen. Doch der Teufel ließ nicht nach in seinem Drängen. Und endlich wurde er sehr laut und drohte dem müden Schmied, falls er das Pferd nicht auf der Stelle beschlüge, würde ihn der Fürst, zu dem er eiligst den Brief bringen müsste, sicher ins tiefste Gefängnis werfen! Was das für einen armen Mann und seine Familie bedeute, könne er sich doch wohl lebhaft vorstellen!

Da erschrak der Schmied so sehr, dass ihm mit einem Schlage alle Müdigkeit verging. Er öffnete die Schmiede und begann das Feuer zu schüren. Er trat den Blasebalg mit aller Macht und fertigte auch bald zwei Hufeisen an.

Als er nun aber die beiden noch glühenden Eisen an die hinteren Hufe anpassen wollte, begann das schwarze Pferd zu sprechen.

„Oh weh, Gevatter Schmied!", jammerte das Pferd. „Oh weh, deine Hufeisen sind ja so glühend heiß, du verbrennst mir die Sohlen der Füße!"

Der Schmied erschrak mächtig, doch da redete das Pferd schon weiter.

„Sei doch vorsichtig, Gevatter Schmied!", jammerte es wieder, „du beschlägst die Fußsohlen einer ehrbaren Wirtin!"

Das brachte den armen Schmied fast um den Verstand

und er erschrak so sehr, dass ihm die Hände zitterten. Dann fielen ihm sogar das glühende Hufeisen samt Hammer und Zange zu Boden!

Da mischte sich der Teufel ein.

„Du sollst dich nicht um das dumme Geschwätz dieses alten Gaules kümmern", brüllte er, „du sollst nur seine Hufe benageln! Und zwar so schnell es geht! Denn noch in dieser Nacht muss ich mit meinem wichtigen Schreiben das Schloss des Fürsten erreichen!"

Halb tot vor Entsetzen über die ungeheuren Dinge, die sich da in seiner Schmiede ereigneten, versuchte der Schmied mit dem Mut der Verzweiflung das schwarze Pferd zu beschlagen. Doch war er in solche Angst geraten, dass ihm sein Handwerkszeug andauernd aus seinen Händen fiel. Er kam und kam in seiner Arbeit überhaupt nicht weiter!

So dauerte es und dauerte immer länger. Und der Teufel wurde immer ungeduldiger und auch immer ärgerlicher!

Doch je lauter, drängender und böser er wurde, desto ängstlicher wurde der Schmied. Und seine vertraute Arbeit, die er seit Jahren tagtäglich verrichtet hatte, ging ihm überhaupt nicht mehr von der Hand!

Da krähte plötzlich ein Hahn. Und im selben Augenblick wieherte das Pferd vor Freude. Als dann der Hahn zum dritten Mal gekräht hatte, da war das schwarze Pferd des Teufels schon wieder zu einer menschlichen Gestalt geworden.

Da stampfte der Teufel mit seinem Bocksfuß so wild auf den Boden der Schmiede, dass ein tiefes Loch entstand. So furchtbar böse war er geworden! Denn mit dem Hahnenschrei und dem beginnenden Tag war seine Macht gebrochen.

Dann stieß der Teufel einen so fürchterlichen Fluch aus, wie ihn der Schmied noch nie zuvor in seinem Leben gehört hatte und auch niemals je wieder hören sollte. Und mit Donner und Blitz und einem grauenhaften Gestank jagte er durch den Schornstein der Schmiede nach draußen!

Doch bevor er im Schornstein verschwand, holte der Teufel noch einmal gewaltig aus und haute der Wirtin so mächtig eins aufs Maul, dass die Abdrücke seiner Klauen schwarz wie Teer für immer auf ihrer linken Wange blieben!

Vom Schlag des Teufels noch halb betäubt, wusste die Wirtin nicht mehr so recht, was ihr geschehen war. Und sie wankte an dem schreckensbleichen Schmied vorbei aus seiner Schmiede hinaus und ging wie im Traum den langen Weg zu ihrem Dorf zurück.

Dort angekommen, machte sie einen großen Bogen um ihre Schankwirtschaft und hat diese seither auch nie mehr wieder betreten.

Der Schmied aber, in dessen Schmiede sich solches zugetragen hatte, der wurde zu einem wohlhabenden und bekannten Mann. Denn es kamen viele Leute von nah und fern, um die Geschichte vom überlisteten Teufel zu hören und jene beiden Hufeisen zu besichtigen, mit denen das schwarze Pferd in jener Nacht beschlagen werden sollte.

Das Gespensterpferd

Einstmals vor vielen Jahren, da soll sich in mancher Nacht an einem der masurischen Seen ein gespenstisches Pferd gezeigt haben.

Dieses Pferd war von einem so strahlenden Weiß, wie man es wohl noch niemals zuvor bei einem Schimmel gesehen hatte. Es war von einer so großen Helligkeit, so berichtet die Sage, dass seine Gestalt weithin durch die finsterste aller Nächte leuchtete.

Der Ort, an dem dieses Gespensterpferd zu nächtlicher Stunde erschien, war eine alte Schleuse, die oberhalb einer Wassermühle lag; an jener Stelle, an welcher ein schmaler Ausläufer des Sees in den Fluss Alle übergeht, der ja durch mehrere Seen hindurchfließt.

Nun erzählt die Sage, dass dieses Geisterpferd sich auch durch ein sehr lautes Wiehern bemerkbar gemacht hätte. Dieses Wiehern habe man noch meilenweit entfernt und überdeutlich hören können. Auch sei ein so wildes und lautes Stampfen der Hufe vernehmbar gewesen, dass manche Menschen erschreckt aus den Betten gesprungen wären, aus Angst, die Erde würde beben!

Um diesem gespenstischen Treiben endlich ein Ende zu bereiten, fragten die Menschen, die um diesen See lebten, ihren Pfarrer um Rat. Der überlegte nicht lange, sondern sagte ihnen gleich seine Hilfe zu. Und er beschloss, genau an jener Stelle, an der sich das Geisterpferd in den Nächten zeigte, des Sonntags einen Gottesdienst unter freiem Himmel abzuhalten.

Die Ankündigung dieses Gottesdienstes in der freien Natur sprach sich bald in der ganzen Gegend herum. Und als die Zeit gekommen war, da lachte die Sonne und kein einziges Wölkchen trübte die Bläue des Sommerhimmels.

So viele Menschen hatten sich an der alten Schleuse versammelt, dass man mit ihrer Zahl ganz bequem hätte zwei Kirchen füllen können! Selbst die allerältesten Leute waren mitgekommen und auch die kleinsten Kinder. Und wer nicht zu Fuß kommen konnte, den brachte man mit dem Pferd.

Der Pfarrer las erbauliche Worte aus der Bibel vor und er segnete auch die Pferde, damit die Worte des Herrn beruhigend in ihren Ohren klängen, wenn wieder das wilde Wiehern des Gespensterpferdes sie in den Nächten erschreckte.

Alle Menschen, die gekommen waren, sangen mit Inbrunst die schönen alten Kirchenlieder. Weithin hallte der Gesang zum Lobe des Herrn durch den sonnigen

223

Sonntagvormittag, dass sogar einige der Pferde mitwieherten.

Als dann der Pfarrer mit solch überzeugender Hingabe predigte wie wohl noch niemals zuvor im Leben, da mussten alle, ob Groß oder Klein, ob Alt oder Jung, vor Freude weinen!

Obwohl dieser sonntägliche Gottesdienst unter freiem Himmel – allseits bekannt auch als „Pferdepredigt" – so wunderschön und gelungen war, wollte das Geisterpferd, so wird jedenfalls berichtet, sein gespenstisches Treiben nicht aufgeben.

Zwar blieb es in Zukunft von jener Stelle fern, an der so viele Leute der Pferdepredigt gelauscht und fromme Lieder gesungen hatten, aber an zahlreichen anderen Orten trieb das weiße Gespensterross weiterhin sein Unwesen.

Es soll zu jener Zeit gewesen sein, als der französische Kaiser Napoleon mit seinen Soldaten durch Masuren ins ferne Russland zog und das Vieh, die Pferde und das Getreide plünderte, dass der Lehrer des Ortes Persing zu Fuß in die Stadt Hohenstein kam. Dort hoffte er sein von den Söldnern Napoleons geraubtes einziges Pferd wieder zu finden. In der Stadt angekommen, suchte und fragte er sehr lange nach seinem Pferd – vergeblich.

Die Sage berichtet weiter, dass der tief enttäuschte Lehrer noch auf dem Rückweg nach Persing gewesen sei, als sich die Nacht über das Land senkte. Und als er in die Nähe eines Sumpfes gekommen war, hörte er ein lautes

Wiehern. Da dachte der Schulmeister, er fände ein ver-
irrtes, herrenloses Pferd, und machte sich schon bereit, es
einzufangen.

In diesem Augenblick kam der Mond hinter den Wolken hervor. Und im Mondlicht sah der Lehrer den Gespensterschimmel. Dessen Fell soll so hell geleuchtet haben, dass sogar das Licht des Vollmondes gegen dieses
Leuchten verblasste!

Doch das Erschreckendste an der geisterhaften Er-
scheinung sei gewesen, dass der leuchtende Schimmel
keinen Kopf mehr hatte. Trotzdem wieherte er wild und
laut! Und dann jagte das strahlend weiße Gespenst ohne
Kopf dem zu Tode erschreckten Lehrer entgegen! Es galoppierte schnell wie der Wind auf den armen Schulmeister zu und hätte ihn beinahe erreicht. Doch da machte
der Lehrer in seiner äußersten Not und im allerletzten
Augenblick geistesgegenwärtig das Kreuzzeichen und
sprach schnell ein Stoßgebet.

Da verwandelte sich von einem Augenblick auf den
anderen der Gespensterschimmel in ein Nebelpferd. Und
schon der nächste Windhauch, erzählte später der Lehrer, hätte den gespenstischen Nebel hoch über die Bäume
geweht. Dann sei er langsam zu den Nachtwolken aufgestiegen und zwischen den Sternen verschwunden!

Seit dieser Zeit, so weiß es die Sage zu berichten, ist
der kopflose Schimmel nie mehr gesehen oder gehört
worden.

Die mutigen Frauen
von Lyk

Als einst vor vielen Jahren das Reitervolk der Tataren aus den östlichen Steppen geritten kam, um plündernd bis in das Land Masuren hineinzuziehen, da verbreitete sich viel Angst und Schrecken zwischen den großen Seen. Denn auf ihren kleinen struppigen Pferden waren die Tataren so schnell und so wendig, dass es kaum jemandem gelang, bei ihrem Nahen rechtzeitig zu fliehen. Und es wird berichtet, dass selbst jene Menschen, die sich in den masurischen Wäldern zu verstecken versuchten, nicht sicher sein konnten, von ihnen unentdeckt zu bleiben.

Eines Sommertages nun erreichte eine große Tatarenhorde auch die masurische Stadt Lyk. Und ohne lange zu zögern begannen die wilden Reiter die Stadt zu erstürmen.

Aber die Bürger wehrten sich mit großem Mut und einem solchen Einsatz, dass alle Versuche der Feinde, diese Stadt in ihre Gewalt zu bekommen, fehlschlugen.

Immer und immer wieder wurden ihre Angriffe von den tapferen Bürgern zurückgeschlagen.

Nachdem sie so Tag um Tag vergeblich gegen die Verteidiger angeritten waren, gaben die Tataren ihre Angriffe auf. Sie lagerten rings um die Mauern der Stadt und hielten auf diese Weise alle Zugänge besetzt. Nichts und niemand konnte mehr in die Stadt hinein und niemand aus ihr hinaus. So dicht belagerten die Tataren die Mauern der Stadt, dass selbst ein Mäuschen keine Möglichkeit gehabt hätte, unbemerkt hinaus- oder hineinzuhuschen!

Um sich die Zeit der Belagerung zu vertreiben, veranstalteten die Tataren wilde Reiterspiele. So geschickt waren sie auf ihren kleinen zottigen Pferdchen, dass sie sogar in wildestem Galopp auf dem Rücken ihrer Pferde stehen blieben! Und für die Bewohner der Stadt Lyk wären diese kühnen Reiterspiele ein erregendes Schauspiel gewesen, hätten sie diese Reiter nicht zu ihren Feinden zählen müssen, die alles daran setzten, die Stadt zu erobern!

Lange Zeit hielten die Bürger der Belagerung stand. Doch mit jedem Tag, der verging, wurde der Hunger größer. Das mussten die Feinde wohl bemerkt haben, denn nun geschah es immer öfter, dass sie rings um die Stadt große Feuer entzündeten, über deren Flammen sie Rehe und Hirsche brieten, die sie in den Wäldern jagten.

Und wenn der Duft des gebratenen Fleisches durch die Straßen der belagerten Stadt wehte, dann jammerten die

227

hungernden Kinder noch mehr nach Speisen, die ihre Eltern nicht besaßen.

Nachdem auch die allerletzten Vorräte aufgegessen waren, wurde die Not endlich so groß, dass der Bürgermeister alle Menschen auf dem Marktplatz versammelte.

„Jeder Krümel Brot ist in unserer Stadt gegessen", sagte er zu den Hungernden, „jedes noch so kleine Zwiebelchen mitsamt seiner Schalen auch. Alle Vorratskammern sind so leer wie die Welt am ersten Tage der Schöpfung! Entweder beschließen wir jetzt, gemeinsam zu verhungern, oder wir müssen die Stadt unseren Feinden übergeben!"

„Der Hunger wütet in den Bäuchen der Kinder wie ein reißender Wolf, mehr noch in unseren Frauen. Und wir selber sind schon so schwach geworden, dass keiner von uns mehr kämpfen kann", sagte der Hufschmied, ein ehemals sehr starker Mann. „Ich fürchte, es bleibt keine andere Wahl, als uns auf Gnade oder Ungnade dem Feind zu ergeben!"

Und da beschlossen die Bürger von Lyk voller Angst, die Tore der Stadt zu öffnen.

Schon strömten ihre Feinde hinein. In wildem Galopp stürmten die fremden Reiter so durch die Straßen der Stadt, dass sich vor Angst alle Bürger in ihren Häusern versteckten.

228 Doch die Tataren durchsuchten jedes Versteck und trieben jeden Mann auf den Marktplatz hinaus. Sie fesselten allen Männern die Hände mit Stricken und ban-

den sie dann aneinander fest, sodass jeder mit jedem verbunden war. So blieb keinem auch nur die geringste Gelegenheit zu entfliehen.

Da fürchteten die Frauen um das Leben ihrer Männer und es war ein solches Jammern in den Mauern der Stadt, dass man es bis zum anderen Ufer des Sees hören konnte.

Aber zu aller Erstaunen ließen die fremden Krieger die Männer am Leben. Sie nahmen die aneinander Gefesselten in ihre Mitte und ritten mit ihnen aus der Stadt hinaus, begleitet vom lauten Weinen der Kinder und dem Wehklagen der verlassenen Frauen.

Angetrieben von den wilden Tatarenreitern schleppte sich der lange Zug der Gefesselten in das Land hinein. Ganz ohne Hoffnung waren die Gefangenen, dass sie jemals ihre Lieben wieder sehen könnten, denn sie sollten als Sklaven fern ihrer Heimat in der Tatarenwelt die allerschwersten Arbeiten tun.

Und als der Abend das Land zu verdunkeln begann, waren die Reiter und die gefangenen Männer auf einer Höhe angekommen, die über das Land hinausragte. Dort oben zündeten die Tataren ein riesiges Feuer an, das weithin bis zu der Stadt Lyk sichtbar war. An diesem erhöhten Ort wollten sie ihren Sieg über die Stadt auf ihre besondere Weise feiern.

Sie brieten viel Fleisch und sie tranken dazu. Sie sangen ihre uralten Kriegsgesänge. Und dann galoppierten sie auf ihren struppigen Pferdchen um die lodernden

Flammen. Und je länger sie ritten, desto größer wurde der Durst und die Wildheit und der Wagemut ihrer Reiterspiele im Freudentaumel über die Eroberung der Stadt!

Die verlassenen Frauen und Kinder in Lyk weinten und klagten noch lange. Zwar gab es jetzt keine Feinde mehr, die sie belagert hätten, aber es gab in der ganzen Stadt auch keinen einzigen Mann, keinen einzigen Vater für die Kinder!

Schließlich wischte sich die Frau des Schneiders entschlossen ihre Tränen ab und sagte zu den anderen Frauen: „Ist es nicht Strafe genug, dass uns der Feind unsere Männer entführte? Sollen wir auch noch die Hände in den Schoß legen und weiter jammern und klagen? Vielleicht sogar bis zum Jüngsten Tag? Die Tataren sind mit unseren Männern fortgezogen, wer hindert uns eigentlich daran, sie zu verfolgen?"

Einige Frauen widersprachen der Schneiderin, doch andere stimmten ihr zu. Und endlich einigten sie sich darauf, den gefangenen Männern zu folgen – in gebührendem Abstand und von den feindlichen Reitern unbemerkt.

Da schlichen die Frauen dem Zug der Gefangenen hinterher. So gut kannten sie diese Gegend und so vorsichtig waren ihre Schritte durch den Wald, dass keiner der Feinde von dieser Verfolgung etwas bemerkte.

Als es dann dunkel geworden war, kamen die Frauen bis in die Nähe des großen Feuers. Und als sie verdeckt von Büschen und Bäumen ganz nahe herangeschlichen waren, sahen sie, was ihre Feinde trieben. Sie hörten die wilden Schreie, die fremden Siegesgesänge jetzt aus der Nähe. Und je weiter sie auf das Freudenfeuer der Tataren zugeschlichen kamen, desto deutlicher konnten sie sehen und hören, wie wild das Gelage der Feinde war – und wie sich die Reiter betranken.

Da lagerten sich die Frauen aus Lyk ins Unterholz und sahen dem seltsamen Treiben zu. Als dann zu später Stunde das Siegesfest seinen Höhepunkt erreicht hatte, da waren die fremden Krieger so betrunken, dass einige von ihnen sogar von den Pferden fielen. Was das bei einem Reitervolk bedeutet, lässt sich kaum sagen!

Nachdem auch der letzte Tatar so betrunken vom Pferd fiel, dass er schon schlief, als er den Boden berührte, da meinte die Frau des Schneiders, nun sei es so weit.

„Worauf warten wir noch?", fragte sie flüsternd die anderen. „Frauen von Lyk, jetzt werden wir unsere Männer befreien!"

Da schlichen die Frauen lautlos wie Katzen an den schlafenden Feinden vorbei bis zu ihren gefangenen Männern und schnitten blitzschnell die Fesseln entzwei.

Kaum waren sie von ihren Fesseln befreit, da stürzten sich die Männer schon auf die betrunkenen Feinde und fesselten sie jetzt ihrerseits. Und dann galoppierten Frauen und Männer auf den erbeuteten Pferden in ihre Stadt zurück; vom großen Jubel der Kinder empfangen, die durch den Mut ihrer Mütter so schnell ihre Väter wiederbekamen.

Schon bald nach diesem denkwürdigen Ereignis, so erzählt es die Sage, waren in Lyk alle Spuren des Überfalls gründlich beseitigt gewesen – nicht zuletzt durch die Hilfe der erbeuteten zähen Pferde. Und die Stadt, die so mutige und kluge Frauen hatte, dass sogar die wilden Tataren überlistet werden konnten, die wurde schöner denn je zuvor wieder aufgebaut.

Dass man den tapferen Frauen von Lyk jedoch ein Denkmal errichtet hätte, davon weiß diese Sage nichts zu berichten.

Der Frosch
auf dem Seidensattel

Es war einmal ein Bauernpaar, das hatte drei Söhne. Die beiden älteren bekamen von den Eltern gute Kleider und konnten auch in die Schule gehen. Der jüngste jedoch, Hänschen genannt, war, wie man sagte, zu dumm zum Lernen und musste in Lumpen gekleidet das Vieh und die Schweine hüten.

Da nun die beiden Älteren herangewachsen waren, sagten sie eines Tages zu ihren Eltern: „Lasst uns in die Welt hinausziehen um etwas Neues zu lernen."

Der Bauer und seine Frau waren damit einverstanden, falls die beiden versprechen würden, nach drei Jahren wiederzukommen, um den Eltern zu zeigen, wie es ihnen in der weiten Welt ergangen sei.

Und sie versorgten die beiden älteren Söhne mit all den Dingen, die man für eine lange Reise benötigt, und gaben jedem auch ein Pferd, damit er ja recht weit in die Welt hinausreiten könnte.

„Ich will mit in die Welt hinaus", sagte da der jüngste

Sohn, der in Lumpen gekleidet das Vieh und die Schweine hütete, „ich will es meinen Brüdern gleichtun!"

Doch seine beiden älteren Brüder lachten und sagten zu ihm: „Bleib du mal schön beim Vieh, du bist zum Lernen doch viel zu dumm!"

Als nun die älteren Brüder in die weite Welt hinausgeritten waren, folgte ihnen heimlich der jüngste zu Fuß. Und er konnte nichts anderes mit sich auf die Reise nehmen als jene Brotreste, die er sich insgeheim vom Munde abgespart hatte. Die trug er in einem alten Sack auf seinem Rücken – und sie waren sein einziges Hab und Gut.

Als er so seinen Weg entlangging, kam er an einen großen Wald, an dessen Anfang sich der Weg teilte. Da bemerkte er die Hufspuren der Pferde seiner beiden älteren Brüder im Sand und sah, dass sie den Weg entlanggeritten waren, der nach links führte. Da entschloss er sich, den rechten Weg einzuschlagen.

Der Weg durch den Wald war endlos lang, doch Hänschen ging unverdrossen weiter. Er ging so lange, bis er auch den letzten Krümel des Brotes aufgegessen hatte. Nun musste er sich von den Beeren des Waldes ernähren, doch das reichte längst nicht aus um seinen großen Hunger zu stillen; und voller Verzweiflung und mutlos geworden, begann Hänschen zu weinen.

„Ach, wäre ich doch bloß zu Hause bei meinen Schweinen geblieben", sagte er klagend zu sich selbst, „dann hätte ich wenigstens keinen so großen Hunger zu leiden!"

Da sah er ein kleines Licht in der Ferne und ging schnell darauf zu. Und als er dann mit letzter Kraft eine Lichtung erreichte, sah er dort eine kleine Hütte stehen.

Voller Hoffnung öffnete er die Tür und trat ein, doch die Hütte war menschenleer. Nur ein Frosch, der auf einem weißen Kissen saß, erwiderte seinen Gruß. Und ehe Hänschen noch darüber staunen konnte, dass er einem sprechenden Frosch begegnet sei, fragte dieser ihn schon, woher er des Weges käme und was er suchen würde. Da erzählte Hänschen ihm alles genau so, wie es sich zugetragen hatte.

„Du kannst bei mir bleiben", sagte der Frosch zu ihm, „deine Arbeit wird leicht sein und zu essen gibt es bei mir auch reichlich und jeden Tag!"

„Was muss ich tun?", fragte Hänschen.

„Du musst jeden Morgen in den Pferdestall gehen", sagte der Frosch. „Dort an der Wand gleich neben der Stalltür wirst du einen kleinen Sattel finden, der ist mit weißer Seide gepolstert. Du nimmst den Sattel und bringst ihn zu mir. Dann hebst du mich vom Kissen, setzt mich auf den Sattel und trägst mich im Haus umher. Wenn du mich dann ein Weilchen herumgetragen hast, setzt du mich wieder auf mein weißes Seidenkissen. Mehr verlange ich nicht von dir."

„Das alles will ich gerne tun", sagte Hänschen und blieb bei dem Frosch in der einsamen Hütte im Wald.

Als nun drei Jahre vergangen waren, wurde der Junge sehr traurig und sagte: „Nun kommen meine Brüder wieder nach Hause geritten. Sie haben sicher viel Neues gelernt, wahrscheinlich auch schon Bräute gefunden und bringen der Mutter schöne Geschenke mit! Ich aber habe keine Braut und auch kein einziges Geschenk, das ich meiner Mutter mitbringen könnte!"

„Nimm diesen Haselnusszweig", sagte da der Frosch zu ihm. „Wenn du damit dreimal fest gegen die Tür des Pferdestalles schlägst, wird ein prächtiger Schimmel heraustraben. Besteige ihn und reite auf ihm nach Hause. Doch merke, wenn du an deines Vaters Landgrenze angekommen bist, musst du das Pferd zurücklassen und zu Fuß weitergehen."

Hänschen tat, wie der Frosch ihn geheißen hatte. Als er den schönen Schimmel bestiegen hatte, rief ihm der Frosch noch zu: „Nimm dieses Päckchen hier mit auf die Reise, es ist ein Geschenk der Braut für deine Mutter."

Und Hänschen ritt davon, ritt den langen Weg durch den Wald zurück, den er gekommen war. Und er kam ihm jetzt so kurz vor, als hätte der Schimmel Flügel.

Als er dort angelangt war, wo das Land seines Vaters begann, stieg er dem Rat des Frosches gehorchend vom Schimmel. Er band das Pferd an einen Baum und ging zu Fuß weiter bis zum Hof seiner Eltern.

Seine Brüder waren schon angekommen, als er sein Elternhaus betrat. Der älteste hatte den Beruf eines Müllers gelernt und er war mit einem Wagen gekommen, vor den zwei kräftige Pferde gespannt waren. Der andere Bruder war Fleischer geworden und auch er kam mit Pferd und

236

Wagen. Sie trugen beide gute Kleider und hatten von ihren Bräuten der Mutter auch schöne Geschenke mitgebracht.

„Hier ist das Geschenk meiner Braut", sagte Hänschen und reichte der Mutter das Päckchen, das ihm der Frosch beim Abschied gegeben hatte.

„Das wird sicherlich was ganz Besonderes sein!", sagte spottend der älteste Bruder. „Du trägst ja noch immer dieselben Lumpen wie vor drei Jahren beim Hüten der Schweine!"

Als die Mutter aber das Päckchen öffnete, da fand sie ein wunderbares Kleid. Das war aus glänzender Seide gemacht, mit purem Gold bestickt und verziert mit diamantenen Knöpfen, die in ihrer Pracht glitzerten und funkelten.

„Das hast du einer Prinzessin gestohlen!", rief seine Mutter erbost. „So ein Geschenk will ich nicht haben!"

Und sie warf ihm das herrliche Kleid vor die Füße.

Da wurde Hänschen über alle Maßen traurig und lief auf der Stelle aus dem Haus seiner Eltern. Er lief mit keuchendem Atem bis zu dem Schimmel am Waldesrand, sprang auf das wartende Pferd und ritt im Galopp den Weg zurück zur einsamen Hütte im großen Wald.

Im Haus der Eltern aber versprachen die Brüder beim Abschied, dass sie in einem Jahr wiederkommen würden. Sie würden ihre Bräute mitbringen, damit die Eltern sehen könnten, wie schön diese seien. Dann rollten ihre Wagen vom Hof.

Hänschen aber kam weinend in die einsame Hütte zurück und klagte dem Frosch sein Leid.

„Ach, Hänschen", sagte der Frosch zu ihm, „sei doch nicht traurig! Alles wird wieder gut, glaub mir, alles wird gut!"

Da nun ein Jahr vergangen war, rüstete sich Hänschen wieder zur Reise. Und wieder gab ihm der Frosch den wundersamen Haselnusszweig.

Doch als Hänschen dieses Mal gegen die Tür des Pferdestalles schlug, da kam nicht der schöne Schimmel herausgesprungen. Dieses Mal kam eine prächtige Kutsche herausgefahren, gezogen von vier herrlichen, edlen Pferden. Und eine wunderschöne junge Frau öffnete die Tür der Kutsche und ließ das Hänschen einsteigen.

„Merke dir jetzt genau, was ich dir sage", sprach sie zu ihm, „wenn wir an deines Vaters Grenze kommen werden, musst du aus dieser Kutsche aussteigen und das letzte Stück des Weges zu Fuß gehen. Und wenn ich nach deiner Ankunft dann bei euch vorfahren werde, trittst du an die Kutsche heran und schlägst alle Fenster entzwei. Das musst du tun! Dann werde ich in das Haus deiner Eltern kommen, und wenn deine Mutter das Essen bereitet hat, musst du mich daran hindern, auch nur die geringste Kleinigkeit von den Speisen zu essen!"

Die Brüder und ihre Bräute waren schon da, als Hänschen zerlumpt bei seinen Eltern ankam. Er hatte kaum den Hof betreten, da nahte auch schon die prächtigste Kutsche, die man in dieser Gegend je gesehen hatte.

238

Doch ehe die Eltern, seine Brüder und ihre Bräute genügend Zeit zum Staunen hatten, lief Hänschen schon der Kutsche entgegen. Und zum Entsetzen aller Anwesenden zerschlug er deren Fenster!

Die schöne Frau sagte keine tadelndes Wort. Sie stieg aus der Kutsche und fragte Hänschens Eltern nur, ob sie die Nacht über hier bleiben könnte.

„Aber wir sind doch nur Bauern, gnädige Frau", sagten diese zu ihr, „wir können Ihnen bei uns überhaupt nichts Besonderes anbieten!"

„Mir soll es schon recht sein", sagte die junge Frau, „denn was bei euch gegessen wird, das sollte auch mir wohl schmecken!"

Sie versammelten sich um den großen Tisch um zu Mittag zu essen. Da fragte die schöne Frau, wo denn der jüngste der Brüder sei.

„Ach, gnädige Frau, der sitzt im Winkel hinter dem Ofen", sagte der Bauer, „wer auf unserem Hof die Scheiben einer so edlen Kutsche zerschlagen hat, der gehört nicht an unseren Mittagstisch!"

Aber die vornehme Fremde bestand darauf, dass Hänschen am Tisch und an ihrer Seite Platz nahm.

Die Mutter hatte eine prächtige Blaubeersuppe gekocht. Als nun die junge Frau den ersten Löffel zum Munde führte, stieß Hänschen ihr gegen die Hand. Die Blaubeersuppe lief vom Löffel und tropfte auf das schneeweiße Kleid aus Seide. Schon bald war das Kleid über und über mit Blaubeersuppe befleckt! Und so sehr sich

239

die fremde Frau auch mühte, es gelang ihr nicht, auch nur einen einzigen Bissen zum Munde zu führen!

Da stand die Edelfrau vom Tisch auf und nahm den ungeschickten Jungen bei der Hand. Sie ging mit ihm in das Dachstübchen des Hauses hinauf, in dem sie die Nacht verbringen sollte.

Dort angekommen, warteten schon mehrere Diener auf sie. Die zogen Hänschen vornehme Kleider an und deckten eine üppige Tafel. Und die schöne Frau setzte sich mit Hänschen zu Tisch um nach Herzenslust zu speisen.

Inzwischen aber war einer der älteren Brüder zum Dachstübchen geschlichen und hatte durch das Schlüsselloch geblickt. Als er den anderen erzählte, was er dort oben gesehen hatte, hielten die es für eine Lüge.

„Du scheinst mir genauso dumm wie das Hänschen zu sein", sagte sein Vater zornig zu ihm. „Wenn sich dort oben eine prächtige Tafel, fremde Diener und ein unbekannter feiner Herr befinden würden, dann hätten wir das doch alle bemerkt! Müssten sie doch hier durch dieses Zimmer hindurchgegangen sein! Ich glaube, du bist noch dümmer als Hänschen – und dazu auch noch ein Lügner!"

Kaum waren diese Worte gefallen, da kam die fremde Frau aus dem Dachstübchen zurück. Und ihr zur Seite schritt ein schön gekleideter junger Herr. Ehe die Eltern, die Brüder und deren Bräute begriffen hatten, dass der stattliche Mann das Hänschen war, waren die beiden schon in die prächtige Kutsche gestiegen und in Windeseile davongefahren.

Nun hielt es die beiden ältesten Söhne und ihre Bräute auch nicht mehr länger und sie kehrten dorthin zurück, wo sie jetzt zu Hause waren.

Die Kutsche war kaum an der einsamen Hütte im Wald angekommen, da verschwand spurlos die schöne Frau. Und in der Hütte saß wieder der dicke Frosch auf seinem weißen Seidenkissen und sah Hänschen aufmerksam an.

„Ach", sagte Hänschen traurig, „nun habe ich wieder keine Braut!"

„Du brauchst nicht zu klagen", sagte der Frosch zu ihm, „denn es liegt jetzt alles an dir! Jetzt musst du selbst über dein Glück entscheiden! Ich werde dich nun für drei Tage und Nächte allein lassen, und in dieser Zeit musst du zeigen, ob du es wert bist, dass eine schöne Frau dein wird für immer!"

Dann erklärte der Frosch, dass in den folgenden Nächten allerlei Versuchungen auf Hänschen zukommen würden; eine immer größer als die vorherige.

„Doch was auch geschehen mag", sagte der Frosch, „nie darfst du ein einziges Wort verlieren. Selbst bei den allergrausigsten Dingen darfst du kein Sterbenswörtchen sagen, sonst ist es um dich und auch um mich für immer geschehen!"

241

Dann war der Frosch so spurlos verschwunden, wie die schöne fremde Frau in der Kutsche.

Das Dunkel einer mondlosen Nacht hatte sich kaum über die einsame Hütte im Wald gesenkt, da öffnete sich die Tür und es kamen junge Musikantinnen und Tänzerinnen herein. Die waren sehr ausgelassen, spielten die lustigsten Lieder und sangen und tanzten dazu. Und alle wollten sie, dass Hänschen mit ihnen singen und tanzen sollte.

Doch der Junge blieb in der äußersten Ecke der Hütte sitzen, stumm wie ein Fisch. Und erst als die Nacht zu Ende ging, war auch der Spuk vorbei.

Am nächsten Morgen bemerkte Hänschen dann, dass ein lichter Streifen sich um die Wände der Hütte ausgebreitet hatte.

In der zweiten Nacht kamen prächtig gekleidete Männer herein, die aussahen wie Grafen und Edelleute oder gar Prinzen. Und diese Männer schmeichelten Hänschen auf allerlei Weise. Sie lobten seine Klugheit, sagten, wie schön gewachsen er doch sei, und sie fanden sogar seine lumpigen Kleider auserlesen vornehm. Und am Ende versprachen sie, dass sie ihn zum König krönen würden, wenn er nur ein einziges Mal „Ja" sagte!

Doch Hänschen gedachte der warnenden Worte des Frosches und blieb auch in dieser Nacht stumm.

Am nächsten Morgen bemerkte er dann, dass der lichte Streifen um die Wände der Hütte noch um ein Vielfaches breiter geworden war.

Die dritte Nacht wurde überaus grausam und schrecklich. Es kamen Folterknechte und Henker ins Haus, die sagten, sie müssten Hänschen dafür bestrafen, dass er sich in der letzten Nacht geweigert hatte, König zu werden! Und sie stießen ihn in der Hütte so umher, dass er sich an den rauen Wänden die Haut zerriss. Doch als er trotz großer Schmerzen kein einziges Wort verlor, da schlugen und quälten sie ihn noch viel mehr. Sie wurden immer grausamer und immer böser! Und je länger er schwieg, desto grausamer folterten ihn die bösen Männer!

Doch trotz aller Schmerzen und tiefer Wunden hielt er die Lippen so fest verschlossen, als hätte er gar keinen Mund!

Erst das Ende der Nacht beendete seine unsägliche Qual. Und da fiel der Junge zu Tode erschöpft in einen so tiefen Schlaf, dass er erst spät am nächsten Tag erwachte.

Er traute seinen Augen nicht, als er sie öffnete. Das Zimmer war voller Licht und er spürte auch keine Schmerzen. Und all die grässlichen Wunden, die furchtbaren Verletzungen seiner Haut, die waren spurlos verschwunden!

Hänschen dachte, er träumte einen schönen Traum. Und während er sich noch darüber wunderte, trat ein Diener an sein Bett. Der verneigte sich tief vor ihm und half ihm beim Aufstehen. Dann kamen noch mehr Diener in den Raum und zogen ihm die prächtigsten Kleider an.

Als Hänschen dann zum Fenster hinaussah, war ringsum der dunkle Wald verschwunden. Überall, wohin

243

er auch blickte, umgab ihn tiefgrünes Land; mit Dörfern und Städten, mit Seen, Obstgärten und saftigen Wiesen, auf denen das beste Vieh weidete und die allerschönsten Pferde und Fohlen grasten. Und aus der kleinen, ärmlichen Hütte im Wald war ein prachtvolles Schloss geworden!

Da kam eine perlweiße Kutsche gefahren, gezogen von acht prächtigen Schimmeln mit einem so weißen Fell, dass sich die Sonne in ihm spiegelte.

Die Kutsche hielt am Fuße einer großen Treppe aus Marmor, die in den Schlosshof führte. Und im Fenster der Kutsche erschien das Gesicht jener schönen Frau, die mit Hänschen bei seinen Eltern gewesen war.

„Steig ein", sagte die junge Frau freundlich zu ihm. „Hänschen, steig ein, ich habe dir viel zu erzählen."

Da schritt Hänschen so schnell und leichtfüßig die Marmorstufen hinab, als schwebe er der Erde entgegen.

Sie fuhren über das Land. Und während die perlweiße Kutsche, gezogen von den acht prächtigen Schimmeln, unter dem Licht der Sonne über die Straßen fuhr, sagte die schöne Frau zu ihm: „Du warst sehr stark, als die Versuchung über dich kam. Und weil du so unbeirrt an meine Worte geglaubt hast, bin ich erlöst worden. Du hast mich durch deinen Glauben an mich vom hässlichen Frosch zur Prinzessin gemacht. So hast du den bösen Zauber für immer gebrochen. Ich bin jetzt deine Braut und alles, was mein ist, das gehört von nun an auch dir!"

So kam es, dass Hänschen, den sie für zu dumm gehalten hatten, um in eine Schule gehen zu können, die schönste Prinzessin zur Frau bekam und ein weiser und mächtiger König wurde.

Leseprobe

„… und das ist mein letztes Wort, Jennifer!" Damit hatte ihre Mutter mit Nachdruck die Zimmertür geschlossen. Noch lange klangen diese Worte Jenny Lake in den Ohren. Sie kannte ihre Mutter; sie meinte, was sie sagte. Hatte Mrs Lake erst einmal einen Entschluss gefasst, war sie ebenso eigensinnig wie ihre Tochter.

Jenny warf sich auf ihr Bett. „Wie ich es hasse, wenn sie mich Jennifer nennt", maulte sie. Madonna, ihre Katze, ließ sich am Fußende des Bettes nieder, und Jenny streichelte sie gedankenverloren. Sie musste sich jetzt etwas einfallen lassen. Ihre Eltern hatten ihr klar zu verstehen gegeben, dass sie an dem Dreitageritt in drei Wochen nicht teilnehmen dürfe, wenn sie wieder so schlechte Noten nach Hause brächte. Dann würden sie nämlich diesen Ausflug nicht bezahlen. Jenny sollte endlich beweisen, dass sie die Schule ernst nähme.

„Ausflug" war leicht untertrieben, dachte Jenny. Der Ausritt in die Berge mit Zeltlager wurde jedes Jahr zum Abschluss der Turniersaison veranstaltet. Seit Monaten war er Gesprächsthema Nummer eins unter den Freundinnen im Reitstall. Hauptsächlich aber sprach sie darüber mit ihrer besten Freundin, Laura Hanson. Sogar ihr Gepäck hatten sie Stück für Stück durchgesprochen. Sie musste einfach dabei sein!

Jenny seufzte. Natürlich konnte sie bessere Noten schreiben, wenn sie wirklich wollte. Sie war nicht dumm, nur tat sie eben lieber das, was sie interessierte. Und das waren nicht gerade die Schularbeiten. Mit Mathe hatte sie allerdings Schwierigkeiten. Zu allem Übel musste sie in drei Wochen ein schriftliches Mathereferat über Dezimalzahlen und Prozentsätze abliefern, das für die Mathenote im Zeugnis ausschlaggebend war. Und dieses Zeugnis gab es genau einen Tag vor dem Ausritt! Aber wie sollte sie ausgerechnet mit einer Arbeit in Mathe ihre Noten verbessern?

Sie grübelte. Vielleicht sollte sie die Arbeit über die Hobbyfischzucht ihres Bruders Michael schreiben und täglich zählen, wie viele kleine Fische hinzugekommen waren? Daraus könnte sie Prozentsätze errechnen und Dezimalzahlen darstellen. Viel zu langweilig, entschied sie und verwarf die Idee. Sie konnte natürlich auch ein wenig im Büro ihres Vaters arbeiten. Er hatte viel mit Zahlen zu tun. Aber dann überlegte sie, welche Folgen es für ihren Vater haben könnte, wenn sie Fehler machen würde. Also auch keine Lösung.

Was konnte sie tun? Gab es denn keinen Ausweg? Doch! Ihre Eltern hatten zwar gesagt, sie würden bei schlechten Noten den Reitausflug nicht bezahlen, aber Jenny konnte doch selbst dafür aufkommen! Sie hatte immerhin ein paar Dollar in ihrem Sparschwein, aber nicht genug für diesen Ausritt mit zwei Übernachtungen. Ihr Taschengeld war regelmäßig in wenigen Tagen verbraucht. Alex, ihr Zwillingsbruder, tröstete sie immer mit der Erkenntnis, dass die Woche eben zu viele Tage hätte. Vom Taschengeld etwas zu sparen war daher unmöglich.

Aber sie konnte doch Geld verdienen und es für den Ausritt sparen! Das war die Lösung! Jetzt wurde Jenny lebendig. Ihr Hirn arbeitete fieberhaft. Es gab doch unzählige Dinge, die sie für die Leute in der Nachbarschaft erledigen konnte. Und dafür würde man sie bezahlen! Zwar hatte sie bis jetzt noch nie versucht, Geld zu verdienen, aber viele ihrer Mitschülerinnen hatten kleine Jobs. Also konnte es so schwierig nicht sein. Jenny ließ ihrer Fantasie freien Lauf. Sie sah sich Einkaufskörbe schleppen, Hunde spazieren führen und auf Babys aufpassen. Sie konnte ihren Freundinnen unangenehme Haushaltspflichten abnehmen oder für Leute, die in Urlaub waren, Blumen gießen. Es gab viele Möglichkeiten.

Madonnas beharrliches Miauen an der Zimmertür riss sie aus ihren Gedanken. Jenny sprang vom Bett und öffnete Madonna die Tür. Die Katze wand sich aus dem Zimmer und ging mit elegant aufgestelltem Schweif die Treppe hinunter. Und auch Jenny, jetzt in bester Stimmung, lief in die Küche und half ihrer Mutter bei den

Vorbereitungen zum Mittagessen. Sie musste nämlich gleich nach dem Essen zur Reitstunde. Darauf freute sie sich immer. Außerdem würde sie dort Laura treffen, die bestimmt auch noch Ideen hatte, wie sie Geld verdienen konnte. Es sah jedenfalls nicht mehr so trostlos aus.

Laura Hanson war bereits im Stall. Ihr Vater, der Oberst bei der Marineinfanterie war, hatte an diesem Nach- mittag Dienst. Da er derzeit in Quantico bei Washington stationiert war, musste er seine Tochter schon zwei Stun- den vor der Reitstunde in Pine Hollow abliefern. Dafür entschuldigte er sich immer bei seiner Tochter, aber Laura beteuerte ihm, dass ihr das überhaupt nichts aus- mache. Sie war immer gern dort; ja sie hielt sich nirgends lieber auf als in Pine Hollow.

Laura gefiel die Reitanlage, zu der 25 Pferde gehörten. Der Stall war u-förmig gebaut; an den beiden Längs- seiten befanden sich die Pferdeboxen. Die kurze Seite bot Platz für die Sattelkammer, in der Sättel und Zaumzeuge untergebracht waren, sowie die Gerätekammer für das Putzzeug, die Heu- und Mistgabeln sowie Stallbesen. Schließlich gab es noch die Futterkammer, wo Hafer und ein paar Ballen Heu lagerten. Laura konnte Stunden da- mit zubringen, von Box zu Box zu gehen, die Pferde zu tätscheln und mit ihnen zu reden. Max Regnery sah darin nur Zeitvergeudung. Max war der Besitzer der Anlage. Sein Großvater hatte sie seinem Vater und dieser ihm vererbt. Auf den ersten Blick wirkte Max locker und sehr ruhig, aber seine Schüler wussten genau, dass ihn nichts so sehr irritierte, als müßiges Herumstehen. Laura durfte sich immer im Stall aufhalten – solange sie sich nützlich machte. Heute arbeitete sie in der Sattelkammer. Sie hatte auf einen Sattelbock vor sich einen Sattel gelegt, den sie mit einem feuchten Schwamm und Sattelseife abrieb. Es gefiel ihr, wie durch die Seife das stumpfe Leder wieder glänzend wurde.

Laura Hanson war, wie Jenny, zwölf Jahre alt. Sie hatte eine zarte Figur und dunkelbraune, lebhafte Augen. Ihre gelockten, schwarzen, schulterlangen Haare trug sie meist offen, nur für Reitwettbewerbe flocht sie sich einen Zopf und steckte ihn hoch.

Pferde waren Lauras ganzer Lebensinhalt. Später einmal, wenn sie erwachsen war, würde sie ihren eigenen Reitstall haben. Das wusste sie jetzt schon.

Ihre Freundin Jenny kam meist in letzter Minute in den Stall, aber Laura war jetzt trotzdem nicht allein. Während sie arbeitete, plauderte sie mit der Mutter von Max, die von allen liebevoll Mrs Reg genannt wurde.

„Dad hat sich doch tatsächlich entschuldigt, weil er mich heute schon so früh hier abliefern musste. Seltsam, immer wieder versichert er mir, dass ihm dies Leid tut und jenes ..."

„Es ist ihm eben so zu Mute, Laura", sagte Mrs Reg sanft.

Laura dachte nach. Es stimmte. Ihr Vater war niedergeschlagen, seit Lauras Mutter vor sechs Monaten an Krebs gestorben war. Auch sie vermisste ihre Mutter schmerzlich.

„Es ist nicht nur Trauer, Mrs Reg", entgegnete Laura.

„Ja, dein Vater leidet darunter, dass er dir nicht gleichzeitig Vater und Mutter sein kann."

„Aber das erwarte ich doch gar nicht von ihm", protestierte Laura.

„Dann musst du versuchen, ihm das zu sagen", riet ihr Mrs Reg.

Laura vergaß den Sattel und überlegte, wie sie ihrem Vater erklären sollte, dass sie durchaus nicht mehr von ihm erwartete, als er ohnehin für sie tat.

„Mrs Reg", sagte sie schließlich mit fester Stimme. Die freundliche Dame sah sie an. „Haben Sie je den Ausspruch gehört: Ein Oberst lässt sich von einem kleinen Soldaten nicht belehren?"

Mrs Reg lachte und nickte. „Okay, dann musst du dich eben gedulden. Mit der Zeit wird er seine Tochter kennen lernen."

Laura nahm den gereinigten Sattel hoch und hob ihn auf den Halter. Dann holte sie das Zaumzeug herunter, das über dem Sattel hing.

„Wenn du das Zaumzeug gereinigt hast, brauche ich dich in der Bahn", rief ihr Max im Vorübergehen zu. Er führte Patch, einen schwarzweißen Schecken, in die Halle. Laura stutzte und schaute ihm nach. Max und dem Pferd folgten ein Mädchen, das Laura irgendwie bekannt vorkam, und eine Dame, die anscheinend die Mutter des Mädchens war. Das Mädchen war zart, hatte welliges braunes Haar und eine kleine Stupsnase mit Sommersprossen. Sie sah niedlich aus und blickte mit klugen Augen um sich.

Jetzt fiel Laura auch der Name der neuen Reitschülerin ein. Sie hieß Julia Atwood und besuchte, wie sie, die Willow Creek Junior High School, nur die nächsthöhere Klasse. Laura hatte sie bis jetzt nur nicht beachtet. In der Schule hatte sie das selbstbewusste Auftreten einer guten Schülerin, aber hier im Stall bewegte sie sich unsicher und schien sich in ihrer Haut nicht sehr wohl zu fühlen. Laura beschloss, das Zaumzeug im Schnellverfahren zu reinigen, um dann zu sehen, was in der Halle vor sich ging.

Zögernd folgte Julia ihrer Mutter in die Reithalle. Sie kam sich fehl am Platz vor. Mrs Atwood dagegen unterhielt sich angeregt mit Mr Regnery über die Reiterei. Sie schwärmte von dem Naturtalent seiner künftigen Schülerin, die den Reitsport über alles liebte, bereits unzählige Lehrbücher über die Reiterei verschlungen hatte und nur noch eines endgültigen Schliffs bedurfte.

„Erst kürzlich hat sie bei einem Wettbewerb ein blaues Band gewonnen", erklärte Mrs Atwood abschließend.

Erst jetzt begriff Julia, dass sie das gepriesene, von der Reiterei besessene Naturtalent sein sollte, von dem ihre Mutter schwärmte. Und der Wettbewerb? Ach, das war ein Ponyreiten im Zoo gewesen. Sie war damals vier Jahre alt gewesen, und alle Kinder hatten blaue Schleifen bekommen!

Julia seufzte. Da sie in der Schule die Klassenbeste war, schien ihre Mutter zu erwarten, dass sie auch sonst überall besser als die anderen war. Jeden Montag besuchte sie eine Ballettschule, am Mittwoch einen Malkurs und am Freitag spielte sie Tennis. Nun stand anscheinend dienstags und samstags noch Reiten auf dem Programm. Noch störte sie die hektische Betriebsamkeit ihrer Mutter nicht weiter, Julia fand sie nur langsam etwas albern. Und manchmal, wie jetzt gerade, schämte sie sich ein wenig.

Auszug aus dem
Ravensburger Taschenbuch 54901
Sattelclub Band 1
„Drei Mädchen gründen einen Club"
von Bonnie Bryant

Pferde – Mädchen – Abenteuer

Bonnie Bryant
Drei Mädchen gründen einen Club
Die Liebe zu Pferden und zum Reiten verbindet Laura, Jenny und Julia, und sie gründen einen Club, den „Sattelclub".
160 Seiten
ISBN 3-473-**54901**-0

Bonnie Bryant
Veronicas Fehler
Nach einem schlimmen Unfall im Reitstall gibt Laura das Reiten auf. Werden Jenny und Julia sie wieder umstimmen können?
160 Seiten
ISBN 3-473-**54902**-9

Gute Idee.

Ravensburger

Pferde – Mädchen – Abenteuer

Bonnie Bryant
Ein Pferd für Laura
Laura pflegt Delilahs Fohlen,
Jenny organisiert ein Reitfest.
Wann haben die beiden wieder
Zeit für Julia und den Club?
160 Seiten
ISBN 3-473-**54903**-7

Bonnie Bryant
Die Neue
Sara verschweigt den Sattel-
club-Mädchen, dass sie erfolg-
reich Turniere reitet. Was ist
das Geheimnis der Neuen?
160 Seiten
ISBN 3-473-**54904**-5

Gute Idee.

Ravensburger

Pferde – Mädchen – Abenteuer

Bonnie Bryant
Freundschaft ist alles
Laura mag die neue Freundin
ihres Vaters nicht – schon gar
nicht als Stiefmutter. Nur das
Reiten macht ihr noch Spaß!
160 Seiten
ISBN 3-473-**54905**-3

Bonnie Bryant
Abenteuer auf der Pferderanch
Laura, Jenny und Julia werden
von Sara auf die Pferderanch
eingeladen. Schon bald fühlen
sie sich wie echte Cowboys!
160 Seiten
ISBN 3-473-**54906**-1

Gute Idee.